ROUTLEDGE LIBRARY EDITIONS:
THE ECONOMY OF THE MIDDLE EAST

Volume 29

SOCIAL AND ECONOMIC DEVELOPMENT IN THE ARAB GULF

SOCIAL AND ECONOMIC DEVELOPMENT IN THE ARAB GULF

Edited by
TIM NIBLOCK

Routledge
Taylor & Francis Group
LONDON AND NEW YORK

First published in 1980

This edition first published in 2014
by Routledge

4 Park Square, Milton Park, Abingdon, Oxon OX14 4RN
605 Third Avenue, New York, NY 10017

Routledge is an imprint of the Taylor & Francis Group, an informa business

British Library Cataloguing in Publication Data
A catalogue record for this book is available from the British Library

ISBN: 978-1-138-78710-0 (Set)
ISBN: 978-1-315-74408-7 (ebk)(Set)
ISBN: 978-1-138-81018-1 (hbk)(Volume 29)
ISBN: 978-1-315-74432-2 (ebk)(Volume 29)
ISBN: 978-1-138-82032-6 (pbk)(Volume 29)

SOCIAL AND ECONOMIC DEVELOPMENT IN THE ARAB GULF

EDITED BY TIM NIBLOCK

CROOM HELM
London and Canberra

ST. MARTIN'S PRESS
New York

and

Centre for Arab Gulf Studies, Exeter

Croom Helm Ltd., Provident House, Burrell Row,
Beckenham, Kent BR3 1AT

British Library Cataloguing in Publication Data

Social and economic development in the Arab Gulf
1. Persian Gulf States – Social conditions
I. Niblock, Tim
309.2'3'09536 HN662.A8

ISBN 0-7099-0422-3

Reprinted 1982

 For information, write:
St. Martin's Press, Inc., 175 Fifth Avenue, New York, NY 10010
Printed in Great Britain
First published in the United States of America in 1980

ISBN 0-312-73145-0

Library of Congress Cataloging in Publication Data
Main entry under title:

Social and Economic Development in the Arab Gulf.

'Initially presented as papers of the inaugural conference of the Centre for Arab Gulf Studies at the University of Exeter, held 9-13 July, 1979.'
Includes index
1. Persian Gulf region – politics and government – congresses. 2. Persian Gulf region – social conditions – congresses. 3. Persian Gulf region – economic conditions – congresses. I. Niblock, Tim. 11. Exeter, Eng. University. Centre for Arab Gulf Studies.
DS326.S65 1980 953'.6 80-13697

Typeset in Great Britain by
Pintail Studios Ltd, Ringwood, Hampshire
Printed and bound by
Biddles Ltd, Guildford, Surrey

Contents

Tables

Figures

Preface

The articles in this book were initially presented as papers to the inaugural conference of the Centre for Arab Gulf Studies at the University of Exeter, held 9–13 July 1979. The editor wishes to extend his thanks to all those who participated in this conference: the lively discussions which characterised conference proceedings have helped to determine both the form and the content of the articles in this book. Dr Aziz al-Azmeh's assistance in organising the conference was highly appreciated. Particular thanks should go to the chairman of the conference and Director of the Centre for Arab Gulf Studies, Professor M. A. Shaban.

Mrs Sheila Westcott has typed the manuscript, displaying her customary resources of patience and good humour – in addition to her competence in typing.

Acknowledgement is due to Frank Cass and Co. for permission to reprint the maps found on page 13 and page 114; to Croom Helm for permission to reprint the maps found on page 12 and page 123; and to John Wiley for permission to reprint the map found on page 85.

It is hoped that this publication will be the first in a series produced by the Centre for Arab Gulf Studies, focusing attention on that crucially important region which has hitherto been so strangely neglected by academic researchers: the Arab Gulf. The Centre wishes to express its appreciation of the generous financial assistance which the governments of Qatar and the United Arab Emirates have provided for the centre's activities.

Tim Niblock

1 Introduction

TIM NIBLOCK

Perspective

The crucial importance of the Arab Gulf region today – which may be defined as comprising the states of Saudi Arabia, Iraq, Kuwait, Oman, Bahrain, Qatar and the United Arab Emirates, with Iran as a non-Arab onlooker – has stimulated surprisingly little interest in academic circles. The few distinguished academic works which have been written on the society and politics of the contemporary Arab Gulf region[1] have by no means filled the need for understanding. Much of what has been written on the Gulf, moreover, focuses exclusively on those aspects of direct concern to external interests. The concern is with 'security', interpreted as the ability of the Western powers to retain access to Gulf oil, with the operation of the oil industry, and with the means whereby petrodollars can be recycled so as to ensure that revenues earned from oil find their way back into the Western economy.

The focus of this book is on the Arab Gulf region as an area with its own problems of social, economic and political development. It examines the dimensions of the attempts by the governments and peoples of the area to create new social, economic and political structures – stemming mainly, of course, from their new-found oil wealth. The ample availability of capital does not by itself solve the problem of formulating and implementing coherent development policies. Indeed, the fact that governments are not restrained by shortage of capital tends to throw into greater relief the other problems confronting the formulation and implementation of coherent policies, and the extent to which the social, political and economic dimensions are intertwined.

Both the desirability of and the difficulty in examining patterns of development and change in the Arab Gulf stem from the speed at which the conditions affecting development potential have been

Figure 1.1: The Gulf Region

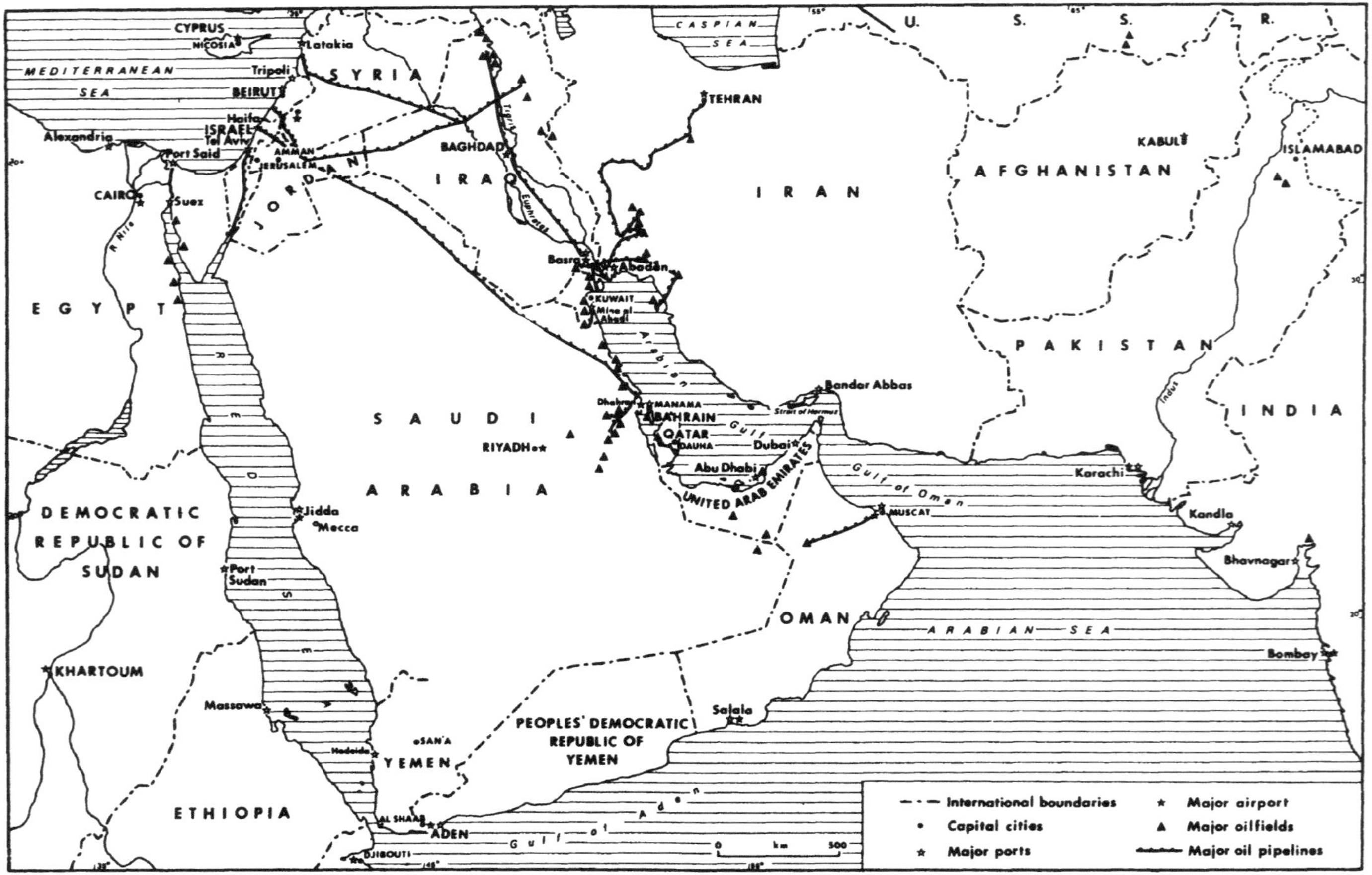

Figure 1.2: Arabia circa 1925

transformed. The availability of ample (and excess) capital for development came upon the states concerned very suddenly. This was most pronounced, of course, for the more recent oil producers – the United Arab Emirates (beginning production in Abu Dhabi in 1962, Dubai 1969 and Sharjah 1973) and Oman (beginning production in 1967). Consequent upon oil production, the late 1960s and early 1970s saw government revenues increase many fold in these states. By 1979, oil production in the United Arab Emirates was averaging 1.5 million barrels a day (b/d), while in Oman average production was running at 300,000 b/d. The small size of the indigenous populations (1975 figures: UAE 200,000, Oman 500,000) ensured that the effects on standards of living were immense. World Bank estimates of GNP *per capita* in 1976 were $13,990 for the UAE and $2,680 for Oman.

Even for those states which had been producing oil over a longer period, however, recent years have seen a sudden increase in the availability of funds for development – resulting both from increased oil production and from the sharp rises in oil prices carried through in 1973 and 1978–9. OPEC had first been formed in 1960, but it was the confluence of political determination (following the 1973 Arab–Israeli war) and demand for oil outstripping supply which enabled OPEC to quadruple prices in 1973. The longer-established Arab Gulf oil producers are Iraq (producing since 1929, reaching in 1979 an average of 3 million b/d), Bahrain (producing since 1934, reaching in 1979 80,000 b/d), Saudi Arabia (producing since 1938, reaching in 1979 9 million b/d), Kuwait (producing since 1946, reaching in 1979 2 million b/d) and Qatar (producing since 1949, reaching in 1979 400,000 b/d). The small indigenous population of Kuwait (1975: 472,100), together with its high oil production, ensured that, in 1976, GNP *per capita*, at $15,840, stood highest in the world. The even smaller indigenous population of Qatar (1975: 67,900) similarly ensured a high GNP *per capita*, at $11,400. Saudi Arabia, with an indigenous population of 4,592,500 (1975), enjoyed a *per capita* GNP of $4,480; Bahrain (1976 indigenous population: 224,700), one of $2,140; and Iraq (1975 indigenous population: 11,124,000), one of $1,390.[2]

The rapid change in the economies of the Gulf States, following from the increased availability of capital, has been accompanied by some change in the political sphere. Here, however, the continuity of traditional structures has perhaps constituted the most prominent feature. Up to 1971, Bahrain, Qatar and the seven Trucial States which came together to form the United Arab Emirates (Abu Dhabi, Dubai, Sharjah, Ras al-Khaimah, Fujayrah, Umm al-Qaywayn and Ajman) were under British protection. The protectorate agreements covering these states had been concluded in the 1820s (for Bahrain and the Trucial States) and in 1868 (for Qatar). While no formal protectorate agreement covered Oman, Britain had been closely involved in supporting the regime prior to 1971 and in handling Oman's foreign relations. The progression towards independent statehood for these entities began in January 1968, with the British government's announcement of its intention to withdraw from its treaty commitments in the Gulf.

As Britain had not been involved in the minutiae of administration in the Arab Gulf states, restricting itself to general support for existing regimes for as long as they catered to Britain's strategic interests in the area, independence did not in itself involve a substantial change in political organisation. The shaikhly families which had held power before independence, relying on alliances with leaders of tribal sections and individual merchants, continued to hold predominant power – the Khalifa family of Bahrain, the al-Thani of Qatar, the Al bu Said of Oman, and in the United Arab Emirates the Al Nuhayyan family of Abu Dhabi, the Al Maktum of Dubai, the Al Qawasim of Sharjah and Ras al-Khaimah, the Al Sharqi of Fujayrah, the Al Mualla of Umm al-Qaywayn, and the al-Nuaymi of Ajman. Independence was none the less significant. The direct contact with the outside world, which was now required, opened up new vistas and posed new kinds of problems. The most immediate problem after the British government's announcement of January 1968 was to determine the form of relationship which should exist among the Gulf states. After a prolonged attempt to form a federation covering Bahrain and Qatar as well as the seven Trucial States, the rulers of Bahrain and Qatar chose separate independence. In the later part of 1971, therefore, Bahrain, Qatar and the federation of the United Arab Emirates (consisting of six Trucial States, joined by the seventh – Ras al-Khaimah – in February 1972) became independent. Co-operation, however, needed to exist on a wider scale – among all the Arab Gulf states – if the security of existing regimes was to be effectively guaranteed; recent years have seen increasing stress on such co-operation and co-ordination replacing the inter-state rivalries of the past.

A further aspect of the political sphere affected by independence was, predictably, the nature of external involvement in the area. The role formerly played by Britain in supporting existing regimes tended to be taken over by a larger grouping of Western powers, within which the United States exerted a particularly powerful influence. The nature and effects of this support have, of course, differed from the pattern which existed before independence, leaving the Arab Gulf states with more scope for manoeuvre. Policies pursued on oil pricing and on control of the oil industry (brought under local control in most of the Arab Gulf states in the mid-1970s) have on occasions proved highly unpopular with the Arab Gulf states' Western supporters. Nevertheless, it is perhaps significant that none of the Gulf states which became independent in 1971 now maintains diplomatic relations with the Soviet Union.

The states in the Arab Gulf which have been constituted as independent entities for longer periods (Kuwait since 1961, Iraq since

1932, Saudi Arabia effectively since the conquest of Hejaz in the western portion of the peninsula by the Saudi rulers of Nejd in 1926) have also in recent years experienced change in the political sphere – although not necessarily affecting basic political structures. The oil wealth has ensured that these states, together with the newly independent, have become more deeply involved than before in international affairs. The value of their resources to the outside world has assured them (especially since 1973) a degree of influence, and the links of mutual dependence between oil producers and consumers (where the processes of production are themselves dependent upon techniques, machinery and expertise provided by consumer nations) have drawn them increasingly into the international arena. Moreover, their attempts at bringing their new-found influence to bear on particular issues, most prominently to bring some redress for the injustices suffered by the Palestinians, have opened up new perspectives on international politics. The rising political consciousness of the populations, the heavy dependence upon foreign labour, and governmental concern with developments in other regional states – for fear of developments which may destabilise their own regimes – have all emphasised the involvement with the wider world.

The basic political structures through which Iraq, Kuwait and Saudi Arabia are governed did not change substantially in the course of the 1970s. In Iraq the Baathist regime, which first attained power under Hassan al-Bakr in 1968, remained in power. There was, however, considerable change in the composition of the government and the higher councils of the Baath Party, the most recent changes following Saddam Hussain's assumption of the national presidency, in place of Hassan al-Bakr, in 1979. In Kuwait, 1976 saw the dissolution of the National Assembly, which had served as the country's parliament since independence (a parliamentary experiment which was briefly copied in Bahrain, 1972–5). While the dissolution ushered in a less liberal policy towards political opposition, predominant power remained where it had always been – in the hands of the ruling al-Sabah family. In Saudi Arabia the assassination of King Faisal in 1975, followed by the accession of his brother Khalid, did not portend any fundamental change in the processes of government.

Dilemmas of Development

The articles in this book centre around five dilemmas which face the societies of the Arab Gulf as they move towards new patterns of economy and society. The first relates to the natural resource base and to the limits which this resource base imposes on feasible (or desirable) development. K. McLachlan (Chapter 5: Natural Resources and Development in the Gulf States) points out that the region is 'rich in hydrocarbon deposits but poor in almost every other natural resource'. The problem, moreover, is not simply that the limited natural resource base reduces potential for economic development in fields other than oil; the development of the oil economy itself has been prejudicial to development in other fields. K. McLachlan shows how, despite public pronouncements by Gulf governments defining their primary objectives as diversification away from dependence on oil, the actual trend has been for the non-oil sectors of the economies to shrink in relative, and sometimes real, terms. The agricultural sectors (of those states which have them) have become steadily less capable of satisfying the food needs of the growing populations.

Some of the reasons for the discouraging effect which the oil economy has had on other sectors, most prominently agriculture, emerge from the articles by D. Cole (Chapter 7: Pastoral Nomads in a Rapidly Changing Economy: The Case of Saudi Arabia) and J. Wilkinson (Chapter 8: Changes in the Structure of Village Life in Oman). D. Cole demonstrates that the subsidies to bedouin paid by the Saudi Arabian government, based on the number of livestock held, have simply encouraged the bedouin to keep more animals and sell less. One of the effects of this has been damage to the ranges through over-grazing. J. Wilkinson contends that the boom economy associated with oil in Oman has drawn labour away from agriculture, leading to the neglect of the irrigation systems (*aflaj*) in the countryside which have traditionally constituted the backbone of the system of agricultural production. Government-sponsored agricultural development consists of a few experimental centres and farms, most of which are run as country estates by the wealthy. These are highly inefficient in economic terms, wasteful of water and draw off labour from villages which are already desperately short of manpower.

The position with regard to the industrial sector is more complex. In the smaller Gulf states this sector is new and, built up through revenues earned mainly from oil, cannot be said to have been 'discouraged' by the oil economy. Nevertheless, J. Townsend (Chapter 6: Problems Confronting the Establishment of a Heavy Industrial Base in the Arab Gulf) sees a threat that the very abundance of government revenue, with the attendant temptation to provide continuing subsidisation for the industrial sector, may be encouraging forms of industrialisation which have no long-term future. States should direct their attention to industrialisation in those fields where their natural resource base gives them an advantage, to producing efficiently for known markets, and to avoiding duplication of effort – where each Gulf state builds up the same range of industries and is then impelled to compete fiercely against its neighbours for international markets.

The second dilemma relates to the social effects of economic policies. The most crucial effect is on the demographic composition of the region. J. Birks and C. Sinclair (Chapter 9: Economic and Social Implications of Current Development in the Arab Gulf: The Oriental Connection) show that current development policies in the Gulf will require an increasing dependence on immigrant labour and that, as the potential for drawing labour from within the Arab world is already largely exhausted, the main part of the labour will be non-Arab – largely from the Far East. The most likely scenario for 1985 is that some 1,600,000 migrants from the Indian sub-continent and the Far East will be required by the capital-rich Arab states, constituting 55 per cent of the migrant labour force. The term 'capital-rich Arab states' here includes one non-Gulf state, Libya, together with Saudi Arabia, Kuwait, Bahrain, Oman, the UAE, Qatar and Oman. The inclusion of Libya causes the percentage quoted for non-Arab labour requirements to err on the side of underestimation when applied exclusively to the Arab Gulf. Moreover, the dependence on non-Arab migrant labour will, of course, be much greater for the smaller Arab Gulf states (such as the United Arab Emirates, where migrant labour already outnumbers local labour by 4:1) than for Saudi Arabia or Iraq. The social and political implications of relying on immigrant labour to this extent are, of course, immense; there are increasing signs of local resistance to the trend of events.

A further social effect of current economic policies is the impact on the fabric of society. J. Wilkinson suggests that the failure to maintain traditional agricultural organisation in Oman is undercutting the value-system of rural Omani life, replacing co-operation and community with individualism, while D. Cole points to the effect of Saudi development policies in relegating the nomadic population to the status of a depressed class. Some evidence of the ability of social values and attitudes to survive economic change, however, is provided by M. G. Rumaihi (Chapter 3: The Mode of Production in the Arab Gulf Before the Discovery of Oil) who argues that contemporary society in the Gulf is still heavily influenced by the relations of production of the pre-oil era.

The third dilemma is in the field of domestic politics. Some assessment is required as to whether the patriarchal form of government, currently prevalent in all Arab Gulf states except Iraq, could really be conducive to serving the long-term interests of the populations. E. Nakhleh (Chapter 10: Political Participation and the Constitutional Experiments in the Arab Gulf: Bahrain and Qatar) argues that only with wider political participation, formally constituted, can the well-being of the populations be served.

The fourth dilemma covers the role of international factors in influencing the pattern of social and economic development and of political change in the Arab Gulf. Historically, international factors have played a highly significant role in determining the limits within which the local economies have been able to operate. This is documented, with emphasis on the period shortly before and shortly after the discovery of oil, by J. Malone (Chapter 2: Involvement and Change: The Coming of the Oil Age to Saudi Arabia) and R. Said Zahlan (Chapter 4: Hegemony, Dependence and Development in the Gulf). The manner in which external influences have impinged upon the Gulf more recently and the international dimensions to the local struggles for power in the area are described by F. Halliday (Chapter 13: The Gulf Between Two Revolutions: 1958–79). The intensified incorporation of the Arab Gulf area into the international capitalist economy, which occurred during the 1960s and 1970s, cannot but affect the framework within which development strategies proceed.

The fifth dilemma concerns the relations which shall exist between the Arab Gulf states. Economic and social development could hardly be meaningful if each of the states currently enjoying independent nationhood retains its ability and inclination to create its own separate social and economic structures. No form of coherent economic organisation, aimed to satisfy the needs of the populations after the depletion of oil, could hope to exist on such a basis. Some of the implications of the problems of intra-Gulf relations are examined by N. Sakr (Chapter 11: Federalism in the United Arab Emirates: Prospects and Regional Implications) and T. Niblock (Chapter 12: The Prospects for Integration in the Arab Gulf).

Notes

1. One of the most useful is J. Duke Anthony, *Arab States of the Lower Gulf* (Middle East Institute, Washington, 1976).
2. Further details of, and sources for, the figures quoted in this paragraph and the previous one can be found in the article by J. S. Birks and C. Sinclair.

2 Involvement and Change: The Coming of the Oil Age to Saudi Arabia*

J. J. MALONE

Introduction

The focus of this article is upon the critical years shortly before and after the exploitation of oil began in Saudi Arabia (roughly 1926–48). It is hoped that a detailed study of this period (drawn largely from United States archival sources) will bring into outline the central factors determining the direction of developments at that time. This is important for two reasons: first, because subsequent, post-oil, development was built upon the basis laid down earlier; second, because some of the factors relevant to the earlier developments are fundamental to later developments also. The relatively less complex situation existing in the earlier period perhaps makes it easier to perceive these factors. The three most central factors shaping social and economic policy shortly before and after the exploitation of oil began were the poverty of the country, the concern of the House of Saud to maintain control of the newly conquered territory of Hejaz, and the machinations of foreign interests. Social and economic developments in later years have also been greatly shaped by concern with security and by the nature of the links with foreign interests.

Background: The Historical Importance of Hejaz to the House of Saud

The refinery, pipelines, gas–oil separator plants and other oil-producing facilities of the Eastern province of al-Hasa, soon to be supplemented by an enormous associated gas-gathering network, are the life force of Saudi Arabian development. Yet it was across the peninsula in the Hejaz that the initial phase of Saudi development was carried out. The Hejaz experience shaped the attitudes and pers-

*For details of locations in Ch. 2, see Figure 1.2 on p. 13.

pectives of the House of Saud, and was no less a determinant of the course of development than were austere religious belief and practice, or the physical environment of Nejd, the heart of Arabia and the Saudi homeland. In Nejd, in the words of the American minister to Cairo who was accredited to the Kingdom of Saudi Arabia, 'a harsh life of desert hardships . . . made these Arabs practical realists'.[1] That practical realism made it possible for the House of Saud to fashion realistic policies to ensure their continued control of the Hejaz.

There is irony in the fact that the oil which fuels the engine of Saudi Arabian development was discovered not far from the oasis of Qatif, forsaken by ancestors of the Kingdom's ruling dynasty for Dariyah, in the Arabian interior more than four centuries ago. It was in the independent city–statelet of Dariyah, one of several in Nejd, that the story of the House of Saud began.

Before oil flowed from beneath Jebel Dhahran, Hasa seldom figured predominantly in the calculations of the rulers of Dariyah. When that eastern region came under a tenuous Ottoman suzerainty in 1590, it was the Banu Khalid tribal confederation – and not the rulers of Dariyah or their tribal cousins – which challenged the intruders and, in 1669, expelled them. While the House of Saud was able to exercise a weak and spasmodic control over Hasa for much of the first two-thirds of the nineteenth century – ebbing and flowing in accordance with the consolidation of their own position in Nejd – eastern Arabia remained peripheral to their real concerns. Eastern Arabia did, however, occasionally constitute a place of Saudi refuge. An errant second son of the great Faisal ibn Ṯurki sheltered in Buraimi before returning to spread anarchy in Nejd in 1870. Abd al-Rahman, the youngest of Faisal's sons, took his family to Kuwait when Riyadh fell to Muhammad ibn Rashid of Hail, intriguer, administrator and field marshal *sans pareil*, in 1891.

It was the extreme disarray of the House of Saud which facilitated re-establishment of the Ottoman garrisons in Hasa (1871–72) as a part of Midhat Pasha's scheme to recover the patrimony of Sulaiman the Magnificent in Arabia. It was inevitable that those garrisons would not long survive the revival of Saudi vigour and sense of purpose beginning with the dramatic recapture of Riyadh by a small band under the inspired command of Abd al-Rahman's son, Abd al-Aziz, in 1902. By 1913 the region between Kuwait and Qatar was under Saudi control, and Hejaz regained its place of priority in the plans and aspirations of the rulers of Nejd. The Hasa 'interludes' were aberrations from the normal pattern of Saudi activities, which emphasised consolidation of their domination of Nejd, and their challenge to the Sherifian domination of Hejaz.

Sherifian rule was long established in Mecca, Medina and Jeddah when the House of Saud was coaxing a living out of the plantations of Dariyah. Indeed, for many centuries before 1744, the year in which the mighty link was forged between Muhammad ibn Abd al-Wahhab's religious fervour and the secular leadership of Muhammad ibn Saud, Nejd was a Sherifian hunting ground. The threat was greatest when the rulers of Hejaz somehow balanced or withstood the pressure of the Yemeni Imams and the Mamluk Sultans of Cairo or, later, when there was more form than substance to the role of Sherifian Hejaz as an Ottoman satrapy.

In the nineteenth century's first decade, Mecca and then Medina opened their gates to the marauding Nejdi warriors of Saud ibn Abd al-Aziz, an expansion made possible by Ottoman embroilments with Bonaparte. When Muhammad Ali's legions pushed the Nejdis out of Hejaz in 1814, in preparation for the Egyptian occupation and destruction of Dariyah (1818), the House of Saud was left with a burden and a challenge. The burden was one of failure, a failure to secure for the puritanical doctrine of *tauhid* (known to the West as Wahhabism) the holy cities of Hejaz. The challenge was to develop the administrative structure without which rule over Hejaz could not be consolidated. For Saud ibn Abd al-Aziz had been compelled to appoint his enemy, Sherif Ghalib ibn Musaid, as chief administrator of 'occupied' Hejaz.

The first evidence of Saudi organisational skills was shown by Turki ibn Abdallah in driving the Egyptian garrisons out of Nejd in 1824. The Egyptians returned in greater strength in 1837 but, after the brief, vigorous and repressive proconsulship of Khurshid Pasha, Saudi control was reasserted in 1840 by Faisal ibn Turki, returned from forced exile and prison in Cairo. Faisal's ascendency inaugurated a 'Hasa interlude', notable for expansion, prosperity and the swiftness of its expiry. The death of Faisal in 1865 led to a crisis over the succession, one of the most profound influences on the House of Saud in the twentieth century. The intra-family rivalry brought Saudi fortunes to a low point, with the Rashidis of Jebel Shammar gaining control of the Saudi capital (al-Riyadh, since 1824) in 1891.

The legacy which passed to Abd al-Aziz ibn Abd al-Rahman when he extinguished Rashidi rule over Riyadh and central Nejd in 1902, therefore, was one in which the Hejaz figured prominently – whether as a Sherifian lair, an Egyptian base of operations, a repository of what was on earth most holy and venerated of Islam, or indeed as the venue of a more advanced civilisation.

Before World War I forced momentous decisions upon Abd al-Aziz, his anti-Sherifian, anti-Ottoman convictions were strengthened mightily. The humiliation of ransoming a brother, held by Sherif Hussain, and the Turkish patronage of the Rashidis of Jebel Shammar were, in their way, policy determinants. The latter brought Abd al-Aziz into relations with the British, once hostilities began in Europe. The comradeship of Abd al-Aziz and Captain Shakespear, formed in northern Nejd before the latter's death near Hail in 1915, was, however, no basis for an enduring political relationship, once the British made common cause with Sherif Hussain in what became known to history as the Arab Revolt.

Anglo-Sherifian co-operation was seen by Abd al-Aziz as a threat, not to be diminished by his own acceptance of a subordinate role in war against the Ottomans. A long-term relationship with the British was unthinkable, in the light both of Abd al-Aziz's vision of the future and of the opposition which such a pact would arouse among the fractious Nejdi *Ikhwan*. In point of fact, clashes between the *Ikhwan* and the forces of Sherif Hussain in north-eastern Hejaz during the war placed further strain upon the fragile relationship between Abd al-Aziz and the British.

In terms of the House of Saud, World War I resulted in the further impoverishment of Nejd through a sharp diminution of the caravan trade, while increasing vulnerability to external threats and pressures. Enfeebled Ottoman administration was replaced by British-backed Sherifian – now better known as Hashimite – control, not only in Hejaz, but in an arc running north and east from western Arabia to Trans-Jordan, curving through the Syrian Desert to Iraq, and down the Shatt al-Arab to the head of the Persian Gulf. The Gulf was virtually a *mare clausum* in which the British writ ran unchallenged. British support for Sayyid Muhammad ibn Ali al-Idrisi, in the key south-western region of Asir, suggested that the London government's goal was to make the Red Sea, like the Gulf, a British lake.

Provision of arms, advisers and subventions to Hashimites and to 'the Idrisi' concealed from Arab eyes the harsh realities of British exhaustion and economic distress. The extension of Saudi control over Jebel Shammar (1921) was a less risky affair than it must have seemed to be, given the decline of British power. Even the illusion of Britain's capacity for shaping events was enough to strengthen Kuwaiti and Iraqi hands in negotiations with Riyadh in the post-war era. Perhaps the former Sherif, now King Hussain of the Hejaz, shared the illusion when he proclaimed his Arab caliphate over the world of Islam in 1924. It was a challenge to everything the House of Saud had stood for from the day in 1744 that Muhammad ibn Abd al-Wahhab came together with Muhammad ibn Saud in Dariyah. There could be no turning back from the task of conquering the Hejaz from a regime considered to be both idolatrous and expansionist.

Problems Following from the Capture of Hejaz

Hejaz put Nejdi pragmatism to a stern test. It was not only that the capture of western Arabia (1926) thrust upon the House of Saud responsibility for the Holy Cities of Mecca and Medina, and thus for the pilgrimage. All of Hejaz had to be made secure against the threats which had eventuated from Trans-Jordan in the north, from Asir and Yemen to the south and, within the region itself, from Hashimite sympathisers and from the fractious *Ikhwan*, the barely manageable engine which powered the war machine of Abd al-Aziz.

The problems facing the country, then, involved establishing security. This, however, had many facets: it required providing adequate facilities for pilgrims (as this would enhance the new regime's international respectability and hence diminish dangers of interference – especially from Hashimite quarters); the establishment of a coherent administrative system to control the area; the development of communications which would bind the country together; catering for the economic well-being of the population as a whole; and gaining acceptance of the new state of affairs from the Great Powers.

Matters relating to the pilgrimage were pressing. Recognition by the new ruler of Hejaz that the annual pilgrimage was the regime's only significant source of income was joined with an awareness of widespread disapproval, in the world of Islam, of the zealotry of the *Ikhwan* in smashing tombs and other evidence of an unallowable intrusion between the believer and God. Such problems called for immediate ameliorative efforts – and these were quickly forthcoming. To discipline the *Ikhwan* was less of a task than to improve the infrastructural and logistical arrangements, mainly in the areas of transportation, food supply and health care, upon which the pilgrimage depended.

Also pressing, but even more elusive, was the attempt to provide the new kingdom with security and status within the Arab world and in the larger family of nations.[2] At an earlier stage, the world beyond the Middle East might have cared little for Saudi cravings for security and status. That the outside world was now rather more responsive to such needs may be understood with relation to the distractions and divisiveness fostered by the inter-war era of European hegemony in the Fertile Crescent, North Africa and Persian Gulf regions. For it was during the inter-war period that the Kingdom of Saudi Arabia's potential as a *place d'armes* and as a petroleum producer was given serious attention. The coming of age of strategic air warfare and of the world petroleum market had the most important ramifications for Saudi Arabia, even before the California Arabian Standard Oil Company – CASOC – (ARAMCO's predecessor) brought in the first well as Jebel Dhahran.

Underlying problems relating to security and international acceptance was the fact of poverty. While the full significance of the fact may not be crystal clear, it is worth recalling that the ruling generation of the House of Saud in the 'petrodollar' era grew to manhood in a period of debt and dependency. The experience has had a shaping but hardly a uniform influence upon the Kingdom's fiscal and development policies.

Respectability, Economy and Security, 1926–33

The interaction of considerations of international respectability, security and economic development may be seen clearly in the policies pursued by Abd al-Aziz ibn Saud in the economic sphere after the capture of Hejaz.

The conquest of Hejaz and the King's assumption of the duties of the Guardian of the Holy Places occurred just as the transportation revolution swept over Arabia. Motor cars, and especially Ford cars and buses, were appearing in the most unlikely places in the Kingdom. They presented opportunities and problems. If properly organised, motor transportation could ease the lot of the pilgrim and thus demonstrate to the world of Islam the superiority of King al-Aziz's stewardship over that of his predecessors. It was important that this be accomplished, because the House of Saud was being pilloried in the Egyptian press and elsewhere for the violent episode during the 1926 pilgrimage, which proceeded from the fury of the *Ikhwan* over the presence of an arms-bearing, music-playing Egyptian escort for the *mahmal* (the carrier in which the covering of the *Kaaba* was kept), to say nothing of the *mahmal* itself, in the Holy City of Mecca.

The effectiveness of motor cars in the 1926 pilgrimage was limited by the sandy, rock-strewn track between Jeddah and Mecca but, having authorised the first motorised pilgrimage of any size, Abd al-Aziz realised that he must turn near-failure into success. The exclusive concession he had awarded for motorised pilgrim traffic was thereupon cancelled and the field was opened to all comers. H. St John B. Philby was the most effective competitor and, not surprisingly, an early and eloquent advocate of paved roads. Early in 1927 construction on the Jeddah–Mecca road, under the supervision of Sulaiman Shafiq Pasha, a former Ottoman minister, began. A single steam-roller which looked 'as outlandish as a camel would . . . in London' was soon augmented by additional equipment shipments.[3] Jeddah, the port of entry, was described as 'the most efficient . . . in the Red Sea, not excepting even Italian Massawah'.[4]

By 1928 the old caravan track from Yanbu to Medina was made passable for motor traffic and regular communication by car was established between Mecca and Medina. These developments and improved medical facilities and security were emphasised by the respected *Ulema*, who were sent to various parts of the Islamic world to promote the pilgrimage.

The King was also aware that the automobile and improved roads could either enhance or threaten security, depending upon who controlled them. He therefore monitored automobile imports and regulated concessionaires very thoroughly.[5] The automobile also conferred an important benefit in allowing him to resist pressures to authorise reconstruction of the Hejaz railway. Better it should remain a monument to the Arab Revolt than reduce the travelling time between Medina and Hashimite Amman.

Abd al-Aziz's Hashimite predecessors had been responsible for the installation of two electric generators in Mecca, for the lighting of the *Kaaba* and the palace, and for the establishment of a telephone link between Jeddah and Mecca. It may not be too much to say that in terms of what is now known as technology transfer, Hejaz conquered Abd al-Aziz and, eventually, Nejd, years before oil brought high technology to Hasa.

An early Saudi interest was the construction of radio stations in Mecca and Riyadh. Inquiries were directed to American companies in 1927 by way of the Consulate General in Jerusalem. The one respondent firm seemingly reversed the modern prequalification process with a barrage of detailed technical questions, which the consular authorities neither understood nor forwarded.[6] The real beginning of a country-wide communications structures came late in 1929 with the award of a concession to the Sharqiah Company Ltd (managed by the ubiquitous Philby) for the installation of a Marconi wireless system, with a central station in Riyadh and fourteen substations. The order was described as

> a great step forward. When King Hussain first talked over the telephone to Jidda from his palace in Mecca, it seemed that Arabia was emerging from a certain mysterious obscurity and swinging into the line of western progress. With fifteen wireless stations scattered over the country, the so-called backwardness of Arabia will seem to be still less pronounced.[7]

Inevitably, the early stage of development in Saudi Arabia was regarded as a contest between 'Westernisation' and the moral arbiters of an austere, closed society with King Abd al-Aziz as the man between.

An American consular assessment, in 1928, was that

> Ibn Saud, in spite of his severe religious tenets, appears to have surprisingly progressive ideas and an eager desire to secure for the Hedjaz the advantages of Western civilisation . . . there is every reason to believe that the Arabian Red Sea littoral is just entering a period of economic awakening, and that it is destined to become a market of ever-increasing importance.[8]

What interested King Abd al-Aziz much more than Western things or Western values were public security, institutional stability and dynastic continuity. Working with what he had or could secure, he enforced public order and punished transgressors promptly and severely. If progress toward his objectives could be made by securing American diplomatic recognition (which came about in 1931), he was willing to organise a lobbying campaign. For the same reason, he gratefully accepted scholarships to colleges and universities for young Saudi men, and sent others with tuition paid from the privy purse.[9] In fact, the characteristics which were 'Western' about King Abd al-Aziz were his directness and pragmatism, which were described as manifestations of 'the practical sense of the Saudi Arabs . . . revealed in their wish to grasp the subject matter rather than to linger over the form of expression'.[10]

Yet by 1932 the fruits of his efforts were meagre. To the west, his country was still a distant, infertile wilderness. When K. S. Twitchell journeyed to the United States a year earlier to recruit interest in the Kingdom's mineral potential, he asked the Department of State for a letter to the effect that 'the Hedjaz does exist and has a competent King and a stable government capable and willing to honour its obligations, financial and otherwise, which government has recently been recognized by ours'.[11]

In 1932, it was apparent that the most significant Western influence in the desert Kingdom was the Great Depression. It seemed as if the few gains made by the House of Saud were about to be nullified. International loans were so heavily laden with conditions as to make acceptance an act of treason; or they were unavailable, as Emir Faisal was later to discover on a journey through Italy, France, Germany and the Soviet Union, during which he discovered that the foundations upon which Western civilisation rested were dangerously eroded.[12] Clearly, the year in which the Kingdom of Saudi Arabia was proclaimed was a turning-point in the history of the House of Saud. New and dangerous initiatives would have to be taken to forestall the break-up of Arabia into a number of warring tribal confederations.

Neither the Depression nor trouble on the frontiers succeeded, however, in bringing the development process to a standstill. Some minor improvement in the water resources of Jeddah was achieved in late 1931 by the installation of a windmill-driven pump, supplemented by a gas engine (another example of the philanthropy of Charles R. Crane).

A greater emphasis was given to investment in security-related installations. By 1933, 28 wireless stations were in place and 19 cities and towns had telephone service. Both means of communication were available in Mecca, Riyadh, Jeddah, Hail, Buraida, Taif, Qatif, Tabuk, Lith and some smaller settlements. The wireless extended the network to (among others) Wejh, Yanbu, Khunfidah, Rabegh and Jizan (all on the Red Sea coast) and Abha and Medina. Two years later, the Soviet Union donated a small semi-automatic exchange in Riyadh; a Russian engineer supervised its installation.[13] But the majority of the network was at Saudi expense, at a time when the Egyptians were still collecting alms for the poor of Medina,[14] and the original Sharqiah–Marconi installation exceeded in cost the £30,000 Abd al-Aziz would receive for signing the Standard Oil concession. A further drain on the exchequer came in the form of payments for guns, ammunition and fuel, and the annual Ramadan subsidy to the tribes, the size of which only became known when annual budgets were drawn up at Anglo-American insistence in World War II.[15]

The Dangers and Dimensions of Foreign Involvement, to 1933

To achieve his security goals, with the consequent economic objectives, King Abd al-Aziz was drawn increasingly into contact with foreign interests. Paradoxically, those contacts frequently threatened, by creating a dependent relationship, to undermine the very security he wished to strengthen.

When the Sultan of Nejd invaded the territory of the Hejaz, he signified his willingness not only to shoulder the sacred burden of responsibility for the Holy Places, but to carry a less exalting burden as well – that of a financial dependency upon foreigners. What he might offer as collateral was unclear. Bahrain's Dukhan field had yet to be brought in and exploration had not begun in Hasa. Years would pass before Issawi's Law ('Where there are Arabs there is oil') could be promulgated.

King Abd al-Aziz had received a modest British subsidy until post-war retrenchment measures resulted in its suspension. When he turned to London again for assistance in 1931, strategic and economic interests outweighed the effects of spreading depression. An American presence in the Persian Gulf – the Standard Oil of California concession in Bahrain and negotiators representing the Gulf Refining Corporation in Kuwait – argued forcefully in favour of including Saudi Arabia in Britain's informal empire. So did Iran's cancellation of Imperial Airways's landing and overflight rights. Hence the conditions on which a £500,000 loan would be granted included not only the assignment of a British national to 'reorganize and control' Saudi Arabian finances, but also overflight and landing rights and some minor concessions.[16] Such an arrangement would have made a British financial 'advisor' the second most powerful, and potentially the most powerful, personage in Saudi Arabia.

The King suspected that the British were using other tactics to further their designs in this matter. The long and costly rebellion of the Billi tribe, sections of which were located in northern Hejaz, Trans-Jordan and Sinai, was a case in point. The Saudis and other observers believed that, leaving aside the personal objectives of Shaikh Hamad ibn Rafada who led the rebellion, the uprising was part of a British-sponsored strategy aimed at placing pressure on Abd al-Aziz to accept the loan and its accompanying terms.[17]

While the proffered British loan was refused, King Abd al-Aziz did respond to one element of the British proposal: Shaikh Abdullah Sulaiman was ordered to reorganise the Ministry of Finance. At the time, the only foreign bank operating in the country was the Netherlands Trading Society. It was therefore to the Dutch that the King turned for assistance. The extent to which reorganisation[18] influenced the decision to remove administrative barriers complicating Nejd–Hejaz relations is not clear, but in the midst of the process the Kingdom of Saudi Arabia was proclaimed (September 1932). The changes constituted the most important development in financial administration until the establishment of the Saudi Arabian Monetary Agency in 1952.[19]

A further aspect of suspected British involvement was the scheme for the establishment of a Royal Arab Bank, the major shareholder of which, former Khedive Abbas Hilmi, had some rather shadowy financial backing. The Bank was a non-starter, but during negotiations it became public knowledge that a British syndicate was to underwrite both Abbas Hilmi's 50 per cent shareholding and the 25 per cent participation of the Saudi Arabian government. The bazaar rumours suggested that the ex-Khedive was the front man for a group of British Zionists. At best it still could be alleged that 'a means has finally been found by the English of extending their influence more surely over the country'.[20]

Commercial relations with the Soviet Union also raised problems, especially relating to a marketing concession granted to Vostgostorg, a Soviet government trading corporation. The establishment of diplomatic relations with the USSR in 1926 had been followed by the inauguration of a steamship service a year later which called at Jeddah and other Red Sea ports on the route between Odessa and the Persian Gulf. No freight was landed until 1931, when the head of the Soviet legation signed an agreement for the delivery of 104,000 cases of gasoline and kerosene from Odessa (described as 'shoddy Soviet petroleum products, defectively packed and short-weight'). The deal was concluded at a time when Shell and Standard Oil were seeking payment of overdue accounts. After the Soviet account went unpaid for two years, protests led to a concession allowing unrestricted entry of Soviet merchandise. The arrangement was soon cancelled, for Vostgostorg had caused much resentment among local merchants because of its underselling and dumping practices; the blame was placed squarely on King Abd al-Aziz.

Further concern with foreign interests in the area followed from domestic unrest and from complications related to Yemen. The efforts of Abd al-Aziz to improve administrative practices provided ammunition to his detractors and rivals, perhaps because they perceived some dilution of Wahhabite fundamentalism and fervour. It is also likely that such modernisation threatened a life in which raids upon caravans and battles over water and forage were as inevitable as drought and the *shamal* (cooling north wind). Best known is the rising of the Mutair, Ajman and Ataiba tribes near the Iraqi frontier in 1928, because their rebellion resulted in a British-led invasion. In re-establishing Saudi control in that quarter, Abd al-Aziz's convictions regarding the indispensability of a country-wide security apparatus were reinforced.

In the south, Abd al-Aziz's problems were centred upon Shaikh Hassan al-Idrisi of Asir, the Imam Yahya of Yemen, and the external involvement of Italy (and possibly Britain). The Western perception was of an Italian strategy aimed at transforming the southern Red Sea into *mare nostrum*. To King Abd al-Aziz, the Red Sea was the most important body of water in the geography of Islam. Moreover, and even more important, a foreign lodgement in Asir, or even in the Yemeni Tihama, was unthinkable. The King frequently referred to Yemen's great contribution to Arab culture, but of greater concern was its large, heretofore unmobilised population and its historic importance as a base for 'strangers' – Ethiopians, Persians, Egyptians, Turks and British.[21] When an Italian (and, some whispered, a British) dimension was added to Saudi concerns in Asir and Yemen, the Kingdom's meagre resources were reluctantly committed to what in modern parlance is described as a pre-emptive strike. The successful conduct of the Tihama campaign, ending in the Treaty of Taif (1934), strengthened the security of the Saudi state while further weakening the economic position.

Rumours of Oil: Problems Raised by and Reactions to the Possibility of Oil Exploitation, 1933–35

The economic problems faced by Abd al-Aziz in 1932–33, and his failure to find adequate solutions to them, suggested to many that the leadership and resolve which had characterised the conqueror of

Hejaz had diminished, and there were predictions of an imminent 'retirement to Nejd'.[22] Instead, the King was for the first time given a glimpse of a future which could be shaped by revenue from oil on a scale which defied comprehension. The concession agreement with Standard Oil of California was important for the optimism and encouragement it provided, and the initial payment of £30,000 was certainly welcome. The King was once again fully in command, and there was an association between preparations for Saudi Arabia's entry into the petroleum era and Abd al-Aziz's assertion of authority in Asir and Yemen.

It was evident, however, that the concession agreement would pose problems in a state based on Wahhabi fundamentalism. The introduction of large numbers of foreigners required that public opinion be shaped in advance of the Standard Oil agreement. Abd al-Aziz, therefore, took the opportunity to propose two schemes specifically geared towards attracting outside Muslim involvement. In March 1933, three months before the signing, but with Standard Oil and Iraqi Petroleum negotiators in Jeddah, Mecca's *Umm al Qura* carried a story on the King's willingness to permit a company, 'preferably of Muslims', to exploit 'the mines of all kinds and the petroleum deposits of virgin Arabia to make it rich and prosperous'.[23] There followed a royal proclamation:

> I declare that whoever of the Muslim Kings, Princes or merchants wishes to undertake *in the Hejaz* [emphasis added] an enterprise of benefit to Islam will be welcome, provided the honour and independence of the country be safeguarded and nothing of our sacred religion be affected.[24]

At about the same time, the Saudi Arabian government announced details of a concession for a 'pilgrim' railway line linking Jeddah and Mecca. It was to be an entirely Islamic enterprise, financed by funds raised from India's Muslim population by a syndicate headed by a Dr Abd al-Kader al-Jilani of Madras. Payment was to be made out of the government's share of receipts and would be facilitated by the absence, as befitting a Muslim undertaking, of interest charges.[25] Despite the elaborate detail and compelling logic of the descriptive material supplementing the concession agreement, the project was no less ephemeral than the majority of the proposals which, since the petroleum era arrived, have weighted the suitcases of Riyadh-bound entrepreneurs and have survived only to accommodate coffee cups and ashtrays in cluttered ministerial offices. In this case, it was the Depression, as virulent in India as elsewhere, which defeated an otherwise feasible enterprise.[26] Once again, the value of the 'pilgrim' railway project was in its timing, which accounted for the publicity received on the eve of another concession agreement which would bring hundreds, and then thousands, of non-Muslims into an Arabia which the Caliph Umar had proclaimed to be an exclusively Muslim sanctuary.

How many non-Muslims would be involved was unknown. The American negotiators had been encouraged by what they considered to be 'the low cost of construction' and presumably thought that the proportion of the Saudi to the non-Saudi workforce would be higher than it eventually proved to be in the major (post-war) construction phase.[27] Just before the agreement was signed, the foreign community in Jeddah numbered 45, 'mostly British, but including Dutch, French, Italian, Persian, Iraqi and an increasing number of Soviet representatives'.[28] Two years later, the granting of a concession to the Saudi Arabian Mining Syndicate Ltd (which had been taken over by the American Smelting and Refining Company) resulted in the introduction of a number of Americans and Europeans into the Hejaz.[29] In urging, yet again, the establishment of an American legation, K. S. Twitchell added up the American presence (four in Hejaz, 17 in Hasa) and wrote '. . . so you see there is quite a colony'.[30]

At least until the first CASOC well was brought in, the arrival of foreign workers was more of a political problem than an economic benefit. Despite the introduction of the radio, telephone and automobile, the purchase of several small steamships and the acquisition of four British light aircraft, the Kingdom remained in a situation of stagnation.[31] The means of developing roads, accommodation for pilgrims and, most important, water resources were absent.

Effects of the Initiation of Oil Production, 1938–45

The immediate effect of the introduction of the first CASOC producer well (1938) was to increase the interest of the Great Powers in Saudi Arabia. In July 1938 a meeting was held between a senior Saudi official and the American leadership – in fact with President Roosevelt and Secretary of State Cordell Hull. The atmosphere in the White House was cheerful and relaxed, as Shaikh Hafiz Wahba, the Saudi Arabian minister in London, and James A. Moffett, Vice President of Standard Oil of California, advised that one 'very large' well had been brought in and others successfully drilled. The potential volume was such that the plan to refine oil at Bahrain would be abandoned in favour of an independent refinery on the mainland. The transformation of Bahrain, which had conferred upon the Khalifahs 'undreamed of wealth and prosperity' was now in prospect for Saudi Arabia. The memorandum of the conversation recorded that 'it seems very likely that Ibn Saud's Kingdom, the most powerful independent state in the Peninsula, will undergo far-reaching economic and social changes'. It was a safe prediction. But then Shaikh Hafiz added a sombre note, stating that Saudi Arabia and other Arab states would not tolerate Jewish immigration to Palestine in numbers 'as to peril Arab control of that land'.[32]

It was an early, and for a very long time the last, word spoken either on Palestine or on incipient prosperity in Saudi Arabia, in the upper echelons of the Saudi Arabian and US governments. But there was no longer any doubt about Saudi Arabia either in terms of potential or as a prize for an aggressor. The American minister in Cairo reported in nervous prose that the Japanese minister, Masayuki Yokayama, and two legation officers had departed for Riyadh in March 1939 to discuss a commercial agreement with King Abd al-Aziz, and hoped to visit the Persian Gulf region as well. The informant, Toshio Katsube, spoke of his own plans to visit Saudi Arabia and Iraq during the following month and concluded, presumably with an inscrutable smile, that 'the people will no doubt suspect that the Japanese have certain petroleum interests in view'.[33]

The Germans had been there earlier. Dr Fritz Grobba, Hitler's rather inept minister to Baghdad, had journeyed to Riyadh to present letters of credence and 'to hunt petroleum concessions'. Upon being expelled from Iraq, he failed to secure the permission of the Saudi government to reside in Jeddah.[34]

The fact of oil production, and the international rivalry which this soon involved, did not by themselves transform the economic situation overnight. On the contrary, as the world was speedily slipping into the Second World War, oil did not effect a positive economic boom in Saudi Arabia until the second half of the 1940s. Nevertheless, the knowledge that oil was in the ground brought Saudi Arabia goods and services during the war years which it might not otherwise have obtained, and which can be classified under the heading of development. Examples of American origin were the agricultural mission of 1942, a sophisticated (for the time) inter-communications system for the Royal Palace in Riyadh, and a C-47 aircraft.[35] Had CASOC drilled a series of dry holes before the Nazi armies began their brutalisation of Poland, Saudi Arabia could have been reduced to the low estate of 1932, or even worse. But producing wells, and E. I. De Golyer's 1943 estimate of proven oil reserves at two billion barrels, indicated reserves above four, and a possible reserve of twenty billion barrels, meant that King Abd al-Aziz should not only be sustained, but that he should be courted.[36] Already in 1940, he shortened his stay in Jeddah 'to remain aloof from potential influences of foreign diplomatic representatives'.[37] In 1945, after a comprehensive reorganisation of the local government structure in the Qatif governate of Hasa province by Shaikh Abdullah Sulaiman and, because ARAMCO was so completely involved, by Shaikh Yusuf Yassin, Acting Minister of Foreign Affairs (to include the introduction of a new team of officials), the King advised ARAMCO officials who called on him in Riyadh that

> when the company and its operations were small, business could be transacted on a personal and informal basis, but with the rapid and increasing expansion, he would insist on proper and official conduct of its governmental contacts by the company.[38]

By 1942 it was obvious to the United States government that the American-held concession in Hasa had to be protected by measures designed to cope with the severe economic dislocation imposed upon Saudi Arabia by wartime developments. Oil company advances against future production could not meet all needs, and early in 1942 the Kingdom became a recipient of aid administered by the US Lend–Lease Administration. British subventions were also generous – if the Americans had the inside track on future oil production, both Britain and the United States had achieved a lively appreciation of the strategic significance of the Kingdom. Moreover, there was always the hope for a turn of events which would confer advantages upon the *Inglezi* that the *Mirkani* now enjoyed. That was fair enough – had not Roosevelt suggested that his second war aim, after the defeat of the Axis powers, was the break-up of the British Empire?

At the end of 1944, the centrality of Saudi Arabia in the Department of State's policy planning was revealed in a memorandum to Roosevelt which argued that, if firm Export–Import Bank support of Saudi Arabia did not supplant the soon-to-expire Lend–Lease assistance, 'undoubtedly it will be supplied by some other nation which might thus acquire a dominant position inimical to the welfare of Saudi Arabia and to the national interest of the United States'.[39]

The Department of State was either too polite or too confident of Roosevelt's perspicacity to attempt an identification of the 'other nation'. It did, however, buttress arguments for a generous loan/grant programme by making the following points:

1. . . . a strong and independent Saudi Arabian government in the Near East, where the two great world powers come in contact, is less likely to fall victim to war-breeding aggression than a weak and disintegrating state vulnerable to economic and political penetration.

2. . . . the vast oil resources of Saudi Arabia, now in American hands under a concession held by American nationals, should be safeguarded and developed in order to supplement Western hemisphere resources as a source of world supply.

3. . . . the military authorities urgently desire certain facilities in Saudi Arabia for the prosecution of the war.[40]

These views won Roosevelt's support and, shortly after the changing of the guard, that of President Truman.[41]

CASOC, moreover, was becoming increasingly involved in general measures to support the economy. CASOC officials had soon realised that King Abd al-Aziz's interest in trees, gardens and farms, based on the exploitation of new water resources, was more than mere altruism. Water was security, that is to say the means of transforming the wandering, raiding bedouin into agriculturalists. Once the promise of oil in commercial quantities became a reality, the digging of artesian wells – both in Hasa and Hejaz – became a priority.[42] In the middle of World War II CASOC became heavily involved in the construction of the Kharj irrigation project, south-east of Riyadh, which was described as 'the first step toward wider assistance to the Saudi Arabian Government by the company in ventures not connected with the production of oil'.[43] The project established a pattern for subsequent ARAMCO–government developmental co-operation, as will be obvious to anyone familiar with the post-war Kingdom.

CASOC's involvement in urban water supply was also a response to a security consideration, as perceived both by the King and the company. Modernisation and development in a desert country are more than fostering security by settling the bedouin, paying them increasingly generous subsidies, or recruiting them into the National

Guard. As the cities expand in an era of rising expectations, so are they likely to become centres of disaffection. In 1940, when CASOC began drilling for water south-east of Jeddah, in Wadi Fatima, drinking water for the poorer classes and washing water for the more affluent was being provided by shallow wells near the city. Those who could afford it purchased condensed sea water from a small government-operated plant, and the weekly Khedivial Mail Line steamer brought Nile water, which must have been relatively free of affluents then, for distribution to the foreign community at the cost of porterage only.[44] Eight years later, the American minister was to write that

> a walk through the streets of Jidda affords ample demonstration of the fact that the King is now devoting an important part of his revenues to the Hejaz. Work on roads, harbour development and civil improvement is proceeding. For the first time in the history of the town, the inhabitants of Jidda have an unlimited supply of pure drinking water which is furnished at absolutely no cost to them.[45]

None the less, the period before oil came fully on stream to fuel post-war reconstruction was one of enormous difficulty. The establishment of the oil industry added to the difficulty, for oil imposed its own priorities and responsibilities, and was a voracious consumer of trained manpower – to produce, administer, monitor and defend it. It was essential that all of those processes be in Saudi Arabian hands as soon as possible, but that meant that many of King Abd al-Aziz's goals, and especially the trees, gardens and farms, would not be achieved in his lifetime. In July 1944, when he met with CASOC's Floyd Ohlinger at Al-Kharj, his frustration must have been especially acute. The oasis was one of Saudi Arabia's best hopes for increased production of foodstuffs which would eliminate the risks and costs of shipping. Yet there were serious food shortages in the Kingdom, a dearth of forage, continued drought, thinning flocks – and with them the threat of starvation and tribal looting. In time, the Middle East Supply Center, the Anglo-American joint venture in the Suez Canal Zone, would adjust its food delivery schedule to meet the emergency. For the moment, CASOC vehicles distributed food, advanced the payment of $500,000 scheduled for 1944 (under the revised concession agreement of 1939), and made a further advance of $1,000,000 to allow the government to approach the tight and high-priced commercial food market.[46] The *suq al-aswad* (the black market) flourished and legitimate markets were empty, waiting to be replenished from Europe. As one observer noted, 'the bazaars are bare; building and expansion are held up owing to the lack of imported materials; transport is at a low ebb owing to the lack of motor vehicles and engines; everything is used up and worn out'.[47]

For the House of Saud, economic uncertainties were unremitting and burdensome, but so were security concerns. The coming of peace, and a modest improvement in Saudi–Egyptian relations, encouraged Hashimite irredentist rhetoric aimed at establishing Abd al-Aziz's unfitness to rule. Exhortations to rise against Saudi corruption and oppression appeared in Mecca, even on the pillars of the shrine of the *Kaaba*. The rhetoric was provided by Emir Abdullah ibn Hussain of Trans-Jordan and by the Iraqi Foreign Minister, Fadhil Jamali. Evidence suggests that the posters and leaflets were a crude Iraqi attempt to foster Hejazi opposition to the Saudi regime and to return relations between Cairo and Riyadh to their 'normal' level of animosity.[48] King Abd al-Aziz saw a British as well as a Hashimite hand in these activities, which reinforced his decision to seek a fuller American partnership in development. Evidence of subversive activity had some role in deciding the forms that 'oil-fueled' development should take.

Thus, for example, the Dammam–Riyadh railroad. When the representatives of Bechtel Brothers McCone International met with the King late in 1946 to discuss the project, they (rather piously) emphasised the need 'to meet His Majesty's objectives with the greatest possible economy to the Saudi Arabian Government'. The King's response was that economy was not a prime objective. The country needed a reliable communications and transportation system. Neither camel nor truck was adequate. The only solution was a railway linking Riyadh to deep water, and it should be built with all possible speed. To the King, true unity – the welding together of his country with indestructible bonds – required trustworthy communications 'to maintain the people of Nejd and . . . ensure the effectiveness of central government authority to prevent the old regime of intertribal strife from again destroying that unity by default of such a central authority'.[49] The same logic which produced reluctance to rebuild the Hejaz railway fortified the King's resolve to establish rail communications between his capital and the oilfields. The railway was an instrumentality of security – in the right hands.

In pressing ahead with the railroad project, according to an American observer,

> the King considers his government to be in a favourable position to liquidate all foreseeable obligations from oil royalties, and therefore he regards it only his own business how his revenues are to be expended. There is little which can be said at this time which would gainsay this point of view.[50]

It was not so much a pattern of development as an attitude regarding the process which became operative at this time. Many years would pass before that attitude would be questioned.

The Onset of Better Times, 1945–46

Throughout the war, the King was provided with translations of both Allied and Axis broadcasts, and often listened to the Arabic services of both sides. He therefore had a clear idea when Saudi Arabian development could be accelerated. A harbinger of better, or at least different, times was the manager of the Swiss trade office for the Near East, who arrived in Jeddah in June 1945. If it is true that 'pas d'argent, pas de Suisses', the period of austerity was nearly over.[51] Where the *argent* should be expended, in the view of King Abd al-Aziz, was identified in a memorandum by K. S. Twitchell which was sent to the Department of State in mid-1945. Whether he had become the King's *alter ego* or an earnest, indeed devout litmus paper test of the intentions of the House of Saud is of less consequence than the unerring capacity of this American mining engineer to translate the King's objectives into proposals. By 1945, Twitchell was associated with the Saudi Arabian American Development Company, a subsidiary of the American Eastern Corporation, the objective of which was 'to promote local industry, improve local conditions and develop trade with the United States'. To put it another way, the objective was to do for Nejd, Hejaz, Asir and Jebel Shammar what oil was doing for Hasa. The memorandum requested assistance in securing information on:

1. US coastguard aids to navigation.
2. Water, light, power and sewage, with layouts for towns of up to 25,000 population.
3. The commercial drying and canning of fish, the extraction of shark oil, the curing of shark skins for export, and the preparations of shark skins for the Chinese market.

4. Preparation of rock salt for the world market, the location of potential markets and the preparation of salt for table use.
5. US markets for hides and skins, carpet wool and camel hair.
6. US government plans for financing farm equipment purchases.
7. Factories for the manufacture of matches.
8. Curing and packaging dates.
9. Coastwise shipping regulations.
10. Construction of wharves and piers for ships having a draft of up to thirty feet.[52]

Had Abd al-Aziz the prospect of less money, and were his security concerns less worrisome than they were in 1945–46, these modest proposals might have set Saudi Arabia on the path toward a more balanced economy than could be envisaged until the petrodollar revolution of 1974. A few months after Hiroshima, the real Saudi Arabian priorities came to light in negotiations with Bechtel Brothers McCone International for the construction of the projects shown in Table 2.1.[53]

In addition, of course, there was the vast ARAMCO-sponsored programme of infrastructure development for oil-related operations, including the Trans-Arabian Pipeline which virtually leapt off the drawing board in 1947.[54] By early 1948, the Saudi Arabian government was spending $500,000 per month on Bechtel Corporation 'goods and services' alone.[55] It was a far cry indeed from the time, only fifteen years before, when a concession payment of £30,000 was regarded as the bridge between disaster and survival. Inevitably, and happily, the King and his government began to hear from more remote settlements, those 'hinterland locales' which 'pass by unnoticed

Table 2.1: Projects Negotiated Between Saudi Arabian Government and Bechtel Brothers McCone International

(self-liquidating)	Jeddah water supply	$892,000
	Mecca electrification	$805,000
	Riyadh electrification	$1,310,000
	Cement plant	$2,925,000
(non-self-liquidating)	Jeddah harbour	$1,170,000
	Irrigation, water conservation	$1,000,000
	Hospitals – Taif	$1,380,000
	– Riyadh	$2,530,000
	Transportation – Railway	$32,418,000
	or – Highway	$13,075,000

in a pre-occupied Saudi bureaucracy ... nonetheless ... they constitute an expression of public opinion, however embryonic, endeavouring to make itself effective'.[56] Jizan sought assistance in completing a water project; Shaqra (Washm) petitioned for a municipal hospital; Tabuk wanted a bus system, especially to link up with Medina, 371 miles away; Wejd needed a new salt-water condenser; and Yanbu, 'unequalled in its vociferousness', wanted virtually everything.[57]

By 1948, the year of the disaster of Palestine, with all its implications for resource allocation and development, to say nothing of deprivation and alienation, it was undoubted that King Abd al-Aziz had 'made known to the world the fact that Saudi Arabia no longer stands hesitant at the crossroads but is now moving ahead rapidly on the path of modernization'.[58] Yet he had not lost sight of the objectives which were consequences of his capture of the Hejaz little more than two decades earlier. Despite the frenetic pace of change, the leader of the House of Saud was

> motivated to launch this comprehensive programme of public works primarily by a desire to make the Moslem world aware of the fact that he is keenly conscious of his responsibility as protector of the Holy Places and that he is doing everything in his power to provide improved facilities for the pilgrims coming to his country ... over three-quarters of the funds committed for the large projects to be undertaken by Bechtel will be spent in the Hejaz. King Abdul Aziz evidently hopes to knit Hejaz more firmly into his kingdom by removing the grounds for criticism that has been evident in the past among some Hejazis to the effect that Hejaz was being neglected in favour of Nejd and Al-Hasa in government schemes for modernization and construction of public works.[59]

The interplay of international factors with concern for domestic security, which characterised King Abd al-Aziz's economic policies during the period of hardship, was to remain a characteristic of later economic policy.

Notes

Author's Note

Two recent articles have covered some of the terrain traversed by this study. However, they more or less look from the outside in, rather than focusing on forces which shaped Saudi attitudes and policies in the era of King Abd al-Aziz. For Philby's early contacts with the King, see Daniel Silverfarb, 'The Philby Mission to Ibn Sa'ud, 1917–18', *Journal of Contemporary History*, vol. 14 (1979), pp. 269–86. See also Barry Rubin, 'Anglo-American Relations in Saudi Arabia, 1941–45', *Journal of Contemporary History*, vol. 14 (1979), pp. 253–67. Rubin attempts to play down British interest in Saudi Arabia, and attributes American concern over a future British role to anti-imperialist zeal and to inexperience. These conclusions do not stand up to analysis. Moreover, King Abd al-Aziz's mistrust of the British and their Hashimite clients is ignored by Rubin. A third relevant but very specialised study recently published is J. E. Peterson, 'South West Arabia and the British During World War I', *Journal of South Asia and Middle Eastern Studies*, vol. II, no. 4 (Summer 1979), pp. 18–37.

1. The National Archives, Washington DC (afterwards NA), 890F. 00/53, 9 March 1940, American Legation Cairo (Judge Bert Fish) to the Secretary of State.

2. Abd al-Aziz ibn Saud was generally considered to be Sultan of Nejd (an imprecise usage, because it included Hasa) until early 1926, when a link was formed with Asir, as a protectorate. The Sultanate of Nejd and its Dependencies became the Kingdom of Nejd and its Dependencies later in 1927, a year after Hejaz was wrested from King Ali ibn Hussain. Abd al-Aziz was thus first King of Hejaz, then King of Nejd and its Dependencies. Some Arabists demoted Hejaz to dependency status, while newspapers were prone to identify the entirety of his domain as the Kingdom of Hejaz. In 1932 such problems were eliminated with the proclamation of the Kingdom of Saudi Arabia, ending what Shaikh Fuad Hamza had styled 'the Dual Monarchy'.

3. The quotation is from *The Near East and India*, the Jeddah correspondent of which was Philby. He was an energetic promoter of the House of Saud – and of Philby. In urging that the United States join Britain, Holland, Switzerland, Turkey and the Soviet Union in recognising the Kingdom of Hejaz and of Nejd and its Dependencies (the Soviet Union having been the first to do so), Philby wrote to the American consul in Aden that 'it would be a very good thing if you could do anything to help in that direction as your country is easily first in the commercial field in these parts thanks to your motor car factories with which no-one can compete'. When Shaikh Fuad Hamza, Acting Director of the Foreign Ministry, wrote at about the same time to Secretary of State Kellogg on the subject of recognition, his request was based upon progress in modernisation, public health, membership in the International Postal Union and Hejaz as a place of pilgrimage for 130,000 persons from overseas, 'including American subjects from the Philippines'. NA, 890F. 00/8, 23 January 1928; 890F. 01/8, 29 September 1928, American Consulate Aden (Clayson W. Aldridge) to the Secretary of State.

4. NA, 690F. 003, 26 May 1926, American Consulate Aden (J. Loder Park) to Department of State. The customs establishment was under the direction of Shaikh Muhammad Bataweel, who clung to his Turkish title, *Jumruk Mudiri*. He was known to be 'just and reasonable' and the customs house was regarded as efficient, indeed 'better than in Turkish days because the Arab is less brazen in his personal requirements from his clientele'.

5. In 1932, it was estimated that King al-Aziz and his family either owned over 550 of the 770 motor vehicles operative in Hejaz, or had a financial share of the transport companies which did. NA, 846A. 9111/44, American Consulate Aden (Walmsley) to the Secretary of State.

6. There was more zeal in Aden, whence it was reported that 'the eyes of the entire Mohammedan world are focused on the Holy City and the erection of an American radio station would undoubtedly become a topic of discussion in many far corners of the globe'. NA, 980F. 008, 23 January 1928, American Consulate Aden (Aldridge) to the Secretary of State.

7. NA, 890F. 74/1, 3 March 1930, American Consulate Aden (Cloyce K. Huston)

to the Secretary of State. It was considered that the network would be used for military, i.e. security and administrative, purposes, 'cases in which news, orders and other communications have hitherto necessarily been carried by the racing camel'.

8. NA 890F. 00/8, 23 January 1928, American Consulate Aden (Aldridge) to the Secretary of State.

9. NA, 890. 01/13, 19 February 1929, American Legation Cairo (Franklin Mott Gunther) to the Secretary of State. Shaikh Hafiz Wahba advised Gunther that 'a considerable number' of government-sponsored and private students from the Kingdoms were attending American schools and universities in Lebanon, Syria and Egypt.

10. NA, 890F. 00/53, 9 March 1940, American Legation Cairo (Fish) to the Secretary of State.

11. NA, 890F. 63A/&, 18 August1931, American Legation Cairo (W. M. Jardine) to Wallace Murray, Near Eastern Affairs.

12. Of all the countries he visited, he was most impressed by the vigour and sense of national purpose of the Soviet Union.

13. NA, 846A. 9111/51, 5 April 1933, American Consulate Aden (Walmsley) to the Secretary of State; 800. 70/52, 16 October 1935, American Consulate Aden (Leo J. Callanan) to the Secretary of State.

14. NA, 883 00 General Conditions/46, 18 November 1935, American Legation Cairo (Fish) to the Secretary of State.

15. NA, 890F. 00/33, 9 March 1940, American Legation Cairo (Fish) to the Secretary of State; 890F. 51/8–1049, 18 August 1949, American Embassy Jedda (Heyward G. Hill) to the Secretary of State. In 1940 it was estimated that the Saudi Arabian government owed £25,000 to British, £25,000 to Polish and £15,000 to Italian armament manufacturers. The Russo–German division of Poland may have been considered as cancelling that part of the debt, although the free Polish legation in Cairo wanted the money for operating expenses. The £30,000 due to Soviets for shoddy petroleum products was still outstanding in 1940. By 1949 the *surrah*, or Ramadan payments of subsidies and 'personal salaries' (cash gifts from King Abd al-Aziz) to the tribes, was budgeted at Saudi Riyals 10,613,890 but went higher because of poor harvests, sparse flocks and other drought-related miseries.

16. There was speculation that the terms included an option to rebuild the Hejaz railway. NA 841. 00 PR/222, 7 March 1932, American Embassy London (Weekly Political, Economic and Financial Report) to the Secretary of State. 800F. 001 Ibn Saud/7, undated, American Legation Baghdad (Alexander K. Sloan) to the Secretary of State. Some analysts ascribed the renewal of British interest in Saudi Arabia to a forceful reassertion of the Iranian claim to sovereignty over Bahrain. The American minister in Baghdad, speculating on negotiations between King Abd al-Aziz and British officials, concluded that H. St John B. (Hajj Abdullah) Philby's public stance of hostility toward his country's Middle Eastern policy was a cover for the promotion of a new British-led Arab alliance, suggesting that 'it is in the purse of this clever merchant that the truth can be found'. In fact, within a few months Philby would be assisting officials of Standard Oil of California in their negotiations with the Saudi Arabian government.

17. See NA, 890B. 00/22, 9 July 1932, American Consulate General Jerusalem (P. Knabenshue) to the Secretary of State. Shaikh Hamad ibn Rafada's base was the small coastal settlement of Wejh, which became a Saudi military garrison once the long-lived insurgency was finally quelled.

18. NA, 846A. 9111/49, 13 December 1932, American Consulate Aden (W. N. Walmsley Jr) to the Secretary of State. Which was carried out 'in such detail . . . that it is safe to assume that a European familiar with the country's problems was the author of the plan'. It was published in the Mecca official journal *Umm al Qura*, which was the most important printed source of information on developments within the Kingdom.

19. NA, 890F. 00/53, 9 March 1940, American Legation Cairo (Fish) to the Secretary of State. The new system provided greatly improved accountability but some years later it was still possible to observe that 'the country's budgetless finance is conducted on "rolling credit", that is, rolling through each Moslem year until the pilgrimage season facilitates an annual payoff effected through the local Dutch Bank at the time when money is plentiful'. It was then that Philby's Ford agency was paid (approximately £50,000 in 1940) as well as 'the leading Jedda firm of Aly Reza, which imports large quantities of foodstuffs from abroad on government account'.

20. NA, 890F. 00/43, 12 April 1933, American Consulate Aden (Walmsley) to the Secretary of State.

21. For example, see NA, 890F. 77/12–1646, 16 December 1946, American Legation Jeddah (Harlan B. Clark) to the Secretary of State, reporting on the King's conversation with Earl F. English, a representative of Bechtel Brothers McCone International, Inc.

22. NA, 890F. 00/43, 12 April 1933, American Consulate Aden (Walmsley) to the Secretary of State.

23. NA, 890F. 6363 Standard Oil/17, 24 June 1933, American Consulate Aden (Walmsley) to the Secretary of State. Three years later Petroleum Development Western Arabia (the Iraq Petroleum Company) signed an agreement for a concession in Hejaz. It cost £50,000 plus 7,500 gold pounds annual rent, but its principal – and unstated – purpose was to exclude the Italians. NA, F.W. 811. 503190 F/9, 13 April 1940, Memorandum of conversation (Wallace Murray), Near Eastern Affairs. *Umm al Qura* concluded its coverage with the thought that 'under our most enterprising King we have entered a new world'. NA, 846A. 9111/51, 5 April 1933, American Consulate Aden (Walmsley) to the Secretary of State.

24. NA, 846A. 9111/51, 5 April 1933, American Consulate Aden (Walmsley) to the Secretary of State.

25. NA, 890F. 6363, Standard Oil Co./9, 26 March 1933, American Consulate Aden (Walmsley) to the Secretary of State.

26. Announcement of the Standard Oil concession was followed by the award of a 'sweeping' concession to Philby's Ford agency. Referring to it and the railroad project, the closest official American observer concluded that, if one succeeded, it would assure the other's failure. The Iron Horse *versus* automobile/truck/bus rivalry would continue in Saudi Arabia until the completion of the Dammam–Riyadh railway (see above). Philby's string of commercial successes, to include his key role in the oil concession negotiations, inevitably brought the sincerity of his conversion to Islam into question. NA, 890F. 797/3, 28 June 1933, American Consulate Aden (Walmsley) to the Secretary of State. Such doubts could be fortified by some of his contributions to *The Near East and India.* At the time of the Ford concession agreement he wrote that the subjects of King Abd al-Aziz 'are extremely fanatical and look upon all occidental devices as instruments of the Devil against which all true Muslims will raise eternal objection ... [but] should these schemes prove successful to the extent of removing some of the wrinkles from the stomachs of his followers, it is believed all antagonism to occidental "kultur" will be removed, and the country may swing its sandy door a little wider'. NA, 890F. 6363, 1 August 1933, American Consulate Aden (Walmsley) to the Secretary of State.

27. Francis B. Loomis of Standard Oil thought it would be possible to request 'the Arabian Government to collect a special tax, the proceeds of which would be used to defray the expenses of construction'. It was a singular example of ignorance of the realities of Arabian life, harsh enough in the best of times, to say nothing of the Depression's effects. Surprisingly enough, K. S. Twitchell was present when this statement was made. NA, 890F. 6363, Standard Oil Co./4, Memorandum of conversation, Near Eastern Affairs (Villard).

28. NA, 890F. 6363/10, 1 November 1932, Memorandum of conversation, Near Eastern Affairs (Villard).

29. NA, 890F. 63/8, 25 July 1935, American Consulate Aden (Callanan) to the Secretary of State. The concession permitted exploration for, and exploitation of, all minerals except petroleum (which became the uneconomic province of the Iraq Petroleum Company) in an area from the Trans-Jordan frontier to a line running east–north-east from Birk on the Asir coast. The interior boundary line ran just west of Medina, roughly parallel to the Red Sea coast.

30. The mining syndicate expected to have from two to four more American engineers shortly. It was estimated that five or ten Americans would be sent to Eastern Arabia if the decision was taken to drill a second well.

31. The Ali Reza Zainal Company had operated a small steamship line for many years before the Saudi Arabian government purchased two vessels from the Lebanese National Shipping Company and installed diesel engines on a number of large dhows. NA, 890F. 50/1, 8 August 1934, Consulate General Jerusalem (Palmer) to the Secretary of State.

32. NA, 890F. 6363 Standard Oil Co. 102, 5 July 1938, Memorandum of Conversation (Wallace Murray), Department of State.

33. NA, 690F. 9415/1, 27 March 1939, American Legation Cairo (Fish) to the Secretary of State.

34. The British government was especially concerned over the possibility of a German breakthrough in relations with Saudi Arabia. Arrangements were made, for example, to block the account of approximately $750,000 that King Abd al-Aziz had in the Bank Misr, Cairo, as well as the *Awqaf* money which was to be transferred to Mecca. It was also noted that the Saudi fleet of twelve aircraft (mostly commercial) was manned by 'native' pilots under the guidance of a Russian pilot and two Russian mechanics, and for the most part based at Jeddah, where the hangar and field were built 'as a friendly gesture' by the Italian government. NA, 890F. 001 Ibn Saud/25, 11 March 1940, American Legation Cairo (Fish) to the Secretary of State. British authorities made much of the provision of asylum in Riyadh to Rashid Ali al-Gailani, leader of the Golden Square rising in Baghdad and (allegedly) a collaborator of the Germans. However, King Abd al-Aziz disapproved of Rashid Ali's action. He would not refuse asylum to an Arab, while being adamant on the exclusion of Dr Grobba, even though their interest in Saudi Arabia stemmed from a chain of events in which they were collaborators.

35. NA, 890F. 61A/68, 10 December 1942, Report of the US Agricultural Mission to Saudi Arabia. 890F. 75/1A and 2, 6 and 15 July, 25 November 1943, Secretary of State to American Legation Jeddah, American Legation Jeddah (Moose) to Secretary of State. Mr Moose also asked that a sporting rifle be secured for the King but warned that 'since he already has a number of guns only a good rifle would make a favourable impression'.

36. Twitchell, NA, 890F. 00/1–648, 6 January 1948. Today the Kingdom's proved and probable reserves stand above 150 billion barrels, the largest share of the Middle East's 376 billion, OPEC's 474 billion and the world's 657 million barrels.

37. NA, 890F. 00/33, 9 March 1940, American Legation Cairo (Fish) to the Secretary of State.

38. NA, F.00/5–2645, 26 May 1945, American Consulate Dhahran (Sands) to the Secretary of State. Growing unrest among ARAMCO's Saudi workforce, based upon inadequate housing, a belief that Indian and Iraqi workers were given preferential treatment, dissatisfaction with medical services and the desire for a shorter working day during Ramadan (*inter alia*) prompted the Sulaiman–Yassin mission. Shaikh Yusuf stated that 'the government is particularly concerned that labourers in this country do not learn to strike, or to employ other Western labour measures, the obvious corollary being that if they are kept satisfied these devices will not occur to them'. But strike they did, first 137 drillers and then 2,000 others only two months later, when tempers and temperatures were high. Neither the government, the workers, nor the company were organised to deal with the situation. ARAMCO did not wish to

negotiate with the five articulate Hejazi clerical workers nominated to the arbitration committee by Emir Khalid al-Sudairi, the Governor of Qatif. The Emir wanted to return the workers to their jobs as ardently as ARAMCO (and probably most workers) did. The negotiations eventually took place between the Emir and ARAMCO, based on the King's intervention calling for equal treatment for all workers and company willingness to raise basic salaries by twenty per cent. Within a year, over-all working conditions had greatly improved. NA, 890F. 5095/7–2845 and 8–1345, 28 July and 13 August 1945, American Consulate Dhahran (W. W. Birge Jr) to the Secretary of State. It is interesting to note that, when fixed custom duties were increased 100 per cent five months later, for the first time since 1938, the Saudi Riyal had declined in exchange value from 25 to the English sovereign (1938) to 65 to the sovereign. Also, fixed customs duties were for the most part on foodstuffs and other consumer goods, so the cost of living was in a steep climb. NA, 690F. 113/11–1445, 14 November 1945, American Legation Jeddah (Sands) to Secretary of State.

39. The first significant US government assistance had been a 1943 loan, repayment of which was deferred until five years after the war, of 5,167,000 ounces of US Treasury silver, which was minted into Saudi Riyal coins at the US mint and shipped to Jeddah. With the loan came a plan for a Central Bank, patterned after the Chinese Stabilization Bank and, inevitably, a proposal to send a US financial expert to the Kingdom. Both proposals were received by Emir Faisal, who negotiated the loan in Washington in the company of his brother, Emir Khalid, and Shaikh Hafiz Wahba, with the undertaking that they would be transmitted to his father for consideration. NA, 890F. 0011/103, 1 November 1943, Memorandum of conversation, Department of State (A. A. Berle); 890F. 516/1–1944, 19 January 1944, Memorandum of conversation, Department of State, Department of Treasury. At the time the British subsidy was about six times the estimated value of US Lend-Lease, and there was 'always the danger that the British will request a *quid pro quo*'. It was therefore urged that joint subsidisation should be on a 50/50 basis, 'as was done recently in providing arms and military equipment to Saudi Arabia for the maintenance of law and order there'. The principal argument in favour of this course of action has an especially nostalgic ring in the wake of the June 1979 OPEC meeting in Geneva and as cars line up at gas pumps all over America. It stated that 'the military authorities of this government are understood to regard the Saudi Arabian oil deposits as essential to the interests of the United States. *Furthermore, in view of diminishing oil reserves in this country, it may be necessary to draw directly or indirectly upon Saudi Arabian oil for normal peace-time needs* [emphasis added]. It would contribute, of course, to the safeguarding of American interests in this concession if the Government of Saudi Arabia were indebted to this Government rather than to the Government of another country'. NA, 890F. 51/4–144, 1 April 1944, Memorandum for Policy Committee, Near Eastern Affairs.

40. The 'facilities' were, of course, airfields and overflight rights, and as much for the prosecution of the peace as for the war. NA, 890F. 51/1–845, 22 December 1944, Department of State Memorandum for President Roosevelt.

41. NA, 890F. 51/5–2845, 28 May 1945. Memorandum of conversation (Assistant Secretary of State Dean Acheson). Secretary of the Interior Harold Ickes favoured a five-year loan beyond the expiry of Lend-Lease, if the British were to be forestalled from 'placing the U.S. in a secondary position' but feared congressional resistance based upon a perception of the loan being 'simply another way of advancing the interest of certain American oil companies'. NA, 890F. 51/1–845, 8 January 1945, Memorandum of conversation, Department of State.

42. NA, 890F. 6363, Standard Oil Co./102, 5 July 1938, Memorandum of conversation, Near Eastern Affairs (Murray).

43. NA, 890F. 6113.1, 22 July 1943, American Legation Jeddah (James S. Moose Jr) to Near Eastern Affairs (Paul Alling). CASOC employees at al-Kharj were on

very bad terms with the Egyptian agricultural mission there, but the latter's dissatisfaction with living conditions, doubtless exacerbated by comparison with the American situation, resulted in an early departure.

44. NA, 890F. 151/2, 21 March 1940, American Legation Cairo (Raymond A. Hare) to the Secretary of State.

45. NA, 890F. 00/1–648, 6 January 1948, American Legation Jeddah (Childs) to the Secretary of State.

46. NA, 890F. 24/7–744, 7 July 1944, Memorandum of telephone conversation (Moose–Leblicher), *Aide Memoire*, British Embassy (Washington) to the Department of State. It should be noted that the 1944 budget indicated estimated revenue as SR 36,500,000 and estimated expenditure as SR 108,768,220. NA, 890F. 51/56, 12 January 1944, American Legation Jeddah (Moose) to the Secretary of State.

47. *The Times*, 'Peace on the Persian Gulf', 22 December 1945. It was noted that a bag of sugar which cost 80 rupees in Bahrain commanded ten times that price on the Persian coast. Wartime changes in diet – after the stocks of Burmese rice were depleted, it was necessary to adapt to wheat – and the increase in the cost of living were the most difficult adjustments.

48. NA, 890F. 00/3–2146, 21 March 1946, American Legation Jeddah (William E. Eddy) to the Secretary of State; ibid. /5–2746, 21 June 1946 (William Sands); ibid. /6–1046, 25 June 1946 (William Sands). None the less, Colonel Eddy described King Abd al-Aziz as 'increasingly the vassal of the British', which suggests that the American representative was somewhat out of touch, as well as out of step. Two years later the Iraqis had the pleasure of providing a platform for Rashidi tribal leaders who had eluded the surveillance under which they were living in Riyadh. In assessing their statements that King Abd al-Aziz was unpopular because of his 'selfish conversion' of oil income, and that the regime would not survive his passing, the American minister noted that there was no serious opposition to the House of Saud. This was especially obvious in Nejd 'where the King's intricate system of tribal relationships has worked well for some time'. As for Hejazis who waxed nostalgic over the Hashimites, they 'have never had a chance to observe the mixed blessings of Hashimite–British rule in Iraq and Trans-Jordan'. The King lived simply and, if he indulged his sons with motor cars, the cost was small by contrast to funds committed to development. It was the American view that development progress was greater than it would have been if Saudi Arabia had a constitutional government, which would mean 'a vast army of civil servants whose venality is proverbial'. NA, 890F. 00/1–648, 6 January 1948, American Legation Jeddah (J. Rives Childs) to the Secretary of State.

49. Shaikh Abdullah Sulaiman told Rives Childs several hours earlier that the railroad was 'wholly uneconomic and that a good highway system could be built for the entire kingdom for less than the Dammam–Riyadh railway would cost'. NA, 890F. 77/12–1646, 16 December 1946, American Legation Jeddah (Harlan B. Clark) to the Secretary of State.

50. Ibid.

51. NA, 690F. 5415/6–245, 2 June 1945, American Legation Jeddah (Eddy) to the Secretary of State.

52. NA, 690F. 1171/7–1545, 15 July 1945, American Legation to the Secretary of State.

53. NA, 890F. 51/9–1346, 13 September 1946, Department of State office Memorandum (Richard Sanger). Although the extension of the railway from Riyadh to Jeddah was discussed, and the route surveyed in the last years of King Abd al-Aziz's life, the enthusiasm which had characterised Emir Saud's meetings on the subject, first with President Truman and Secretary of State Byrnes in January 1947, and then with Secretary of State Marshall and Loy Henderson a month later, had evaporated. There was no further possibility of an Export–Import Bank loan, ARAMCO sought to avoid further involvement, and cost-effectiveness arguments

were, at the time, compelling. NA, 890F. 51/2–1847, 18 February 1948, Memorandum of conversation, Department of State. The Bechtel Corporation, it should be noted, produced statistics in 1947 supporting the theory that the railroad was more feasible in economic terms than highway construction. NA, 890F. 6363/2–1747, 17 February 1947, American Legation Jeddah (Childs) to the Secretary of State.

54. Ibid.

55. NA, 890F. 00/1–648, 6 January 1948, American Legation Jeddah (Childs) to the Secretary of State.

56. NA, 890F. 00/1–3149, 31 January 1949, American Legation Jeddah (Childs) to the Secretary of State.

57. Ibid. On Yanbu 'no similar settlement is as successful in making itself heard, admittedly not always effectively, above the din of everyday Jidda–Mecca affairs, reminding harassed government officials of its existence, desires and requirements'. The 1948 wish list includes a central telephone exchange, a water system linking up the springs of Wadi Yanbu and Nakhl, two doctors (one woman) and authorisation for the debarkation of pilgrims (who then could only use Yanbu as a point of departure for home), despite the water shortage, since they were 'not as yet denuded of funds'.

58. NA, 890F. 15/1–1948, 19 January 1948, American Legation Jeddah (Childs) to the Secretary of State.

59. Ibid.

3 The Mode of Production in the Arab Gulf Before the Discovery of Oil

MOHAMED G. RUMAIHI

Contemporary Relevance of the Pre-oil Mode of Production

This article is written in the belief that the social relations which exist among the peoples of the Arab Gulf today are heavily influenced by the mode of production which obtained in that area before the discovery of oil. It contends that an understanding of that mode of production is essential to an understanding of the social, economic and political structures which exist today.

The framework within which this study is situated is set by the belief that the mode of production in any society imposes a certain pattern of relations of production, and that these in turn provide the guidelines within which social, political and legal relations develop. The predominant values and moral principles can also be traced back to the necessities imposed by the mode of production and its resultant relations. By studying the mode and relations of production we are able to identify the main components of the social structure.

Many of the most crucial aspects of the social, political and legal structures, however, are determined not by the mode of production currently existing but by a previous mode of production which still exerts its influence. This, the writer contends, is relevant to what has occurred in the Arab Gulf. Although the introduction of the oil economy transformed the mode of production, integrating this region closely into the international capitalist system, the effects which this had on the social, political and legal structures were limited – confined to superficial adaptations. For historical, economic and technical reasons the populations of the Gulf states have not been central to the establishment or maintenance of the oil industry, nor to the related fields of economic activity. In many respects the introduction of the oil economy was a foreign imposition on Arab Gulf societies – it was operated mainly by foreigners, with production geared largely to foreign interests. The source of many of the problems with which Gulf societies are currently confronted may, the writer contends, be found in the alienation of those societies from the new mode of production – the tension arising from the social, legal and political structures relevant to one mode of production continuing to dominate social relations while the economy has in fact shifted into a new mode of production.

It is hoped, therefore, that a study of the mode and relations of production before the initiation of oil production will shed some light on the social phenomena prevailing today within the societies of the Gulf.

The Traditional Economy

The geography of the Gulf area – the bare nature of the land and the lack of rain – meant that Gulf peoples traditionally had a hard struggle against nature. To earn a living from a barren environment was difficult. The primary resource upon which the economies came to concentrate was the sea, which supported pearl-diving, fishing and trading activities. On a more limited basis, agriculture was carried out in the oases, with nomadic production predominating in the inland areas. Trade played a significant role in the economy, whether internally, between villages and the trading centres, or externally, between the Gulf area and India, Iran, Africa and Iraq.

The element of the traditional economy upon which this article will concentrate is the pearl industry. As the pearl industry constituted the main base of the economy in the nineteenth and early twentieth centuries, the pattern of relations of production within this industry was crucial in setting the framework of social relations generally. The centrality of the pearl industry is reflected in the Gulf proverb, 'Pearl diving is a habit, praying is worship of God' (these are synonyms in Arabic, '*al-salat ibadah wa al-ghaws adah*'). By linking pearl-diving synonymously with the act of worship the proverb emphasises the importance of pearl-diving to Gulf peoples. Moreover, early Arab historians referred to the Gulf area as a place where pearls could be found,[1] with generation after generation inheriting the job of pearl-diving as their main source of living.

Estimates of the size of the Gulf pearl industry in the early years of this century have varied. The main centres were Kuwait and Bahrain, and S. Mallory provides a picture of the flourishing state of the Kuwaiti pearl industry at this time: 'Kuwait was an important centre for pearl-diving and in 1911 there were eight hundred ships with approximately twenty thousand men on board. The men were not only Kuwait natives, they came from different places.'[2] It seems likely that this estimate of the size of the industry was reasonably accurate. In the 1920s the Bahraini pearling fleet seems to have consisted of some five hundred ships.[3] The rapid decline of the pearl industry began in the 1930s with the international monetary crisis and the growth of the cultivated pearl industry (primarily in Japan); the decline gathered momentum during the 1940s until in the 1950 Bahrain population census no one was recorded as being employed in the pearl industry (the same was true of Kuwait).[4]

The details given here of the operation of the pearling industry are taken mainly from the case of Bahrain. Most aspects, however, hold true for the pearling industries in the other Gulf states. The main diving season was from the beginning of June to the beginning of October, the water then being at its warmest, and was known locally as *al-ghaws al-kabir*. The ruler normally issued a proclamation fixing the date of the start of the season. There were, in addition, some minor seasons, such as the *khanjiah* in the few weeks before the major season began, and the *riddah* or *ardidah* covering a few weeks in the winter. Most of those active in the pearling industry, however, worked only in the major season, and so most of the labour force was active for only one-third of the year. For the rest of the year, unless they were able to find some work on the land, the divers remained idle. The annual income of a large proportion of the Gulf labour force was thus the product of four months' work.

Each pearling boat was under the command of a captain (*nokhudah*) and would have a team of divers (*ghawas*), usually from ten to 40 in number, depending upon the capacity of the dhow. There would be an equivalent number of pullers (*sib*), whose responsibility was to raise the diver from the sea bed. Sometimes in the larger boats there were assistant pullers (*radif*), who helped when the diver was working in deep waters. The complement of the ship was made up by one or two boys known as *tabbab*, who provided the captain with meals and refreshments. Some of the latter would in due course train as divers. The choice of pearl beds (*fasht*) for fishing depended to a large extent on the captain's experience, although divers who had a considerable knowledge of the pearl beds advised him in his choice.

The working day of the diver started at sunrise and continued until sunset. Each diver had two ropes; the one on which he descended was weighted with a large stone to take him quickly to the bottom, and he carried the second rope with him, tied around the waist. As soon as he reached the bottom the puller raised the weighted rope ready for the next dive; the second was used to pull him to the surface. He carried an open-weave basket around his neck, in which the oysters were placed. On his nose he wore a clip which kept the water out of his nose and enabled him to hold his breath longer and at the same time left both hands free for work. Sometimes the diver would stuff cotton or beeswax in his ears for protection. He also wore a set of leather finger thimbles to protect his fingers from coral and other sharp objects. Apart from these items, and a loincloth, the diver was naked.

The diver, once on the bottom, collected as many shells as he could, and when ready to ascend signalled on the rope tied around him. The puller, standing on the gunwhale, having received the signal, immediately raised the diver by means of the rope. Once raised to the surface, the diver's catch (an average of 8 to 12 shells) was taken from him and he rested for a few moments by hanging on to the side of the boat, after which he repeated his dive. The time spent below the surface, which was normally one minute, was known as *tabah*. After completing ten dives the men came on board to rest. Ten dives would normally occupy about three-quarters of an hour, after which the diver was dragged out of the water and manhandled to some spot on the ship to recover, often looking more dead than alive. After a period of rest and refreshment, usually coffee, he began again. The diver usually performed 40 to 60 dives per day in waters ranging in depth from 30 to 70 feet. For the deeper dives the puller was given assistance in raising the diver.

The diver experienced great danger and discomfort not only from the attacks of sharks and sawfish but also from the masses of stinging jellyfish. The diver often suffered physical damage as a result of driving himself past the limits of human endurance. The 'bends' were a common affliction amongst the divers and produced severe pains in the joints, paralysis or even death. Suppuration of the ear drums and rheumatism were also common amongst divers. If the diver stayed down too long he often suffered from severe bleeding from the ears and nose. A few seconds' neglect by the pullers could mean the difference between life and death to the diver and therefore great co-operation and attention were needed. The divers never ate while working and took only small sips of either coffee or water, as food would cause nausea.

As soon as he had finished diving for the day, it was customary for the diver to have a meagre meal of fish, dates and rice and then go to sleep. These small meals were generally insufficient to sustain the energies of the divers throughout the season. The small meals, combined with the extremely poor living conditions aboard the boats, took their toll of the divers' strength and by the end of the diving season they were usually in poor physical condition.

The shells collected were usually left overnight so that they might be more easily opened at the start of the next day. The shells had been put into a pile in the middle of the deck as they were brought from the sea bed, so that no diver knew exactly which was his catch. The opening was performed with a small knife, the flesh searched for pearls and the empty shells and flesh thrown back into the sea.

Less than one-third of the shells opened yielded pearls, most of which were small and irregularly shaped. These pearls were known locally as *lulu* and were of comparatively small value. The next in size and value was known as *danah* and, whilst it was still of irregular shape, it was more valuable. The rarest and most prized of pearls was the *hasbah* which was large and perfectly formed. The captain watched the opening procedure closely so that no pearls were secreted. Stories were often told of divers swallowing a valuable pearl, but the experienced captain usually noticed this and recovered it by his own means. After the last shells were opened the captain then collected the pearls and tied them in a red flannel cloth which he put in his sea-chest or *bishtakhtah* on the poop deck. The business of the day's diving then began once more.

Finance for Pearl-diving and the Distribution of the Gains

The distribution of the gains from pearl-gathering was calculated on the basis of long-established practice. This practice in effect gave the main part of the gains to the merchants who financed the pearling trips and to the owners of the ships. Although the divers performed very difficult work and constituted the only element in the process which was actually producing wealth, their share in the product was minimal. While the Gulf did not experience feudalism in the European sense, the relationship between the divers and the merchants and shipowners was akin to a feudal relationship – the diver was trapped within a system of clearly defined duties and marginal rights, which gave him little opportunity of bettering his position and which effectively transferred the economic surplus into the hands of his masters.

The details given below about financing of trips and distribution of gains refer to major-season pearling; slightly different arrangements were made in the other seasons. The pearl-diving trip, *al-tarshah*, was financed in a number of ways. Most crucial to the whole operation, naturally, was the ownership of the boat. The boat could be owned by the captain, the *nokhudah*, or it could be owned by a merchant. Some merchants owned a considerable number of boats. The merchants who owned the boats could also be the dealers who bought the pearls at the end of the season to sell in international markets – in India, or else in Europe with the help of intermediaries. Such a dealer was known as a *tawwash*. Naturally, the social class to which the *nokhudah* and *tawwash* belonged was limited in number and effectively constituted the dominant class in society.

The running and financing of the pearl industry throughout its history proved to be disastrous socially to various sections of the community, but no one suffered more than those most directly involved in the pearl-gathering: divers, pullers, etc. The social impact of the pearl industry did not die with the pearl fleets, but long continued to cast its shadow over the lives of the former pearl industry employees. The evil of the system lay in the method in which the expeditions were financed.

The abuses of the system were made manifest at the lower level, namely with relation to the divers and pullers, who comprised the largest proportion of those employed in the industry and who virtually mortgaged their lives and livelihood to the pearl industry. This was due to the fact that they were not paid wages as such, but were entitled to a share in the profits, something which rarely enabled them even to cover the costs of their own subsistence.

A diver, starting the season, was usually given a cash payment, *salafiah* (credit), which was intended to support his family while he was away; at the end of the season, after the sale of the pearls, he was given another payment called *tisgam*, or maintenance, and in the winter, when no diving took place, he was given *kharjiyah*, pocket money, in anticipation of his diving for the same captain the following year.

All of these cash advances were recorded against the diver's name in the captain's logbook, but it was only very rarely that a diver would earn enough to cancel his debt to the captain. When a diver did not earn sufficient to cancel these debts, the amount outstanding was carried forward to the following year and interest charged upon it.

Having once taken an advance from the captain, a diver was compelled to work for that captain throughout the following season, and in effect the divers doomed themselves to work until their death in an effort to repay these debts. Until 1923, when the general reforms in the administration were started in Bahrain, even death was not an exit for the Bahrain diver, as his debts were then inherited by his sons or brothers, who were forced to enter the pearl industry themselves unless they had money or property with which to clear the debt. Some of the more inhuman of the captains would insist on marrying the widow of the diver as payment for the debts, and in doing so obtained for themselves the children of the diver to act as servants in the house and later to be trained as divers themselves.

The divers, however, were not the only people in debt, as the captains themselves were often forced to obtain financing from the merchants in the towns in order to equip and provision their boats and pay the advances to their divers. The shore merchants charged interest on their money and the captains passed this on, in turn, to their divers.

The charging of interest is contrary to Islamic law, but the merchants circumvented this by a system known as *mukalabah* or turn-over. The merchant sold to the captain certain goods or provisions, for a fixed sum; the goods were immediately resold by the captain to the merchant for a cash payment which was appreciably less than that originally specified. The difference between these two prices formed the interest payment to the merchant.

When the season came to an end, the captain deducted from the sale of the pearls the cost of the crews' food and provisions. The remainder represented the profit and was shared according to certain rules, depending on whether or not the captain was the owner of the boat. If the captain owned the boat, one-half of the profits were retained by him and the remainder was divided amongst the crew after the deduction of any advances made, with the divers taking two shares to the pullers' one. The *tabbab*, or boys, received nothing. If the captain was not the owner, he was entitled to one-fifth of the profits, the remainder of his normal 50 per cent being paid to the owners or financiers of the boat. The other half was paid to the crew on the previously mentioned share system.

The merchant who put up the money for the expedition was entitled to buy the pearls at 20 per cent below the market value and this obviously further reduced the profits of both captain and crew and had the effect of putting them further into debt, especially after a bad season.

The fact that the divers were illiterate led to many abuses by the captains; it was possible for captains to falsify the accounts so that divers were permanently in debt to them, and it was not unknown for the accounts of the best divers to be regularly falsified in order that their services were retained for future seasons.

The position of the diver was summed up by Harrison who wrote in 1924:

> The diver is known as a slave for the rest of his life. It is probably easier for a negro slave on the pirate coast to escape, than it is for a Bahraini diver to regain his freedom. As long as he is in debt he cannot change his employer, no matter how badly he is treated, nor can he leave the town, except under bonds to return before the diving season begins and he will never be able to get out of debt, he cannot read or write, there is no witness to the transactions that take place between the captain and himself. It is the recognised thing for the divers to receive a loan of rice. . . . The sum written into the books is regularly about 50 per cent greater than the market value of the rice. If necessary entirely false entries are written in. The upshot of the matter is that their men never get out of debt, not one in a thousand of them.
>
> In seven years residence in Bahrain, I have never yet met a diver who had escaped from the account book as the Arabs put it.[5]

The decline of the pearl industry brought further problems for the people working in it; the captains went bankrupt and the divers fell further into debt. In spite of selling all their properties the debts were still not met or liquidated, and it was not unusual to find people working in the oil industry and at other jobs for up to two decades before the debts were cleared.

As if this were not enough, the control of these properties and lands passed into the hands of the merchants and financiers who profited greatly from them and became even richer during the time of economic growth and development following the discovery of oil.

In summary, the means of production in the pearling industry were mainly in the hands of the merchants, who drew substantial benefit from the operations. The desire to restrict ownership of the factors of production turned the merchants into a semi-class with a strong and powerful social base. The *nokhudah*s were closely linked with this class; as supreme commanders on the boats they sometimes had the right to decide whether a diver or puller should live or die, and this shaped their relationship with divers and pullers on land also.

The relations of production in agriculture were similar to those in the pearling industry. The farmers in the traditional Gulf societies did not know ownership of land in the full sense: namely the presence of perpetual rights of control and the ability to buy and sell. The farmer had the right merely to use the land. The actual ownership of the land was vested either in a shaikh or in a big merchant who had acquired the land from a shaikh. The shaikh or merchant would stipulate the conditions according to which the land could be used, including the percentage of the product which should accrue to him. This latter stipulation implied great risks to the farmer. If he failed to fulfil what he had promised to the landlord his private property was confiscated.

In trade also, the conduct of business was so arranged as to enable the shaikh and the bigger merchants to extract a large part of the economic surplus. The shaikh would usually nominate a merchant as his agent in collecting taxes from ships entering port, and the merchant would then levy taxes to satisfy both the shaikh's greed and his own financial needs.

Social Effects of the Traditional Mode of Production

The relations of production, as has been shown, involved the principal means of production being owned by a restricted grouping of shaikhs and merchants, with whom the majority of the population maintained a semi-feudal type of relationship. Class struggle, however, was not a sharply noticed phenomenon. Many factors account for this: the small size of the Gulf societies meant that personal relationships could help to conceal the realities of economic and social inequality; the labour force had little alternative; the economic surplus was meagre, such that even the merchants and shaikhs were not conspicuously wealthy; the absence of modern education meant that social consciousness was retarded; and the dependence on uncertain sources of income caused the populations to harbour deep superstitions, believing that existing conditions were determined by fate and were thus unchangeable. Nevertheless, the absence of class struggle does not detract from the reality of the mode of production determining social structures.

A situation where the means of production were severely limited meant that those who did own these means had a powerful base within their own extended families. The heads of families, in other words, had considerable power over the other members: the others could be employed within the 'family' business with minimal economic rights.

The head of the family had authority over the marriage of family members and would manipulate the traditional marriage customs (dowries, etc.) to ensure that the family's wealth was maximised. In Kuwait, intermarriage between the more prosperous families and the less prosperous was obstructed by a social distinction with a potent economic base: it was regarded as unbecoming for families who classified themselves as of noble origin (*asil*) to intermarry with those who were classified as of foreign origin (*baisari*). Under such a system, where women were used to enhance the family's wealth only by marriage and played no part in the process of production, women naturally enjoyed very little freedom – whether to choose their husbands or to express an opinion. Shaikh Yousif ben Eisa al-Genai wrote about this:

> A woman represented no value to men, especially the old ones. She was a worldly pleasure that one should avoid. If you mentioned her in your speech you should say to your listener, 'May God grant you honour'. A girl was compelled to marry her man, especially if he were her cousin. It does not matter if he were ugly or immoral. A man who was 80 had the right to marry a 20 year old girl.[6]

There was no codified legislation before the early years of this century. Effective power to judge lay in the hands of the shaikh, the tribal chief or, at sea, the *nokhudah*. When laws were first codified, moreover, it is significant that they were concerned initially with pearl-diving. The legislation, issued in Bahrain and on the Oman coast in the 1920s and 1930s, was evidently intended to reinforce the position of the merchants and *nokhudahs*; it was in fact based on traditional conventions. The courts to enforce the legislation on pearl-diving were called *al-salifa* courts, and the judges in these courts were themselves prominent *nokhudahs*. The ability of such judges to give an objective judgement when disputes arose between divers and *nokhudahs* was, of course, limited. Legislation, in fact, was simply a means for protecting the interests of the ruling class.

The political regime in the Gulf states, before oil, evolved in an increasingly dictatorial direction. The tribal structures which had existed in the earlier period after the tribes settled in Kuwait (eighteenth and early nineteenth centuries) involved continuous consultation between the ruler and the various tribal sections. An economy which was still largely pastoral necessitated widespread consultation, for the main economic resource – the herds – could not be brought under the direct control of the ruler. In the words of Amin al-Raihani:

> The rule which existed before Sabah the second was of a democratic nature, where the chiefs of the tribal sections all participated. Sabah would not carry out a plan without consulting them. The chiefs of the tribal sections would also consult their own wise people. This consultation weakened after the reign of Sabah until it completely disappeared during the reign of Shaikh Mubarak.[7]

The increasing importance of the pearling industry involved effective power being concentrated more and more in the hands of the ruler. The ruler's ability to draw revenue from the pearling industry and, through his control over the industry, to affect the economic well-being of all those who worked in it ensured that wider consultation was not necessary. He could operate by forming shifting alliances with different merchants, never becoming dependent on any one. The link with the 'protecting' power (Britain) further reinforced the ruler's position.

The political authorities had no interest in encouraging education, for the spread of modern education could undercut the whole social structure upon which their power rested. The only education which was acceptable was that based on the reading and recitation of the holy Koran, together with some simple mathematics. When modern education did come to the Gulf, with schools being established in Kuwait, Dubai and Bahrain in the 1920s and 1930s, it was initiated mostly by the more enlightened *nokhudah*s and merchants, who felt that educated personnel would enable them to organise their businesses better and widen the range of their international contacts. The attempt to establish these schools encountered considerable resistance from those who feared their effect on the social structure. The attitude towards education, therefore, was one of extreme wariness, coupled with an emphasis on utilitarian training – i.e. where education was brought in, it was geared towards training people for specific economic roles.

The values and customs of Gulf societies, as elements of superstructure, were predominantly products of the relations of production. These values and customs needed to be installed so as to maintain the whole structure. Yet superstructural elements did themselves exert some influence over the nature of economic relationships. On Islamic principle some *nokhudahs* refused to carry debts forward from season to season, or even to take interest from their divers. The system of religious education and the existence of Islamic preachers helped to soften the harsher aspects of the socio-economic system. The idea of working for the next world, and the idea of the fear of God, functioned as psychological barriers which prevented some merchants from exploiting those who worked for them. In the long term, this alleviation of the harsher aspects possibly contributed to the longevity of the system.

Conclusion

This article has attempted to describe the nature of social relationships, values and attitudes which were associated with the traditional economy in the Gulf. It is suggested that the relationships, values and attitudes which exist today in Gulf societies are heavily influenced by the pattern inherited from the earlier mode of production. The extent to which the inherited pattern has continued may be accounted for by the nature of the economic change which has occurred: the oil economy has, in effect, been an external imposition, employing only a small proportion of the population and thus having little direct effect on basic relationships and attitudes.

Notes

1. Among others, al-Masudi and Ibn Batuta both mentioned pearl-diving in the Gulf. For a longer discussion of the historical references, see Saif Marzouq Shamlan, *Tārīkh Al-Khaws al-Lu'lu' fi al-Kuwait wa al-Khalij al-Arabi* (*History of Pearl Fishing in Kuwait and the Arab Gulf*) (Kuwait, 1975 and 1978, 2 vols).
2. Taken from *The Diary of Dr Stanley Mallory*, translated into Arabic by M. G. Rumaihi and published as *al-Kuwait qabl al-Naft* (*Kuwait before Oil*) (Basim Sarhan, Kuwait, 1975), p. 12.
3. See M. G. Rumaihi, *Bahrain: Social and Political Change Since the First World War* (University of Kuwait, 1975), pp. 58–60.
4. Ibid., p. 60.
5. P. W. Harrison, *The Arabs at Home* (Thomas Y. Crowell Co., New York, 1924), p. 80.
6. Y. I. al-Ganai, *Tārīkh al-Kuwait* (*History of Kuwait*) (Kuwait, 1968), p. 78.
7. A. al-Raihani, *Mulūk al-'Arab* (*Arab Kings*) (Beirut, 1951), vol. 2, pp. 172–3.

4 Hegemony, Dependence and Development in the Gulf

ROSEMARIE SAID ZAHLAN

Introduction

The purpose of this article is to provide the historical dimension that could serve as an important guideline in the formulation of strategies for the socio-economic development of the Gulf region. The article will deal with the context within which strategies and policies have to function rather than with the specifics of planning. Generally speaking, the design of policies for national development is based both on the historical record of the nation concerned and on a comparative study of the experiences of other nations with similar circumstances. Thus most countries today evince a strong interest in the study of their own historical experience, as well as that of others. In the case of the Gulf states, a thorough study of the past has been inadequate due to a number of reasons: the lack of sufficient local records and the failure to develop and document oral history; the weakness of local institutions of advanced study; the recent preponderance of well-paid literature that is merely propagandist; a curious prevailing attitude that the lean years had best be forgotten; and the rapid transformation of the society at large that calls for a particularly sophisticated body of scholars. This has led to a dangerous situation whereby planners are hampered by the absence of sound historical analyses. The situation is exacerbated by the fact that comparative studies are only marginally relevant in view of the unique characteristics of the social, political and economic conditions of Gulf society today.

The Arab side of the Gulf is made up of a small number of tiny states. They have low populations with a basically tribal construction and are the recipients of tremendous wealth that accrues from one single resource. During the past three decades their societies have undergone a rapid transformation that has been motivated by two principal events, each occurring independently of the other: the demise of the British Empire, and the discovery and exploitation of large petroleum resources. Thus comparative studies must necessarily be cautious as far as Gulf countries are concerned. It is my personal belief, however, that the history of the region itself is sufficiently rich, diverse and relevant to merit the attention of planners of future policies.

This article will attempt to demonstrate this relevance with respect to one dimension that has been, and continues to be, of primordial importance to the region: that of dependence and interdependence.[1] It is clear that the economic activities and/or the exploitation of the resources of the Gulf states are dependent on the international market. A definite relationship therefore emerges between a country and its people, on the one hand, and the rest of the world on whose markets it depends, on the other. This equation necessarily develops special characteristics over different periods of time, with well-defined qualities which may be examined and analysed. Here we will concentrate on three periods in the twentieth-century history of the Gulf region: the pre-oil, transition to oil, and post-oil periods. These periods will be schematised. The pre-oil era covers the time span before the possibility of the existence of oil resources became known; the transition to oil era takes in the period when the preliminary oil concessions were being signed; and the post-oil era will be considered as having started when the receipts from petroleum began to accrue.

The Pre-oil Period

It was during the pre-oil period that the Gulf region became of great strategic importance to Britain. It lay on the route to India and the oil supplies of Persia. Its geo-political nature, therefore, became a resource with negative assets for the people of the region, since it led to British domination. The treaties that were imposed on the local rulers, first by the British government of Bombay and later by the government of India, subsequently restricted the behaviour of their people. They became confined to a parochial existence that greatly limited their potential development on the internal, regional and international levels. The only major resource left for them to exploit was the rich sea that produced oysters. Thus the pearling industry became their principal economic activity.

The industry as such was extremely arduous, and sophisticated methods for its development had emerged locally over the centuries. Its importance as the economic mainstay of the different shaikhdoms along the Gulf shores can best be shown by the figures supplied by Lorimer[2] on the pearling manpower of each shaikhdom (see Table 4.1).

These figures indicate the high percentage of the participation of adult males in the pearling industry. Since 50 per cent of any population is made up of males, and since at least 50 per cent of these were under fifteen years of age, a demographic characteristic that still prevails in the Gulf states today, a labour force figure approximating 25 per cent of the total population would indicate the deployment in the industry of practically every adult male in each shaikhdom. The figures also point out certain basic differences between Bahrain and Kuwait on the lower side of the median, and Qatar and the Trucial States on the higher. Both the former shaikhdoms had other, often complementary, economic activities, trade and boat building being the most important. It would seem that Bahrain was the main supplier of boats for the Trucial States and Qatar, and in 1903/4 it exported a total of 130 to these places. At the same time Kuwait produced around twenty to thirty boats per annum. In Qatar and the Trucial States, by contrast, there were no local industries and there was no significant trade, except in Dubai which began to develop as an entrepôt in the early years of this century. Thus, a greater percentage of the population in these states was active in the fisheries; moreover, both places, and Qatar especially, still retained slaves (single, without families) for work in the pearl banks. It is clear, then, that pearling provided the main source of both employment and income to all these shaikhdoms and in some cases, Kuwait in particular, pearl fishing was even extended to the Ceylon pearl banks during the off-season period in the Gulf.

Most of the shaikhdoms had a resident foreign community, largely Persian and Indian. The latter were merchants involved in various

Table 4.1: Pearling Manpower of the Shaikhdoms

	Total Population	Labour Force Engaged in Pearling	Percentage of Population in Pearling
Bahrain	99,075	17,633	18
Kuwait	37,000	7,200	20
Qatar	27,000	12,890	48
Trucial States	72,000	22,045	31

aspects of the pearling business; as British subjects they enjoyed special privileges, privileges that they were wont to abuse locally, thus often causing resentment, particularly as they were mostly wealthy and lent the money for the pearling expeditions. Indian colonies were prevalent in Kuwait, Bahrain and Dubai, another indication of the nature of these places as trading centres. Qatar alone had no Indian resident by the beginning of the present century. This was a reflection of the local animosity towards the Indians which had culminated in their wholesale exodus in 1883 and the fact that Qatar did not enter into treaty relations with Britain until 1916. Even then, the British government agreed to allow the clause in which the ruler was bound to allow British subjects to reside in that place and to protect their lives and property, to remain inoperative in order to obtain Shaikh Abdallah bin Qasim's signature to the treaty itself. The presence and special privileges of the Indian traders in the Gulf towns were facets of interdependence.

The British played the central role in guaranteeing the structure on which the pearling trade was based. Not only did their Indian subjects enjoy special rights which Britain, if necessary, intervened to uphold. Their treaty relationships with the rulers were also responsible for allowing these rulers to remain in power, for these relationships constituted the main factor in the maintenance of the political fabric of the shaikhdoms. The reliance of the rulers on the trade was also an established fact, because it enabled them to raise the money necessary to wield their individual power locally. The taxes they levied on the pearl boats were one aspect of this income. Far more important were the customs dues levied on the goods which the merchants imported with the profits they made from pearling.[3]

The functions of the different levels of workers in the industry have been described at length elsewhere.[4] The various definitions of their roles, from the lowliest puller and diver to the wealthiest *tawwash* (pearl merchant), became stratified with usage, emphasising the highly organised state of this pivotal activity. The financial regulations were as well defined as the actual fishing, and the complicated system of debts around which the industry revolved provided untold hardship for some, great wealth for others. It was, however, the sale of the pearls to the Indian dealers in Bombay that determined the success or failure of a season, the life and death, so to speak, of the community.

The dependence of this industry on the international market was thus strong. The pearl merchants in Bombay were the principal agents who transmitted the exquisite Gulf pearls to the jewellers of Paris, London and New York. The pearls were luxury items, expensive, and the perfect ones rare. The contrast between pearls as the main source of livelihood for the Arabs of the Gulf and as a luxury item for their ultimate owners is striking and gave the interdependence between producer and consumer a highly unequal character. The almost total collapse of the industry as a result of the world economic depression after 1929 is well known.

The industry was also adversely affected by the introduction into the international market of the cultured pearl which had been developed by the Japanese. The decline in the demand for the expensive Gulf pearl coincided with the production of a cheaper version of the same product, and the economy of the Gulf was dealt a shattering blow, one that would have been almost impossible to overcome had the strange hand of fate not stepped in.

The collapse of the pearling industry occurred within living memory. From it, many questions can be raised, others answered. The people of the Gulf had been deeply integrated into the international market, their very subsistence strikingly linked to its ups and downs. Yet their knowledge of this market and their ability to forecast its changes were in no way commensurate with their dependence on it. When the decline set in, they were caught unawares, largely incapable of reacting favourably or positively to its force.

The actual technology of pearling was largely indigenous, although foreign manpower had been brought in to the labour force. It was technically autonomous, therefore, yet its dependence on the international market was crucial to its entire existence. The question inevitably arises whether, given a reasonably accurate knowledge of both the international economic depression and the production of the cultured pearl, the same people who had evolved the pearling techniques of the past could have then adapted them to be competitive with those of Japan. Why is it that there were no serious attempts to stave off the economic ruin that ensued by diversifying the economy in time? When did the society become fully aware of the reasons for its own economic decline? It might be interesting to note here that, in 1908, Lorimer foresaw the repercussions of a possible collapse in Bahrain when he remarked that it would be probable that 'if the pearl beds were to fail, the Shaikhdom would shortly be reduced to comparative insignificance'.[5] But the pearl banks did not fail; the market collapsed.

Transition to Oil

Although Lorimer reflected some British apprehension on the consequences of the stoppage of the industry, little material aid was forthcoming, whether from Britain or from other concerned countries.[6] The shaikhdoms were left to cope for themselves. Although the decline set in slowly, the increasing poverty of the region was striking. The internal response to the situation differed from place to place. In Dubai, Kuwait and Bahrain, the earlier diversification stood the people there in good stead, and trade began to play a leading role in their respective economies. Harbours were developed, ships which had been used for pearling were used increasingly to carry cargo, and a new merchant class began to grow in number as well as in influence and experience. These changes were not without concomitant sociopolitical shifts, and the movements of 1938/39, calling for a reform of the old order in all three places, were the obvious results.[7] Within the Trucial States themselves, a fair amount of internal migration, particularly to Dubai, took place, an indication of the new centre of economic activity in the lower Gulf. During the period between 1908 and 1939, the population of Dubai doubled, from around 10,000 to 20,000, while that of Sharjah dwindled from approximately 15,000 to 5,000.[8] The emigration of Qataris to Bahrain was to take place throughout the 1930s as a result of Qatar's great financial hardship; even the ruler, Abdallah bin Qasim, was so badly affected that he was forced to mortgage his house for some 17,000 rupees.[9]

But a new factor was beginning to emerge at this time, one that was radically to alter the course of events. This was, of course, the possible existence of substantial reserves of oil in the region. Although, at first, British interest in the likelihood of the oil potential was lacking, this interest grew after the discovery of oil in Bahrain in 1932 and the award of the Saudi oil concession to the Standard Oil Company of California (SOCAL) – the same company that held the Bahrain concession. The British government then sought to channel all remaining concessions in its sphere of influence to British-owned or British-controlled companies. The latter, however, were slow to act, and the Kuwait concession was finally awarded in December 1934 to two companies, the British-controlled Anglo-Persian Oil Company and the US Gulf Oil Corporation. That left Qatar and the Trucial States. By now, the British authorities had become deeply concerned about the entry into Arabia of American companies, and their fears and suspicions about American commercial interests in the Gulf began to assume large proportions. They wished to consolidate their hold over these shaikhdoms not so much because of the implicit financial gains – of which they were not truly aware – but for political reasons. The local resistance to their new forward policy prompted the Political Agent in 1939 to express his regret 'that we seem reluctant to use the means we possess to deter a crew of feeble but ill-conditioned shaikhs from treating the wishes of His Majesty's Government with quite such persistent disrespect'. He then put forth his view on how to deal with the problem:

> Let us make it perfectly clear that when we say we want a thing we are going to get it . . . and without undue delay; and that obstructive tactics do not pay . . . We certainly do not want to administer their disgusting territories and people, *but* if they happen to be on the air route or there is oil underground they have got to behave.[10]

A different form of dependence began to emerge. This was further complicated by the new importance of the Gulf's geo-political position as an essential stage on the air route to India. Although we will not dwell on it here, particularly as this element did not lead to an economic relationship between Britain and the Gulf shaikhdoms, it strengthened British imperial interests in the region.[11] Petroleum, however, was of much greater importance. In striking contrast to the relationship created by the pearl trade, the dependence on the petroleum factor was not formed by choice; it was forced on the people of the shaikhdoms. Furthermore, it was not an outcome of an economic activity that had existed before the British first sailed the Gulf waters; it was the result of a unilateral decision of British political and commercial policy regarding the possibility of the existence of a new resource, about which the people of the Gulf had little knowledge. How the shaikhdoms, particularly Abu Dhabi and Qatar, were forced to submit to this dependence, and what the impact of the new order on both the shaikhdoms themselves and with each other was, will now be examined.

Shaikh Shakhbut bin Zayid of Abu Dhabi for a long time resisted pressure to sign an oil concession with the company chosen by the British authorities. He had heard of the vastly superior terms offered by the American company, and could see no reason why he should lose such a golden opportunity. Together with some of his fellow rulers in the Trucial States, he had held out so long (from 1935 to 1937) that the Political Resident issued an ultimatum: His Majesty's Government approved of only one company (Petroleum Concessions Ltd – PC Ltd – a subsidiary of the British-controlled Iraq Petroleum Company) and was therefore not 'prepared to consider permitting negotiations with any other company'.[12] Shakhbut's reaction to this statement was to shrug it off defiantly as *hawa* (hot air). Whereas the ultimatum brought the rulers of Sharjah and Ras al-Khaimah to the discussion table, Shakhbut flatly refused to accept the terms of PC Ltd, causing much anxiety in London, Bushire and Delhi, particularly as the company's geologists were aware of the oil potential of his shaikhdom. But Shakhbut also seemed to know of this, and resisted for as long as he could. He finally capitulated in 1939 after the Political Resident, who had been waiting for the opportune moment, seized on a report regarding an instance of the slave trade, which had been furnished by the representative of PC Ltd, on the Trucial Coast.[13] The Resident withdrew 'the good office of His Majesty's Government', i.e. the travelling papers of all people from Abu Dhabi, including the ruler's, were cancelled until further notice. When Shakhbut had 'the impertinence' to ask why this had been done, he added insult to injury by also asking for proof of the existence of trading in slaves in his shaikhdom. But his defiance had adverse effects on his people, and could weaken his own position with them considerably. He probably did not realise that the Resident was also contemplating much more severe punishment which, however, the India Office in London ultimately rejected.[14] Shakhbut finally had to admit defeat, and in the early days of 1939 he signed a concession with PC Ltd.

A different strategy was used with Shaikh Abdallah of Qatar to induce him to sign on the dotted line. Qatar had been the last of the Gulf shaikhdoms to have been drawn into treaty relations with Britain. Even then, the negotiations had lasted for one year, for Abdallah had encountered a fair amount of family opposition to the impending treaty and had to placate his relatives before affixing his signature. Percy Cox, who had been negotiating with him on behalf of the government of India, finally gave in to many of Abdallah's terms, and the treaty was signed in November 1916 on condition that certain clauses in the treaty (such as those concerning the protection of British residents, the establishment of British postal and telegraph offices, and the stationing of a British agent in Qatar) would remain inoperative until further notice. But the most important concession Abdallah obtained was that, in contrast to the treaties of the other shaikhdoms (which were only given protection from attack by sea), the British government undertook to grant the ruler its 'good offices' should he or his subjects be attacked by land.[15] Five years later, Abdallah, in an oblique reference to his fears of Wahhabi expansion in Qatar, questioned the Political Resident about the kind of security he could rely on according to the treaty. The Resident told the startled ruler that all he could expect with reference to 'good offices' was diplomatic help.[16] Abdallah had become increasingly nervous about Saudi machinations in his shaikhdom; Ibn Saud was deliberately courting the disaffected members of his family, who were in turn openly defying Abdallah's authority at home. He warned the British authorities more than once that he might have to leave Qatar, and urged them to provide the assistance they had promised him in 1916. He also asked that the British government formally recognise his son Hamad as his heir, for he needed a powerful tool with which to fight his enemies. But he was told firmly that the government of India had no desire 'to get mixed up in the internal affairs of Qatar'.[17] So Abdallah was obliged to pay Ibn Saud a secret subsidy of 100,000 rupees a year to ensure his own security.[18]

He eventually found a way to obtain stronger British protection, this time in the form of a bargain. In early 1934, the British authorities had become extremely nervous about the obvious attractions to Qatar of SOCAL, which was offering much more generous terms than the British-controlled Anglo-Persian Oil Company (APOC). They were particularly worried about rumours that Ibn Saud had warned Abdallah about signing a concession with APOC, and that Abdallah and his son Hamad had gone to Riyadh to sign an agreement with the King to the effect that the hinterland of Qatar, and therefore the oil in it, belonged to Saudi Arabia. Their anxiety was exacerbated by reports that SOCAL had already made Abdallah a very generous offer and that he had no further desire to negotiate with APOC.

Although the Resident warned Abdallah in no uncertain terms that he could negotiate only with APOC, he was nervous about the situation and eager to finalise it. To make matters worse, an official at the India Office in London suddenly realised that the 1916 treaty had been made personal to Abdallah, and was not binding to his successors. If the ruler were suddenly to die, the treaty would have to be renegotiated, a most undesirable situation. In their obvious desire to see the Qatar oil concession concluded with APOC, the Political Agent in Bahrain and the Political Resident made an unprecedented number of visits to Doha. Abdallah became acutely conscious of the political rather than the commercial importance of this agreement, for it is clear that he had little inkling of the tremendous wealth he stood to gain from a discovery of oil. He therefore asked for, and obtained, all that he had been pleading for since 1921.

In exchange for signing an agreement with APOC in May 1935, Abdallah was formally assured that he could expect protection from the British government against 'serious and unprovoked attacks' and that the government also recognised Hamad as his heir, provided Hamad were to accept the 1916 treaty on his accession.[19] Thus Abdallah assured the succession of his son and obtained additional British protection in exchange for accepting British conditions on the oil concession itself.

Repercussions of the Oil Agreements: Aspects of Dependency

The Gulf shaikhdoms had entered into an area completely foreign to them, on terms imposed by Britain. They had little vision regarding the outcome of their commitments, yet the impact of these commitments on their external and internal affairs was great. Maybe the most outstanding were the boundary disputes which came into being almost immediately after the concessions had been won. Kuwait was spared many of these problems, having had its borders delimited during the conference of Uqayr in 1922. But Bahrain, Qatar and the Trucial States became deeply involved in the precise delimitation of their respective territories as a result of the anxiety of both the oil companies and the British government. The whole concept of defining exact boundaries was foreign to the shaikhdoms; but with the coming of the oil companies every square mile of land became important financially. The greatest problem was the definition of the exact borders of the shaikhdoms under British 'protection' with Saudi Arabia. The concession in Saudi Arabia having been placed in the hands of SOCAL, the entire exercise became more complicated, drawing in, as it did, the United States government.

The subsequent correspondence; the presentation of the Blue Line, the Riyadh Line, the Red Line and the Green Line; the London Conference; and the British Committee of Imperial Defence's proposal that Abu Dhabi be induced to cede a part of its territory, Khawr al-Udayd, to Saudi Arabia – all came to nothing. The well-known Buraimi crisis of the 1950s resulted, with claim and counter-claim still being produced as evidence. The undefined borders of the UAE with

Saudi Arabia today are testimony of the intricacy of the situation; they are also illustration of the alien nature of the new impositions.

Another example of the radically different approaches to territorial disputes exhibited by Western and Arab methodology was the territorial dispute between Bahrain and Qatar regarding the Hawar islands. Here it must be noted that, in 1937, following a visit by representatives of PC Ltd to Zubarah on the north-western coast of Qatar peninsula, a dispute arose between Bahrain and Qatar regarding ownership of Zubarah. The Al-Khalifah of Bahrain had long refused to relinquish their claim to Zubarah, and the 1937 crisis resulted in a serious armed clash. The Zubarah dispute, a long and drawn-out saga, continued on and off for the next decade. Zubarah, of course, belonged irrevocably to Qatar, but the hard feelings the dispute created between Qatar and Bahrain constituted a dramatic reality in the 1930s and 1940s.

Zubarah was not the only cause for territorial dispute between the two shaikhdoms. The Hawar islands, which lie about three kilometres off the west coast of Qatar, also became the centre of controversy between the two emirates as a direct result of the Qatari oil concession. The small population of the islands was made up of fishermen, and ownership had never been questioned before. Suddenly, in 1936, aware of the new importance of territory, the ruler of Bahrain posted a military garrison there. Two years later, the Bahrainis began drilling for water, an ominous sign to Shaikh Abdallah of Qatar. He complained to the Political Agent in Bahrain, obviously regarding the islands as part of Qatar.

The Agent then reported to the Political Resident in Bushire that Bahrain had a *prima facie* claim to the islands because of the 1936 military garrison; Abdallah, if he wanted to claim sovereignty, had to put forward his statement of ownership to the Agency for consideration.[20] The implication was that Abdallah had to present a portfolio of his historic ownership of the islands and of the tribal loyalty owed to him by the local fishermen. The concept of a portfolio was in itself entirely alien to Abdallah, and he did not know how to cope, for he was clearly ill equipped to present a highly documented file to prove his sovereignty in the form demanded by Western law. The ruler of Bahrain, on the other hand, had a British Political Adviser, C. Dalrymple Belgrave. It was the latter who presented a sophisticated treatise that included photographs and the testimony of local fishermen to substantiate the Al-Khalifah claim. Abdallah's letters to the Political Agent in Bahrain reveal his bewilderment, and are a good indication of the traditional Arab approach to such matters: Hawar was an integral part of Qatar; everyone knew that; Bahrain had no right over it despite the *prima facie* claim to which the Agent referred; truth and justice would prevail; and he had confidence in the fair play of the British government. When Abdallah finally agreed to present a file with his claims, Belgrave responded with a new set of counter-claims. Bahrain presented the more sophisticated case so, in July 1939, Fowle, the Political Resident, 'awarded' the islands to Bahrain. His successor, Prior, viewed the award as having been most unfair to Qatar and remarked that the 'case had been decided according to Western ideas, and no allowance has been made for local custom and sentiment'.[21] Qatar consistently refused to accept this verdict, and the Hawar islands case is still outstanding today.

Although Prior regarded Fowle's verdict on Hawar as unjust, he did not reverse it, on the grounds that such a reversal would not have been 'practical politics'. It was the consideration of practical politics that determined much of British policy during the 1930s and 1940s, following the signing of the preliminary oil concessions in the Gulf states. The imposition on local structures of the demands of an alien system, whereby the oil companies needed to know exactly where their concessions started and ended, had repercussions which are still being felt today. Abu Dhabi and Dubai, strong rivals, neighbours and fellow members of the Bani Yas tribe, had a long and protracted war over their boundaries from 1945 to 1948; this occurred as a direct outcome of the oil concession, and the residual effects of the war are still felt today with strong rivalry between the two shaikhdoms in the UAE.

An examination of the British response to local needs during this period further reveals the inequality of the relationship. Despite the above-mentioned examples of the British role in Gulf affairs, British policy was formally against interference in local affairs. As we have seen above, this could be argued away or reiterated when the need arose. As long as the *status quo* was preserved, Britain had no interest in intervening; once this was upset, it had to act. The British involvement in the reform movements of Kuwait and Dubai is a particularly good example of the latter practice. A further example may be given of the British disregard for local needs which had no bearing on imperial interests. The son and heir of Abdallah bin Qasim of Qatar had become a very ill man during the late 1930s and, together with other Qataris, had to rely on foreign medical treatment, there being no hospital in the shaikhdom. The medical care that had been supplied in the Arabian peninsula by American missionaries of the Dutch Reformed Church had not been extended to Qatar,[22] but the missionaries agreed to help Abdallah establish a hospital in Doha in 1945. The ruler's resources were limited, however, both financially and with respect to qualified manpower. He consequently turned to the British authorities in the Gulf for help, asking for assistance in the completion of the actual construction of the hospital and in the purchase of certain medicines. The Political Agent in Bahrain, close to the realities of the Qatari situation, recommended that help be given; but the Political Resident did not want to give away something for nothing, he saw it as a good opportunity to further British political interests. He therefore suggested that Britain offer Abdallah the services of a British (preferably Indian) doctor rather than help in the construction; this doctor could also be secretly engaged in political work for Britain, since Abdallah had still not permitted the entry into Qatar of a British political agent.[23] The suggestion came to nothing.

Another example of the unequal relationship reveals the misapprehensions under which some of the Gulf people laboured with reference to British power. Although Orders-in-Council for the jurisdiction of foreigners existed in Kuwait, Bahrain and Qatar, none existed in the Trucial States until 1946. British treaty relations with these states did not technically claim any over-all right by the British government to make laws for peace and order, but the Political Resident did exercise a certain jurisdiction. This had no legal basis and had grown up by long usage. The same applied to British jurisdiction over foreigners. Although the latter jurisdiction was technically in the hands of the rulers, they did not seem to be aware of this fact. The Political Resident underlined the situation when he noted with relief in 1936 that 'I believe that the Shaikhs are under the wholesome impression that they cannot touch British subjects'.[24]

A further illustration of the internal impact of the new type of dependence is provided by the 1938 disturbances in Bahrain. Bahrain was the first of the Gulf states to have received an income from oil, and the transformation of its economy began in 1934, considerably before its neighbours. Its revenues, albeit small with the hindsight of 1979, were large enough to allow an expansion to take place, and with it employment opportunities in the oil company and the newly formed civil administration. These opportunities were a welcome relief from the economic depression and in 1938 there was widespread local resentment when a large number of Indians were brought in as employees, particularly of the oil company. This resentment unified the Bahrainis into a gathering anti-government movement. The ruler's son, Salman, took on the leadership of the movement which then listed its demands for reform. In order to pledge their support for these demands, the Bahraini workers at the oil company planned an organised strike. The government reacted by arresting the leaders of the planned strike; a wave of protest followed which reached its climax in a national strike.[25] Although the demands were not to be realised for some time, the movement in itself characterised the local reaction to the imposition of the new order; it was not without its positive qualities, having acted as a cohesive factor between both Shia and Sunni in the islands.

The arrival of the oil companies brought divisive tendencies. Discontent within the ruling families, particularly in Dubai, Ras al-Khaimah and Qatar, arose because of the added income supplied to the ruler according to the terms of the concessions. Although the sums were infinitesimal, particularly by today's standards of oil revenue, and although the money paid to the rulers was not for revenues but as an annual payment until petroleum was discovered, it was sufficient to warrant the envy of the impoverished members of the ruling families. This feeling was the initial motivating force behind the 1938 reform movement in Dubai, and it brought about sufficiently serious disturbances in Ras al-Khaimah in 1948 and in Qatar in 1949 for the rulers there to be obliged to step down from their respective positions.

In the more densely populated emirate of Bahrain, the oil company's activities fostered the growth of a new middle class. This was made up of the petty merchants whose trading activities grew with the expansion of the economy, the employees who were recruited into the civil service and the oil company, and the students who were sent for training to foreign countries (Egypt, Lebanon and the United Kingdom). In Kuwait, Qatar and the Trucial States, sparsely populated and still poor in the 1930s, a parallel formation was not as marked. A few individuals, however, did rise to prominence as local agents of the oil companies. Although the income they gained in these positions was not very great, the influence they wielded was substantial for they were openly bolstered by the British authorities. The most outstanding example of this kind of individual was Abdallah Darwish of Qatar who grew from his position as the closest friend and adviser of the ruler's son Hamad to being the agent of the Anglo-Iranian Oil Company, as the APOC became in 1935. Yusuf bin Ahmad Kanoo enjoyed a similar role in Bahrain. Over and above this genre there were the 'secret agents' recently employed by the British authorities. They were recruited locally and employed for different purposes: to verify whether or not the slave trade was being carried out in Abu Dhabi;[26] to assess the allegiance of the tribes in the Buraimi oasis; and to discover whether Shaikh Abdallah of Qatar was negotiating privately with SOCAL.

The above examples have been selected to illustrate the local repercussions caused by the impact of the oil concessions on the different shaikhdoms. In all of them, the importance of the British role in the changes overtaking the states is clear.

It is interesting to note that, despite the discovery of oil in Bahrain in 1932, followed by its discovery in Saudi Arabia, Kuwait and Qatar during the same decade, there was still no corresponding awareness of the great financial potential of the shaikhdoms. The strikingly unequal status between Britain and the Gulf states remained, surprisingly, until the 1940s, and it is perhaps fitting to conclude this section with an illustration of this status that seems particularly ironic in 1979 when the international financial assets of the Gulf states are so well known. After the Bretton Woods meetings (which took place to establish a structure for the international financial and economic system after World War II and which agreed on the creation of the International Monetary Fund and the World Bank) it was Britain's duty to convey the decisions to the Gulf states, since it was responsible for them, according to the agreements reached. The Political Resident was, however, against informing the rulers of the details of the new agreements since 'they have no currency of their own . . . and it seems extremely unlikely that either the International Monetary Fund or the International Bank will have representation or own assets in the Shaikhdoms'.[27] Deciding that the possibility of any relationship between Bretton Woods and the Gulf states was extremely remote, the Resident concluded that:

> For the sake of formality, I suggest that we merely inform the Rulers that His Majesty's Government have accepted certain international obligations under the Bretton Woods Agreements, which will have effect in their territories in all areas linked with the British financial system. It seems preferable for our action to take the form of an announcement rather than a request for their agreement as the subject would be extremely difficult to explain and most of the Rulers are unlikely to understand it despite the most detailed of explanations.[28]

A Perspective of the Post-oil Era

The speed with which circumstances changed once oil was discovered is brought into sharp relief if it is recalled that the above statement was made a mere thirty-three years ago. The swiftness of change is especially striking when compared with the impact of oil revenues on the neighbouring states of Iraq and Iran where the size, rate and cost of petroleum production, plus the large populations, considerably slowed down the process.

The socio-economic transformation of the Gulf region, which started during the 1940s and which continues to the present day, has been attested to and widely documented. The setting up of civil administrations, the widespread health and education services, the rapid infrastructural expansion and the diversification to industry are but a few examples. These have all been made possible by the income available from the receipts of petroleum sales. Yet in practice each one has depended on a foreign executing agency – individual, collective or corporate – for its planning and implementation. Moreover, the exploration, extraction, processing, shipping and marketing of oil in the Gulf states today are virtually all undertaken by foreign technology. The national oil companies have to use this foreign technology, whether directly or indirectly. This situation is in sharp contrast to the days of the pearling economy which was all native to the region and thoroughly absorbed into its day-to-day life. Yet, in the pre-oil days, the pearls that were such an essential part of the region's economy were luxury items in the international market. The situation is radically different today. The petroleum resources of the region are vital to the social stability and economy of the rest of the world, and a relative luxury to the small and sparsely populated Gulf states. Once again, in the equation describing the relationship between the Gulf and the rest of the world, there are new and obvious changes in the degree and nature of dependence and interdependence. The perspective is sharpened in view of the recent announcement of the establishment of a US military force to respond to crises in the Gulf if the oil flow is interrupted.[29]

In the pre-oil era, trade, shipping and pearling constituted the dominant economic activities in the region. All three were centred on the sea and constituted the area where the most crucial decisions regarding the productive process had to be made: what to produce, by whom, how and for whom. It was this economic activity that determined the political, social and cultural institutions of the region. The tribal structure contributed the required organisation, discipline, loyalty and trust essential for the conduct of these activities. In the face of British power and technological changes in the production of cultured pearls, the traditional activities gradually died out. They were followed by a totally new economic institution based on oil. We have already noted the force with which this new mode was inflicted. The new era has generated considerable affluence, however, of which a fraction has been utilised to provide extensive social services. Here, as in all other domains, dependence ushered in totally new life styles. A central point of dependence is the disintegrating effects it has on the economic and cultural fabric of a society. Each activity, then, becomes separately dependent on a foreign influence. One finds, for example, no relation between the rate of exploitation of a depletable resource, on the one hand, and local needs or long-term national aspirations, on the other. If the oil resources were to run dry within two generations, the people of the Gulf would have had little chance of acquiring the needed technology to become masters of their own resource, as they had been in the pearling economy. But the present rate of petroleum exploitation is determined by foreign demand rather than by national needs: this is the hallmark of a dependent relationship.

Economic diversification in the Gulf states is currently based on widespread expansion in industry (which again is dependent on foreign expertise) and investment in Western enterprise, both of which render the states subject to fluctuations and change beyond their control. The Gulf communities have historically been closely involved with international commerce and banking, and the contemporary experiences of Kuwait, Bahrain and Dubai prove that these traditions were never entirely stifled. If the Gulf states were to concentrate on activities in these fields, they would be relying on their traditional skills and would reduce their dependence on foreign expertise. The key factors for these activities to constitute the prime sector of the economy exist: capital and manpower. By closely integrating them within the fabric of society, a large measure of independence could be achieved at minimal cost. This form of independence would provide the states with considerable leverage in other domains – e.g. defence – in times of crisis. The history of the Gulf in this century is made up of a sequence of phases that reflect increasing dependence. This growing dependence was relentlessly resisted by past rulers of the different shaikhdoms. Although irreversible changes have already taken place, the role of the development planner must be to seek a strategy that is consistent with the personality and vocation of the Gulf communities.

The energy crises that the US, Japan and Western Europe are encountering at this moment are but the beginning of the future crises that could transpire when the petroleum resources are depleted. What will happen to the Gulf states when this occurs? Will their economies undergo the collapse of the 1920s and 1930s? Without the foreign manpower and technology on which they are so heavily dependent today, will their social and economic plans all grind to a halt? As the 1938 reform movements were the repercussions of an economic depression, will there be upheavals in response to affluence? Certain lessons from the past can be drawn. First, international help is unlikely to be forthcoming, so they will have to rely on themselves alone. Second, a sound knowledge of the international market and serious research into alternative sources of energy, and alternative resources to utilise, are vital. Greater knowledge and awareness in these matters would strengthen independence in decision making. Above all, it would allow the Gulf states to be more effective masters of their own destinies.

Notes

1. Extensive attention has already been given to external dependence in development studies. The Latin American school has been particularly prominent in this field. See Osvaldo Sunkel, 'National Development Policy and External Dependence in Latin America', in Yale H. Ferguson (ed.), *Contemporary Inter-American Relations, A Reader in Theory and Issues* (Prentice-Hall, NJ; Osvaldo Sunkel, 'Transnational Capitalism and National Disintegration in Latin America', *Social and Economic Studies*, vol. 22 (1973); Martin Godfrey and Steven Langdon, 'Partners in Underdevelopment? The Transnationalisation Theses in a Kenyan Context', *The Journal of Commonwealth and Comparative Politics*, vol. 14 (1976).

2. J. G. Lorimer, *Gazetteer of the Persian Gulf, Oman and Central Arabia* (Calcutta, 1908–15, republished by Gregg International, Westmead, UK), vol. II, pp. 2256–9. The figure for the Kuwaiti labour force does not include the 2000-odd men who were Persians and who went to Kuwait specifically for the pearling season.

3. To give an example of the income of the rulers, the case of the ruler of Kuwait will be cited here. In 1904, his income from pearl dues was estimated at 20,000–60,000 Maria Theresa dollars; from customs dues, this was estimated at 150,000. Lorimer, Gazetteer, vol. II, p. 1076.

4. For a succinct presentation of these, see the article by M. G. Rumaihi, *Bahrain: Social and Political Change Since the First World War* (New York, 1975), pp. 42–9.

5. Lorimer, *Gazetteer*, vol. II, p. 245.

6. It is interesting to compare this fact with the aid programmes offered by Gulf states today. See *OAPEC Bulletin* (April 1979), p. 35, for a listing of the total authorised capital of a number of Arab funds, viz. the Kuwait Fund and the Abu Dhabi Fund.

7. For details of these movements, see M. G. Rumaihi, 'The 1938 Reform Movements in Kuwait, Bahrain and Dubai' (in Arabic), *Journal of the Gulf and Arabian Peninsula Studies*, I, no. 4 (October 1975); and Rosemarie J. Said, 'The 1938 Reform Movement in Dubai', *Al-Abhath* (December 1970).

8. R. Said Zahlan, *The Origins of the United Arab Emirates* (London, 1978), p. 4 (henceforth, *United Arab Emirates*).

9. R. Said Zahlan, *The Creation of Qatar* (London, 1979), p. 75 (henceforth, *Qatar*).

10. India Office Records (IOR) L/P&S/12/3747: PZ 1724/39, Political Agent, Bahrain, to Political Resident, 5 February 1939. Enclosed in Political Resident to Government of India, 21 February 1939. Unpublished Crown Copyright material in the India Office Records transcribed here appears by permission of the Controller of Her Majesty's Stationery Office.

11. This was not without local repercussions, however, the most outstanding being the creation of a new shaikhdom, Kalba, on the Trucial Coast. For an account of the establishment of the air route, see R. Said Zahlan, *United Arab Emirates*, pp. 92–106.

12. (IOR) I/P&S/12/3836: PZ3833/37, India Office to Political Resident, 17 June 1937 (telegram).

13. Abu Dhabi's treaties with Britain bound the ruler to suppress and abstain from the slave trade in his shaikhdom. Although this curtailed the traffic considerably, it did not suppress it entirely. The British government, moreover, reserved the right to issue manumission certificates to any slave who wished to be freed.

14. The Resident, T. C. W. Fowle, had wanted to extract 8,000 rupees from the ruler which would be repaid to him in instalments if it could be ascertained that he had put a halt to the slave trade. If Shakhbut were to refuse, his forts would be destroyed by bombing. R. Said Zahlan, *United Arab Emirates*, pp. 121–3.

15. This was Article XI. C. U. Aitchison, *A Collection of Treaties, Engagements and Sanads*, vol. XI (Delhi, 1933), p. 260.

16. R. Said Zahlan, *Qatar*, p. 62.

17. Ibid., p. 64.

18. (IOR) L/P&S/11/222: P. 5875/30, Political Agent, Bahrain, to Political Resident, 2 August 1930.

19. This Hamad promised to do in writing. See R. Said Zahlan, *Qatar*, Ch. 6.

20. Since Qatar and Bahrain were bound by their treaties with Britain not to enter into relations with any foreign country except Britain, it was the latter that channelled all their foreign affairs, even between each other.

21. (IOR) R/15/2/547: Prior (Political Resident) to Peel (India Office), 26 October 1941. See R. Said Zahlan, *Qatar*, Ch. 7.

22. Hospitals existed in Kuwait, Bahrain and Muscat.

23. (IOR) R/15/2/608: Political Resident to Government of India, 21 December 1946.

24. (IOR) R/15/2/1865: Political Resident to Political Agent, Bahrain, 5 July 1936.

25. M. G. Rumaihi, 'The 1938 Reform Movements in Kuwait, Bahrain and Dubai'.

26. With respect to the accusation levelled at Shaikh Shakhbut as narrated earlier in this paper, the 'secret agent' discovered that he was completely innocent!

27. (IOR) R/15/2/374: Prior (Political Resident) to Donaldson (India Office), 3 April 1946.

28. Ibid.

29. See *The Guardian*, 23 June 1979.

5 Natural Resources and Development in the Gulf States

KEITH McLACHLAN

Introduction

The countries lying on the littoral of the Gulf are caught in a difficult dilemma in their selection of strategies for national development, given the two basic factors affecting their domestic economies – that they are generally rich in hydrocarbon deposits but poor in almost every other natural resource. Oil exports from the area have earned increasingly large incomes but few governments have been able to transfer these revenues into productive assets of significant size to modify the essentially immature economic structures inherited from the pre-oil era. The underlying realities of limited natural resources remain much as they were in the early 1960s:

> natural resources are in general very small as compared with those of other regions, and the sparse natural wealth that does exist is only too often inefficiently or incompetently utilised. Thus the economic potentialities . . . are not large and it is regrettable that . . . there should have appeared . . . inflated estimates of possible future development.[1]

It can be argued that the augmenting flow of oil revenues to the Gulf states has diminished rather than enhanced the potential for exploitation of those few non-oil resources found in the area and that the imbalance between the contributions of hydrocarbons and other sectors of economic activity to national income and employment has been exaggerated by changes in the volumes of, and payments for, oil exports over recent years. This article sets out to review a selection of the literature concerned with the changing nature of the Gulf economies, with special reference to the use made of, or the damage suffered by, the resource base other than hydrocarbons.

Regional Strengths and Weaknesses in Natural Resources

Evaluation of natural resources in this area is recent and as yet incomplete. For the region as a whole there is no comprehensive or consistent survey of water resources, soils, land classification or land use. While this situation is improving, progress is slow[2] despite the introduction of new techniques into the process of resource evaluation.[3] Estimates of the quantities and qualities of basic natural resources are inevitably, therefore, imprecise and open to different interpretations. Those who wish to flatter propose that 'les possibilités d'extension de la production sont enormes',[4] while others viewing the same scene take the position that 'unfortunately, the deterioration of the land in Iraq over the last few centuries has been so severe that carefully planned large-scale schemes will be necessary to ensure any major improvement'.[5] Similarly polarised assessments of the other states surrounding the Gulf add to the confused perceptions of the resource endowment of the area.[6] Even where there is recognition that strong environmental constraints have limited economic development in the past, there is a tendency for future potential to be seen in over-optimistic terms, as if scientific economic planning and high allocations of oil revenues to industrial projects were themselves able to 'buy "development" like a commodity'.[7]

Available, albeit imperfect, estimates of the basic resources of the Gulf area demonstrate clearly that, while geology has been kind to the states of the area, geography has been ungenerous to extremes. The limestone and sandstone geological formations aligned around the Gulf contain some 55 per cent of the world reserves of crude oil, but the surface environment is 'located in the most extensive arid zone in the world'.[8] Gischler provides one of the most comprehensive reviews of water resources and their potential use in the Arab Middle East but points out in objective hydrological terms that in Qatar, as an example of the situation in much of the western Gulf Coast area, there is 'impotence to reverse the critical (adverse) imbalance in the groundwater regime. In other words it is already too late to solve completely the (water) problem.' Current and future water demand for the main Arab states of the Gulf, as estimated by Gischler, is given in Table 5.1.

The over-all trend in water use in the Gulf area is for rapidly increasing demand to be met by short-term and expensive water provision systems. Sub-surface water resources are being heavily pumped in a number of states, to the detriment of water quality and longevity

Table 5.1: Water Use and Future Demand in the Arab States of the Gulf

Country	Current consumption (km^3/year)	Forecast consumption (year) (km^3/year)
Bahrain	0.199	0.182
Iraq	42.820	67.400 (1995)
Kuwait	0.169	2.930 (1995)
Oman	0.430	n.a.
Qatar	0.056	n.a.
UAE	0.362	0.442 (1990)
Saudi Arabia	2.330	3.098 (1980)

Source: C. Gischler, *Water Resources in the Arab Middle East and North Africa* (Menas Press, Cambridge, 1979), pp. 98–118.

of reserves. Increments in water supply are increasingly being made available through desalination techniques, especially for domestic and industrial water requirements. Desalination is not only costly in most cases, but Gischler warns that

> The problem is not if water can be made available at a certain site, but rather, primarily, if it can be obtained cheaply enough to fit into the budget which handles it, and secondly, if it can be supplied in such a way so as to be assimilated as a new cultural amenity by the consumers.

In effect, there is doubt whether governments in the Gulf are educating their populations adequately in the costs and means of utilising new and expensive water sources in a way that will both protect the environment from ill-considered ventures into irrigated agriculture leading to soil salination and also constrain demand for water so that the energy sources used in desalination processes are not wastefully diverted from higher-value operations.

The extremely limited nature of the basic resource is shown in Table 5.2. If anything, this table tends to overstate the agricultural area, since Saudi Arabia, Kuwait and Oman all have substantially less than one per cent of their cultivable lands under irrigation: in Iraq much of the irrigated area carries only one crop each year. Rainfed agriculture is unreliable except in a few favoured locations in north-west and

Table 5.2: Cultivated Area of the Gulf Countries

Country	Total surface area – km^2	Proportion of land cultivated (percentage)	Proportion of cultivable land irrigated (percentage)
Saudi Arabia	2,260,000	1	80
Iran	1,648,000	14	20
Iraq	438,446	18	50
Oman	272,000	1	
UAE	32,000	5	100
Kuwait	16,900	1	80
Bahrain	662	5	100

Source: US Government, *Issues in the Middle East* (Washington, 1973).

northern Iran. Attempts to intensify agricultural production in the irrigated zone have been far from successful. In Iraq, allocation of development funds to new water control and drainage projects have failed so far to stem a loss rate of agricultural land from the irrigated area estimated at between 25,000 and 30,000 hectares each year from alkalinity and salinity problems. Spreading into the extensive margin has been equally disappointing. Iranian experience in Khuzestan has indicated that great social disruption and high rates of investment are unjustified in view of the poor returns to modern technological farming systems.[9] Even schemes that have had technical success, as, for example, the Sadiyat Island complex, have operated on a small experimental scale, have largely been dependent on expatriate skills, and have been divorced from local agricultural communities.[10] Agricultural activities in most of the smaller states of the Gulf are supported by extensive subsidies from government organisations and must be seen as expressions of faith, optimism and cosmetic landscaping. As oil wealth makes an increasing impact on Ras al-Khaimah and Oman, so these agricultural areas will lose their current serious commercial basis in response to rising wage rates, rural depopulation and the opening up of more rewarding and less burdensome ways of earning a living.

While there is little evidence that production has declined on a dramatic scale, even in Iran, it is clear that there is a growing relative decline in the proportion of foodstuffs in the Gulf in relation to total consumer demand. As late as 1968 the Gulf region was importing only modest volumes of agricultural products, valued by the US Department of Agriculture at $528.5 mn (Table 5.3) and almost insignificant in *per capita* terms other than in exceptionally poor agricultural years. By 1977, the situation was totally changed. Imports of agricultural commodities by the Gulf countries in that year were valued at $6,322.0 mn, by which time *per capita* imports were some $200 for Saudi Arabia, $475 for Kuwait and $75 for Iran. Within a decade, the Gulf states, in company with most other countries of the Middle East, had become deeply, if not irretrievably, dependent on foreign suppliers for their basic foodstuffs, including grain. Worse, the majority of Gulf states were able to pay for only a small fraction of their food imports by their non-oil exports, indicating a degree of vulnerability for the distant future.

Richness in hydrocarbon deposits in the Gulf area is in no way matched by wealth in other minerals, though increasing levels of exploration may reveal new deposits. Discovery and development of the Iranian Sar Cheshmeh copper fields indicates that past generalisations concerning the sparsity of non-hydrocarbon minerals must be treated with care. None the less, the main concentration of minerals is confined to the Iranian mountain systems of Alborz and Zagros, with smaller areas of deposits in the central districts of Saudi Arabia.[11] With the exception of the Sar Cheshmeh copper fields, most mineral deposits are limited in quantity and quality, are expensive to exploit and costly to transport to export terminals or to established industrial areas. In Iraq problems of isolation have been met by construction of

Table 5.3: Imports of Agricultural Goods by Gulf States – 1968 and 1977

Country	1968	1977
Iran	142.5	2,550.0
Saudi Arabia	147.6	1,285.0
Iraq	86.7	1,180.0
Kuwait	103.0	525.0
UAE	27.1	465.0
Oman	11.4	147.0
Bahrain	20.0	90.0
Qatar	10.2	80.0

Sources: Bureau of Census, US Department of Commerce and Economic Research Service, US Department of Agriculture.

Figure 5.1: Mineral Deposits in the Gulf Region

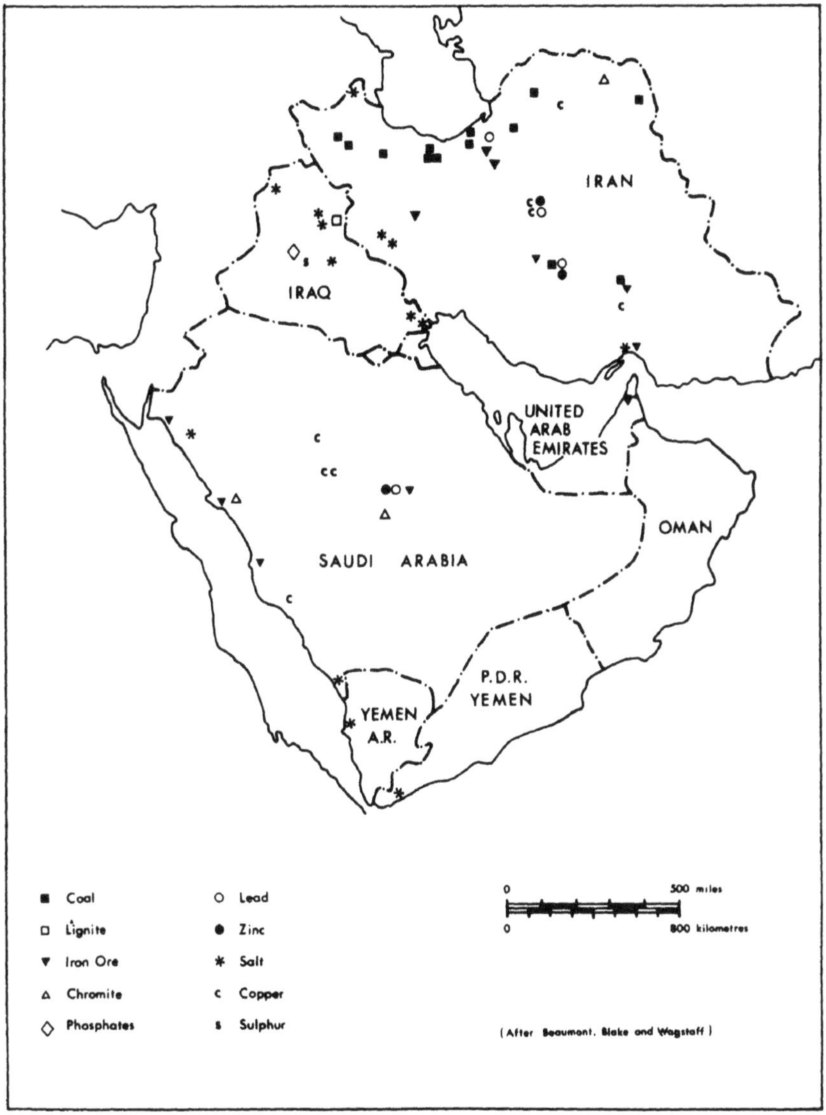

a new town at al Qaim, where a chemical complex is under construction to utilise the local sulphur deposits and phosphates from Akashat, though this is an expensive solution only possible in an oil economy and not necessarily one that could be sustained without open and hidden subsidy. The distribution of major non-hydrocarbon mineral deposits is illustrated in Figure 5.1

This brief and incomplete survey of basic physical resources in the states surrounding the Gulf has sought to bring out the very significant contrasts between an area overwhelmingly rich for the most part in crude oil and natural gas reserves but severely lacking in any other appreciable natural resources. It follows, from this, that creation of new productive assets by the oil-exporting states will be very considerably inhibited by the constraints of a difficult and hazardous environment. Oil wealth may be used to buy ways round some of the difficulties. Water can be produced from desalination plants at a price for domestic, industrial and agricultural use. Soils can be cultivated at the cost of high inputs of fertiliser, human skills and energy. It may be questioned, however, whether these activities are appropriate to anything but an extremely capital-rich oil economy and whether any will survive the passing of oil wealth.

A Review of Typologies of Oil-based Economies

Assessment of the current position of, and future prospects for, the oil-exporting states of the Gulf has tended to polarise, on the one hand, to a view where regional diversity is seen as so intense as to exclude generalisation or, on the other, where the oil states are seen as some kind of unity with more or less identical economic problems.[12] Certainly, the varied nature of the Gulf states is a deterrent to the creation of typologies, with wide differences in surface areas, populations and resource endowment (see Table 5.4).

Possibly one of the most valuable contributions to analysis of the economies of the Gulf states, representing a first step towards use of economic criteria correlated with environmental factors, is that put forward by Katouzian.[13] This typology suggests two main categories, including the desert states in one and the agricultural countries in the other, the former characterised by low population bases and insignificant agricultural sectors, the latter with relatively large populations, significant proportions of which are engaged in rural occupations. Katouzian classifies countries such as Abu Dhabi and Kuwait

Table 5.4: Areas and Populations of the Gulf States

Country	Surface area in km²	Estimated population (1976)	Persons per km²
Iran	1,648,000	33,592,000	21
Iraq	438,446	11,505,000	27
Saudi Arabia	2,260,000	9,235,000	4
Kuwait	16,900	1,093,000	65
Oman	272,000	770,000	3
UAE	32,000	656,000	21
Bahrain	662	267,000	403
Qatar	5,200	182,000	35

Sources: United Nations Yearbooks; Official Country Reports; *Europa, Middle East and North Africa* 1976/77; Economist Intelligence Unit, Quarterly Economic Reviews.

as desert oil economies and states such as Iran and Iraq as agricultural economies. He makes the valid point that

> the oil-exporting countries, though extremely fortunate in comparison with many of the non-oil developing countries, do face serious problems in the development of their economies which arise from the logic of their situation and which, therefore, cannot be entirely considered in a purely abstract and technical framework.

Another Iranian economist[14] takes the point further, indicating that, in the case of an 'agricultural' oil-exporting state, Iran, the oil sector is truly an economic enclave and the income of the state becomes largely of a 'rent' variety, divorced from the structure, the productive capacity of the mass of the population, and the poverty of the natural resource base.

It would seem an interesting exercise to press the typology further to take account both of the changes in scale in oil income arising from escalating oil prices since 1973 and also the demonstrated skill or lack of skill on the part of the oil-exporting states in elaborating linkages between the petroleum sector and other areas of the economy and in utilising physical and/or human resources to expand non-oil activities of a serious commercial kind. In essence, the question must be asked whether the division proposed by Katouzian between 'desert' and 'agricultural' types of economy can be sustained in the light of changes over the recent past. It might be argued, too, that comparison of typologies of the Gulf states in the period before 1973 with one appropriate to the end of the 1970s would reveal the dynamic strengths of the typologies and usefully indicate likely modes of future change.

A Geo-economic Typology

Whereas it would be naïve to assume that any typology could possibly please anything other than a small minority of those with expertise in the Gulf countries and it must be acknowledged that variations within individual states are so considerable as to call into question generalisations even at the national level, the creation of typologies, by intuitive or analytical means, has the beneficial function of forcing an appraisal of the regional states on a comparative basis. In philosophical or real terms, is the view of the Arabian peninsula taken by Thesiger[15] in the 1960s, that 'Men live there because it is the world into which they were born; the life they lead is the life their forefathers led before them; they accept hardships and privations; they know no other way' going to remain just as true in the era after oil exports lose some of their importance as it was before? Or will 'This bitter and desiccated land' be permanently converted into one that knows gentleness and ease?

For the period before 1973, the division put forward by Katouzian between desert and agricultural states has much to recommend it, though the number of categories will be increased here to provide some shades of change between the two extremes. The desert economies are classically exemplified by Kuwait and, latterly, by Abu Dhabi. By definition, these states have an extremely poor relative endowment of natural resources. Kuwait has an absolute shortage of water and, other than hydrocarbons, has no mineral deposits of major importance. Crude oil exports dominate the economy and it is to oil income that all other activities ultimately return for financial sustenance. Oil sector contributions to national income, to foreign exchange earnings and to direct and indirect employment are high. *Per capita* incomes even by 1973 were appreciable: Kuwait's stood at $4,125 and Abu Dhabi's at $3,850. Absorptive capacity is low in relation to the high levels of oil income, constrained by the lack of real domestic resources, and Kuwait especially was steadily accumulating financial assets overseas before 1973. Reliance on foreign labour was high and increasing, while the national population was concentrating in a few urban areas at an accelerating pace. As early as 1973, before oil prices rose dramatically, it was apparent that opportunities for the elaboration of the domestic economies of the desert states were severely limited and that only sustained export of oil and natural gas offered a certain future.

Different by degree from the purely desert economies, yet by no means agriculturally based states, were Saudi Arabia and Qatar. Before 1973 these marginal desert economies were characterised by the presence of modest non-oil resources – some agriculture in favoured rainfall or oasis areas, involvement in international trade, tourism (through the *haj* in Saudi Arabia) and some small-scale but locally important industry. *Per capita* incomes were not high in 1973, when Saudi Arabia's stood at some $1,360. Saudi Arabia and Qatar did, however, share the problem of low absorptive capacity with their desert neighbours, while the proportion of national income and foreign exchange earnings from oil were beginning to grow to levels only marginally less than those of Kuwait. Yet there could be a justified measure of optimism in the early 1970s that the Saudi Arabian and Qatari economies might be elaborated, slowly and with difficulty, into something rather more complex than simple oil-based structures.

Different from both previous categories were Bahrain, Dubai and Oman, which were at that time oil-exporting states only partially dependent on the petroleum sector of their economies. Their characteristics were that oil made up a comparatively small proportion of national income and oil reserves were expected to be of short duration. In this situation, oil income was large enough to stimulate development activity in the non-oil areas of the economy, to which aim government policy was forced by the short-term nature of the oil industry. Oman had opportunities in agriculture of sizeable magnitude, and Bahrain and Dubai were making intensive use of available geographical and economic advantages, including traditional entrepôt functions in trade and commercial services. Bahrain and Oman were separated from the other oil states in having only minor reliance on imported labour in the period up to the end of 1973.

A final category is that recognised by Katouzian as 'agricultural states', which in the Gulf area includes Iraq and Iran. With oil representing less than 40 per cent of national income (33 per cent in Iraq and 30 per cent in Iran in 1973), these states were clearly more economically elaborate than were most of their neighbours. A comparatively wide spread of non-oil resources could be identified, led by fertile land, large quantities of water, the presence of some non-hydrocarbon mineral deposits and large, if ill-trained, labour forces. Although agriculture had been losing ground as a generator of national income and employer of labour over a number of years, it still accounted for 13 per cent of GDP in Iraq and 16 per cent in Iran in 1973. Industrial development, too, was exhibiting a certain growth in both countries, with 10 per cent of GDP in Iraq and 16 per cent in Iran arising from manufacturing industry. At the same time *per capita* incomes were low, at $509 in Iraq and $380 in Iran. The nature of economic development in both states gave rise to questions of the appropriateness of policies and the degree to which real new resources were being created in the early 1970s. But it did not require a complete optimist to believe that Iraq and Iran could, with dedication and stability, establish viable and large non-oil sectors to their economies; that the relative role of oil in their economies could be kept to controllable proportions; and that they would make a transition when ultimately required to do so to an economic regime no longer reliant on large volumes of oil revenues.

The typology proposed above for the early 1970s cannot be regarded as altogether satisfactory. Oman and Dubai might be considered to be strange bedfellows, while the shade of differentiation between, say, Qatar and Bahrain will not find universal support. A mixture of economic and geographic criteria might offend purists from both disciplines. It is equally a problem that typologies deal with static and essentially historic situations. What, then, has the response been of these various categories outlined above to the changes in the Gulf that have taken place since late-1973, stimulated by rapidly rising oil income in the wake of the Arab–Israeli war of October 1973?

All states of the Gulf area have shared in a period of unrestrained growth in imports and 'development' activity, have experienced extremely high rates of inflation and have undergone large increases in domestic wage rates. In other spheres effects have been more varied. The desert economies of 1973 have experienced a heightening of their characteristics – *per capita* incomes have risen (Kuwait recorded an income per head of $12,500 in 1977) and the problems of absorptive capacity have been much enhanced (Kuwait failed to absorb 65 per cent of foreign exchange income in 1976 and 10 per cent in 1977/78). Meanwhile, reliance on foreign labour has increased, with Kuwait currently dependent on a labour force almost 75 per cent non-national. For the desert oil economies there were never many options available other than elaboration of a welfare state: after the events of 1973/74 and 1979, which have pushed up the price of oil, it must be finally acknowledged that income from oil and from investments overseas will remain the financial props of their economies and that all other forms of development will be functions of the governments' need to inject funds into the domestic economies to create employment and to appear to be concerned with establishment of alternative productive assets to the oil industry. It follows that, without a large income from oil and overseas investments, the desert economies could sustain neither the population numbers nor likely standards of living expected during the early decades of the twenty-first century, and that ultimate adjustment to a non-oil economy could be difficult.

The marginal desert states have ceased to be marginal since 1973/74. The contribution of the oil sector to national income has risen above 65 per cent and foreign exchange earnings are now almost entirely dependent on oil exports. Saudi Arabia and Qatar have witnessed a rapid increase in import dependence. Those small non-oil contributors to national income that appeared, on aggregate, to be capable of expansion to the stage where they might compete, however unequally, with petroleum as sources of national wealth and employment have been entirely dwarfed by the growth of the oil sector during the 1970s. There has, too, been a surge in urbanisation, with demographic concentration replacing a formerly diffused population. The foreign labour force in Saudi Arabia and Qatar has been much augmented in recent years with four out of five of the workforce in Qatar being of foreign extraction. In essence, these economies have become in almost all respects indistinguishable from the desert states, as a result of the changes affecting the petroleum sector since 1973, and their future prospects appear to be as limited as those foreseen for Kuwait and Abu Dhabi.

In the cases of Bahrain, Dubai and Oman (especially the former two countries), the increase in oil wealth in the recent past has been used with some effect in a conscious drive towards the creation of new assets, such as the Jebel Ali development in Dubai and the aluminium smelter in Bahrain, or the reinforcement of existing business in entrepôt and service functions. While the current profitability of, and future prospects for, all new schemes initiated in these states is by no means certain, many are already commercially viable and the others will need to be so at some stage if they are to survive. Urbanisation has strongly affected all countries in this category, while an expansion of foreign components in the workforce has been appreciable, particularly in Dubai, bringing them into positions not altogether dissimilar from the desert states in this regard. Over all, however, the three states are not oil-dependent at the present time, despite the economic convulsions of the mid- and late-1970s.

For the resource-endowed states such as Iran and Iraq, changes wrought to their economies during the 1970s have significantly altered their status within the typology. In the case of Iran, political change has brought further disruption that has accentuated purely economic trends. The degree of change affecting Iran and Iraq is debatable. By 1976 agriculture still contributed 12 per cent to GDP in Iran and 11 per cent in Iraq, with industry at 16 per cent in Iran and 8 per cent in Iraq, representing an apparent continuation in structural maturation of their economies. Income per head had ceased to be quite so modest: \$1,600 in Iran and \$2,100 in Iraq indicated an important change in this area by 1976. The structure of the economy and of employment, however, have altered sufficiently to make them more arguably marginal or partially dependent oil economies. The aspects which give evidence of this are the pattern of spending of oil revenues in the two countries since 1973 – in which allocations for industrial and agricultural development took lower priority than expenditure on state and private consumption[16] – the growth in the petroleum sector to 30 per cent of GDP in Iran and 39 per cent in Iraq, and the severe levels of rural migration to the cities.

The outcome of the so-called oil booms of 1973/74 and of 1979 would appear, therefore, to have changed the positions of the oil-exporting states within the typology proposed, though not the typology itself. Without pressing the case too strongly at this stage when statistical detail is mainly lacking, it would seem that the typology arrived at for the pre-1973 situation in the Gulf represented an apparent continuum through which many of the states in the area are progressing, regardless of the official aims of economic policies which specifically propose a stabilisation or reduction of the role of the oil sector. Continuing enhancement of the oil sector through rising prices of crude oil or augmenting levels of crude oil exports in the future would, it could be argued, result in all the states of the Gulf surrendering their option of creating non-oil domestic production assets as the basically poor resource endowment other than hydrocarbons plays a diminishing part in the generation of national income and employment. In Iran, a combination of economic failure since 1977 and political disruption since 1978 may well have brought about an absolute decline in the participation of agriculture and industry in GDP – a development which might not be redeemable[17] and which would accelerate Iran's shift towards the mainly oil-dependent status of an 'oil-exporting state partially dependent on oil'.

A summary of the tentative typology and the location of states within it at the present time would be as follows – in the category 'desert economies' Kuwait and Abu Dhabi have been joined by Saudi Arabia and Qatar, while Oman might be deemed to have become the sole resident of the category 'marginal desert economies'. The third grouping of the typology, 'oil-exporting states partially dependent on oil', includes two of the original members, Bahrain and Dubai, together with Iraq and Iran. As a result of the relative changes noted above, the category 'resource-endowed states with oil' ceases to be relevant. Such conclusions are unlikely to be seen as flattering: they are certainly harsh. But if this view of the economies of the Gulf and their confined base in natural resources either assists in a move towards a more realistic assessment of the area and its prospects outside the petroleum sector or distinguishes advertised national aims of diversification into non-oil activities from apparent trends in the opposite direction, then no apologies are needed. Doubtless alternative and better typologies will be elaborated, possibly, and more usefully, taking in the remaining areas of the Middle East and North Africa. Meanwhile, this article has sought to enlighten one small area of debate and enter a necessary caveat on the prospects for development of non-oil potential in the countries of the Gulf region.

Notes

1. W. B. Fisher, *The Middle East* (Methuen, London, 1963), p. 7.
2. J. A. Allan, 'Renewable Natural Resources in the Middle East' (1979), in J. I. Clarke and H. Bowen-Jones (eds), *Change and Development in the Middle East* (Methuen, London, forthcoming).
3. J. A. Allan, N. D. E. Custance and J. S. Latham, 'New Era for Landsat', *Geographical Magazine* (London, 1979), p. 431.
4. *Industries et Travaux d'Outre-Mer* (Paris, April 1979), p. 239.
5. P. Beaumont, G. H. Blake and J. M. Wagstaff, *The Middle East* (Wiley, London, 1976), p. 342.
6. Cf. F. Langer, *Iran – Oil Money and the Ambitions of a Nation* (The Hudson Letter, Paris, 1975), p. 14, and M. Rouhani, 'Agricultural Development Policy', in *Iran* (Times Newspapers/Confederation of British Industry, London, 1973), p. 10, with respect to potential resources for agriculture in Iran.
7. E. Penrose, 'Industrial Policy and Performance in Iraq', in A. Kelidar (ed.), *The Integration of Modern Iraq* (Croom Helm, London, 1979), p. 163.
8. C. Gischler, *Water Resources in the Arab Middle East and North Africa* (Menas Press, Cambridge, 1979), p. 3.
9. E. Ehlers and G. Goodell, *Traditionelle und Moderne Formen der Landwirtschaft in Iran* (Marburg/Lahn, 1975).
10. FAO, *Agricultural Development in the UAE – Report on Present Position, Prospects and Priorities* (Rome, 1973).
11. Beaumont, Blake and Wagstaff, *The Middle East*, p. 241.

12. Y. Sayigh, *The Determinants of Arab Economic Development* (Croom Helm, London, 1978), p. 46.

13. M. A. Katouzian, *The Political Economy of Development in the Oil-exporting Countries: An Analytical Framework* (paper delivered to a Conference on the Impact of Oil on the Social and Economic Life of the Oil-producing Countries, Sussex University, 1976).

14. H. Mahdavy, 'Patterns and Problems of Development in Rentier States – the Case of Iran', in M. A. Cook (ed.), *Studies in the Economic History of the Middle East* (Oxford University Press, London, 1970).

15. W. Thesiger, *Arabian Sands* (Penguin, London, 1965), p. 15.

16. K. S. McLachlan, 'Development – the Disaster of the Oil Boom', *Middle East Annual Review* (Saffron Walden, 1979).

17. K. S. McLachlan, *Iran – Political Crisis: Origins and Development* (paper delivered to UAE Ministry of Foreign Affairs, Abu Dhabi, forthcoming).

6 Problems Confronting the Establishment of a Heavy Industrial Base in the Arab Gulf

JOHN TOWNSEND

Introduction

The objective of this article is to analyse the broad strategy of the oil-producing nations of the Arab Gulf for the establishment of a heavy industrial base and to interpret the major constraints standing in the way of a rapid transformation of the Arab Gulf into an industrial region. It is particularly concerned with markets and prices, with management, with skills and with labour. A detailed discussion of every heavy industrial project in Saudi Arabia, Kuwait, Iraq, Bahrain, Qatar and the United Arab Emirates will not be provided, but for ease of reference an indicative list of the major heavy industrial projects in operation, proposed, planned or under construction, in the general area of the Arab Gulf may be found at the end. This list has two important qualifications: first, it makes no mention of industry in Iran. Even though much of Iranian industry is under a cloud of uncertainty at the moment, it must never be forgotten that industry in the Arab countries of the Gulf is likely to be in competition with Iranian industry over the course of the next two decades. The second qualification is that, although great care has been taken in compiling the list, it is not necessarily comprehensive nor does it give an up-to-the-minute status report on individual projects. Whereas much publicity is given to projects when they are first mooted, or when a feasibility study is commissioned, very little is said when projects are cancelled or deferred.

It must be stressed that a number of heavy industrial projects, for example the Arab Ship Repair Yard in Bahrain, the ALBA aluminium smelter in Bahrain, the fertiliser and steel plants in Qatar, and many refineries and smaller industries are operating successfully and making a profit. Most of these projects have had the inevitable start-up problems and management problems. In some cases, these problems have been serious, but in no case has there been a failure to solve the problems and overcome the difficulties. It is only to be expected that industrial projects incorporating advanced technology will have problems during the implementation stage. Attention will not be concentrated on these problems.

Rather, the concern is with understanding the basic environment of the Arab Gulf and with examining the industrial development strategies of the Gulf states as they seek to master their environment and to harness their basic resources in a way hitherto undreamed of by their peoples. Policies for industrialisation, being radical in the geographic and social environment, have inevitably brought into the open contradictions and constraints, some of which will doubtless be mastered. Others are so fundamental that they could either emasculate plans for the establishment of a heavy industrial base or, being resolved, change the basic character of the societies of the states of the Arab Gulf.

Plans for broadening the economic base of any oil-producing nation in the Arab Gulf start with a simple and impeccable statement of principle: to invest oil revenues today in such a way that tomorrow, when oil revenues may no longer be important, they will not be missed. More precisely, governments have set out to spend oil revenues in such a way that modern science, technology and management may be applied to all resources in the Gulf countries, including resources in the agricultural sector, so that the over-all productivity of these resources should be permanently raised. In other words, they are setting out to create an industrial base. The resources which are plentiful are capital, energy, raw materials for petrochemical industries, and certain building materials. The resources which are extremely scarce are water and labour.

Making Optimum Use of Existing Resources

The most prominent reason given to justify industrialisation as a means to ensure long-term prosperity in the Gulf is that in this way the best use can be made of existing resources and the value of raw materials can be enhanced. Let us now consider what is involved in seeking to achieve such objectives. The most abundant raw material in the countries of the Arab Gulf, after crude oil, is natural gas. This gas, which is also a cheap energy source, is the basic input for capital-intensive petrochemical plants which produce ethylene and ethylene by-products. Ethylene is the basic feedstock for the international petrochemical industry, and Saudi Arabian plans call for the production of two million tons of ethylene equivalent by the early 1980s, all intended for export. Iraq, Abu Dhabi and possibly others are also planning ethylene plants and would intend to export production.

Natural gas is also a fuel for metallurgical industries, such as alumina and iron ore smelting. The value added in each case is likely to justify the import of the necessary ores. The principal market for the aluminium ingots produced in the Arab Gulf is a world market, although local and regional markets can be expected to take an increasing share of production. The production of steel bars and billets in the Arab Gulf is intended for local and regional markets. In addition to the aluminium smelter planned for Saudi Arabia, there is already a smelter operating in Bahrain. Dubai's smelter is due to start production in 1981 and Iraq's at about the same time. As far as steel is concerned, the Qatar steel mill started operating in August 1978, and Iraq's mill in January 1979. Qatar's mill is intended to serve a regional market, Iraq's a local market only.

In a sense, the strategic location of the Arab Gulf countries *vis-à-vis* world trade routes, and especially tanker routes, is an economic resource. Dry docks and ship repair yards form an important element in the Gulf countries' plans for creating a heavy industrial base. The market for tanker and ship repairs is, of course, international. The governments of the Arab Gulf countries, with the exception of Oman which is not a member of OAPEC, are all shareholders in the Arab Ship Repair Yard (ASRY) in Bahrain. Dubai's dry dock and ship repair yard complex was formally opened in February 1979, but has not yet started operating. The Dubai yard was built in direct competition with the Bahrain yard and has a theoretical capacity of three times the latter.

These examples, which are not intended to be exhaustive, reveal the major problems confronting the governments of the countries of the Arab Gulf as they try to establish a heavy industrial base. The examples point to the problem of markets and of prices and, allied to these, the problems which could arise from regional duplication. With these problems must be considered questions of imported technology, management and manpower generally.

Let us start with the question of markets. As far as the export-oriented industries are concerned, there is no reason why Arab Gulf producers of ethylene, ethylene-equivalent products and aluminium ingots should not ultimately sell all their products profitably on world markets. Aluminium Bahrain (ALBA), for example, established over seven years ago, is now making money after a long period of losses. This profitable operation is due mostly to increasing demand on world markets for aluminium, but a managerial shake-up and a determined attack on production costs by management have also contributed to this favourable situation.

ALBA is a joint venture in which the government of Bahrain has held 77.9 per cent of the equity, with foreign companies with international reputations in the aluminium business holding the balance. The Saudi Arabian Basic Industries Corporation (SABIC) has this year agreed to buy 20 per cent of the equity in ALBA from the government of Bahrain, so that Bahrain's experience can benefit SABIC in Saudi Arabia's plans for a smelter. Dubai's Shaikh Rashid, the moving spirit behind his Emirate's Dubai Aluminium Company (DUBAL), believes that the present buoyancy in world markets for aluminium will continue into the 1980s when the DUBAL smelter comes into operation. At that time, Iraq's smelter should also be competing for a share of the market. The problem is obvious: no one can predict with confidence the likely state of the world market for aluminium throughout the 1980s, and four Arab Gulf producers will be competing with each other for a share of this market.

There is no reason why these four producers should not each win and keep a market share. This will require the best in professional production and marketing management, with a tough cost discipline. Production costs in the Gulf countries tend to be high compared with the international competition because distance and a harsh physical environment add a significant factor both to initial plant construction and to plant maintenance costs. Local labour shortages tend also to put up production costs, and distance can add a factor to distribution costs. None of these problems is incapable of solution but, it should be stressed, the solution lies in good management. Any temptation on the part of Arab Gulf governments to subsidise production costs to maintain competitiveness may give short-term benefits, but could not be compatible with the longer-term establishment of a viable heavy industrial base.

The joint venture as a means of establishing heavy industry is much favoured by countries such as Saudi Arabia, Bahrain, Qatar and the United Arab Emirates. The theory is simple: a joint venture permits an Arab Gulf country to maintain control of its heavy industries whilst obtaining from the joint venture partner the management, technology and access to markets deemed essential for successful heavy industrial projects. Equity participation by the joint venture partner, up to a maximum of 49 per cent, is favoured rather than a straightforward management contract because it is believed that a foreign joint venture partner who is prepared to stake his own money in a project is, in effect, locked in and hence will be more likely to exert every effort to ensure the profitability and the success of the project.

Foreign partners are possibly less happy with the concept. The Saudi Arabian steel joint venture with West Germany's Korf Stahl A.G. took a considerable time to negotiate. Korf wanted only a management contract, whereas SABIC wanted them to take 49 per cent of the equity. Korf finally agreed to take a share in the equity of the project after the Saudi–West German Joint Economic Commission agreed to a scheme for guaranteeing private West German investment in the Kingdom.

There is an apparent lack of confidence by potential foreign joint venture partners in the viability of Arab Gulf heavy industrial projects. This lack of confidence would appear to be behind the reluctance of international companies to finalise joint venture agreements which have been on the drawing boards for some years. One which seems now almost certain to go ahead is a Saudi–Japanese joint venture to build a 310,000-tons-a-year ethylene plant. Originally conceived as a joint venture between SABIC and Mitsubishi, the project now will be between SABIC and a Japanese company to be known as the Saudi Petrochemicals Development Company, a consortium led by Mitsubishi and including no fewer than 54 Japanese companies. The role of the Japanese Ministry of International Trade and Industry has not been formally announced, but it seems probable that the Ministry is offering some form of guarantee to the Japanese investors. In short, some foreign joint venture partners seem to be seeking guarantees from their own governments before they are prepared to invest in heavy industry in the Arab Gulf.

This reluctance by foreigners to invest is not a major hurdle, though it may require a certain amount of rethinking of policies on the part of Arab Gulf governments. The government of Iraq does not favour joint ventures. The ASRY shipyard in Bahrain has no foreign capital invested in it, and nor does the Dubai dry dock project. ASRY in Bahrain is managed by a Portuguese shipyard operator under a ten-year management contract, and the Dubai yard will have a similar arrangement with another foreign shipyard manager.

Just as difficulty in finalising joint venture agreements with foreign investors should not be an insurmountable problem in the way of establishing a viable heavy industrial base in the Arab Gulf, nor should the apparent duplication of projects be allowed to become a stumbling block. Much is talked about regional co-operation in the Arab Gulf. Many institutions have been set up to further this co-operation, for example the Gulf Organisation for Industrial Consultancy, but the plain fact is that competition is more apparent than co-operation, in spite of regional organisations like Gulf Air and ASRY.

ASRY is worth examining in a little more detail, as it is an example of regional co-operation which risks being made less viable by the potential competition from the Dubai dockyard. Saudi Arabia, Kuwait, Bahrain, Qatar and the United Arab Emirates are equal major shareholders in ASRY, with Iraq and the Libyan Jamahiriya each having a small shareholding. Although the shareholders do expect some financial return on their investment, a commercial return is less important for them initially than the fact of an Arab-owned shipyard which can act as a catalyst for wider industrial expansion in the region of the Arab Gulf. Their immediate commercial objective was to establish an efficient dockyard operation which would attract international shipowners because of the price and the quality of the work carried out. In this objective they have succeeded and the ASRY yard has a full order book. Yet this comparatively satisfactory state of affairs could be upset by competition from the Dubai dockyard, which is equipped to carry out the same work as the Bahrain yard and which has three dry dock basins to Bahrain's one. The ASRY management is deeply concerned at the prospect of regional over-capacity and has indicated that it is ready to work out a formula for co-operation with the Dubai yard.

The question of regional co-ordination of industrial plans is not as simple as it looks. Apart from the obvious political considerations, there is a fear among some Arab Gulf governments that state capitalism, which they have been obliged to adopt to get heavy industries launched and which inevitably tends to be less efficient than the private enterprise which is at the heart of Arab Gulf successful business, would naturally be strengthened at the expense of private enterprise and hence of over-all commercial competitiveness. The question of state as opposed to private sector ownership of Arab Gulf heavy industries is not an issue at the present time, but it is likely to be one uppermost in the minds of Arab Gulf leaders over the course of the next few years as heavy industry competes with government for the best Arab Gulf minds and abilities.

Associated Problems in Industrialisation

The dimensions of the Arab Gulf's likely dependence on foreign labour as a result of industrialisation are discussed in detail by Birks and Sinclair elsewhere in this book. Here it will simply be stressed that this dependence would hold serious political and social implications for the states of the Arab Gulf. Local governments face a dilemma: they do not want to have such large numbers of foreigners, but at the same time the present and future economic health of their communities would seem to depend on foreigners.

Apprehension for a future where Gulf nationals constitute a steadily diminishing proportion of the total population is one factor causing some Gulf citizens to question whether heavy industrialisation is really desirable. There is an increasing tendency to listen to voices which contrast the present pattern of development unfavourably with the past. Such voices contend that the traditional communities of the Arab Gulf were not really underdeveloped before the oil era brought such sweeping changes in its wake. The traditional communities were certainly poor but, it is argued, they had great moral strengths, were balanced and had simple effective rules of social justice which were understood and accepted by all. Each community was recognised as being the best judge of its own interests, and communal rules at once permitted communal wishes to be optimised and precluded much interference by rulers and officials in communal activities. The organisation of each community's institutions, economic structures, markets and administration was simple but in general adequate for the needs of the members of the community. With very little contact with the outside world, the obvious differences between the life patterns of the Arab Gulf communities and the outside world were scarcely noticed and, if noticed, were not valued. There was no deeply felt need to 'modernise' or to 'catch up'; these are concepts which have been imported from the industrialised nations, along with a taste for a wide range of consumer goods.

The policy prescription following from this attitude is that each Arab Gulf nation should produce just enough oil to generate revenue for its own immediate needs. Such a policy would have added advantages, so it is argued, in that it would put up the price of oil and conserve the depleting resource. From this point of view, the question is not whether the purchase of modern capital-intensive technology to create an industrial sector will be effective, but rather whether the attempt should be made at all. This attitude must be counted among the problems confronting the establishment of a heavy industrial base in the Arab Gulf.

Appendix: Indicative List of Heavy Industrial Organisations and Projects Operating, Being Constructed or Planned

N.B. This list is intended to give an indication of the nature and scope of projects. It is not necessarily comprehensive, nor does it claim to give a status report on any one project.

(i) *Regional Industries*

(a) Owned by the Organisation of Arab Petroleum Exporting Countries (OAPEC):
- Arab Maritime Petroleum Transport Company (AMPTC); operating.
- Arab Ship Repair Yard, Bahrain (ASRY); operating.

(b) Owned by Arab Gulf Governments:
- Gulfair (international airline); operating.
- Gulf International Bank (wholesale bank); operating.
- Gulf Organisation for Industrial Consultancy (industrial consultancy); operating.

(ii) *Saudi Arabia*

(a) Oil refineries:
- Jeddah refinery, 240,000 b/d; planned.
- Petromin/Shell Jubail refinery, 250,000 b/d; planned.
- Petromin/Chevron–Texaco lube oil refinery, 120,000 b/d; planned.
- Petromin refinery, Riyadh, 120,000 b/d; planned.
- Petromin/Mobil refinery, Yanbu, 250,000 b/d; planned.
- Petromin/Mobil petrolube refinery, Jeddah, 3,000 b/d; operating.
- plus ARAMCO refinery at Ras Tanura; operating.

(b) Petrochemical plants:
- SABIC/Mitsubishi–Japanese consortium, 310,000 tons p.a. ethylene; being constructed.
- SABIC/Shell, 656,000 tons p.a. ethylene, linked to Petromin/Shell refinery, Jubail; planned.
- SABIC/Exxon, 240,000 tons p.a. low density polyethylene, linked to SABIC/Shell ethylene plant; planned.

- SABIC/Mobil, 450,000 tons p.a. ethylene, Yanbu, linked to Petromin/Mobil refinery; planned.
- SABIC/Dow, 440,000 tons p.a. ethylene; planned.

(c) Methanol plants:
- SABIC/US consortium, 660,000 tons p.a.; planned.
- SABIC/Japanese consortium, 600,000 tons p.a.; planned.

(d) Metal smelting plants:
- SABIC/Korf iron ore and steel, 850,000 tons p.a.; being constructed.
- SABIC/ALBA; SABIC has bought 20 per cent of the equity in ALBA, Bahrain, as a probable preliminary to an aluminium smelter in Jubail.

(e) Fertiliser plants:
- SABIC/Taiwan Fertiliser Company, 500,000 tons p.a.; planned.

(f) Other industry (not comprehensive):
- steel rolling mill, Jeddah (Korf now has management contract); operating.
- aluminium extrusion plant; operating.
- Mercedes truck assembly plant, Jeddah; operating.

(iii) *Kuwait*

(a) Oil refineries:
- Kuwait Oil Company (KOC) refinery, Ahmadi.
- Kuwait National Petroleum Company (KNPC), refinery, Shu'aiba.
- KOC gas liquefaction plant, inaugurated early 1979, to produce 4.4 m. tons p.a.
- KOC bitumen plant, inaugurated October 1978, capacity 250,000 tons p.a.
- Refinery projects being discussed with Romania, Jugoslavia, Indonesia, and Ras al-Khaimah (see UAE section).

(b) Petrochemical plants:
- Kuwait Petrochemicals Company, aromatics plant to produce benzene and xylene. Capacity 300,000 tons p.a.; being constructed.

(c) Fertilisers:
- Kuwait Petrochemicals Industries Company, started operations 1970, produced 668,200 tons urea and 522,900 tons ammonium 1978.

(d) Shipping:
- Kuwait is base for AMPTC (see Section (i)) and also operates its own shipping line, the Kuwait Oil Tankers Company (KOTC), which was operating 12 tankers in 1978.

(e) Other industry:
- Kuwait has established private sector light industries including a flour mill and various engineering assembly plants.

(iv) *Bahrain*

(a) Ship repair yard:
- ASRY (see Section (i)); operating.

(b) Metal smelter:
- Aluminium Bahrain (ALBA), joint venture owned 57.9 per cent government of Bahrain, 20 per cent SABIC, 17 per cent Kaiser Aluminium of US and 5.1 per cent by Breton Investments of West Germany. 20 per cent of output now sold to Saudi Arabia for Saudi extrusion plant. Plant operating.

(v) *Qatar*

(a) Oil refinery:
- Umm Said Refinery, 50,000 b/d; operating.

(b) Petrochemical plant:
- Qatar General Petroleum/CDF Chimie, 280,000 tons p.a. ethylene; under construction.

(c) Metal smelter:
- Qatar Steel Company/Kobe Steel 380,000 tons p.a. sponge iron reduction and steel plant; operating. 70 per cent production for export to Gulf, 30 per cent for domestic market.

(d) Fertiliser plant:
- Qatar Fertiliser Co./Norsk Hydro–Hambros Bank ammonia/urea; operating.

(vi) *United Arab Emirates*

(a) Oil refineries:
- Abu Dhabi (Ruwais) Abu Dhabi National Oil Co. (ADNOC) 120,000 b/d refinery; planned.
- Dubai (Jebel Ali) 150,000 b/d refinery; proposed.
- Ras al-Khaimah – possible joint venture refinery with Kuwaiti interests – unlikely to go ahead.

(b) Metal smelters:
- Dubai/Southwire (DUBAL) aluminium smelter being constructed.
- possible iron ore/steel plant in Ruwais.

(c) Fertiliser plant:
- possible urea/ammonia plant in Ruwais.

(d) Ship repair yard:
- Dubai dry dock complex (completed early 1979).

(e) Other industry:
- Dubai has other lighter industry, for example a successful joint venture producing glass-reinforced plastic piping which is exported throughout the Gulf.

(vii) *Iraq*

(a) Oil refineries:
- Al Doura refinery, Baghdad; operating.
- Basra refinery – being expanded to 300,000 b/d with Japanese participation.
- smaller refineries in various parts of country.

(b) Petrochemical plant:
- Basra ethylene and by-product plant, 138,000 tons p.a.; for completion 1981.

(c) Metal smelters:
- sponge iron/steel plant; operating 1979.
- plans for aluminium smelter deferred.

(d) Fertiliser plants:
- complex totalling 5 nitrogenous fertiliser and urea plants operating or being built in the Basra/Khor al-Zubair area.
- phosphatic fertiliser plant being built at al-Qaim.

(e) Other industry:
- much smaller-scale industry, especially in building materials sector.

7 Pastoral Nomads in a Rapidly Changing Economy: The Case of Saudi Arabia[1]

DONALD P. COLE

Socio-economic Development in Present-day Saudi Arabia

The aim of this paper is to examine and explain the socio-economic situation in which pastoral nomads, the bedouin, find themselves in present-day Saudi Arabia. It is evident that the role of the contemporary bedouin can only be understood within the context of the wider socio-economic framework. We must first, therefore, sketch out the essential features of that wider socio-economic context. In this section a brief overview will be given of what seems to be the way in which development has been taking place in Saudi Arabia in recent years, as gleaned from a review of selected Saudi Arabian government documents and from conversations with a number of government officials in the Saudi Arabian Ministry of Planning.

The fundamental long-term strategic goals of Saudi Arabia's development have been stated in the Kingdom's *Second Development Plan for 1395–1400 AH : 1975–1980 AD*. These include the following seven objectives: to maintain the religious and moral values of Islam; to assure the defence and internal security of the Kingdom; to maintain a high rate of economic growth by developing economic resources, maximising earnings from oil over the long term, and conserving depletable resources; to reduce economic dependence on the export of crude oil through diversification of the economic base; to develop human resources by education, training and raising standards of health; to increase the well-being of all groups within the society and to foster social stability under circumstances of rapid economic change; and to develop and utilise the physical infrastructure to support the achievement of the above-mentioned goals.

Indications from the Ministry of Planning are that these objectives are still valid and will govern the direction of *The Third Development Plan for 1400–1405 AH : 1980–1985 AD*. However, the Third Plan is expected to put greater emphasis on the utilisation of physical infrastructure than on its development, along with an increased emphasis on the development of human resources, a new emphasis on the development of economic resources, and a continued emphasis on the well-being of citizens and the stability of society.[2]

At present, mid-point in the period of the Second Development Plan, Saudi Arabia's economy is essentially dualistic, consisting of two interacting systems – what we might call the 'modern' and the 'traditional'. The modern economic system includes some industry, elements of large-scale modernised agriculture, financial and other services, capital-intensive trade and government. The oil industry is obviously an important element in the modern economic system. Other important elements are its very large foreign reserve holdings, probably the greatest in the world, the fact that it is the largest single provider of new investment funds flowing into the world's economic systems, and its possession of one of the world's largest foreign aid programmes. It is also a vital supplier of funds to international lending and development agencies. At the same time, it is a highly significant consumer of the exported goods and services of industrialised nations. Because of its recognised responsibilities and the tasks of managing its oil reserves and production and because of the need it feels to protect and manage its extensive and growing overseas investment holdings and aid programmes, a very significant amount of top quality Saudi Arabian managerial manpower and ministerial time is required.

Alongside the modern economic system, which mainly operates from metropolitan centres, is the traditional economic system prevailing in rural areas and small towns and even in parts of the metropolitan centres. This system is based on peasant subsistence agriculture, nomadic pastoralism, petty trade, and various services which support and supply these activities. The Ministry of Planning estimates that some 35 per cent of the Kingdom's labour force (excluding nomads and all women) is engaged in the low growth, low productivity, and low wage sectors of agriculture and personal and community services.

More or less straddling the traditional and modern economic systems are the construction sector and the traditional service sectors. The construction sector draws manpower from the traditional system and employs it in the development of the modern system. Many of the service functions of the modern system, especially trade and transportation, are provided by enterprises from the traditional economic system, using labour-intensive, low-capital, small-scale and relatively inefficient ways, yet receiving great cash income because of high demand from the modern system. Both the construction sector and the traditional service sectors essentially draw manpower out of the traditional productive sector of agriculture (and pastoralism)[3] without transmitting it into modern productive sectors. Instead, it is kept in economically inefficient but relatively well-paid employment. Some 57 per cent of the Kingdom's labour force (excluding nomads and women) is estimated to be engaged in government, construction, transport, and trade – all throughput rather than productive output sectors. This leaves only eight per cent of the Kingdom's labour force to be engaged in productive output sectors.

As already mentioned, the traditional economic system is operative mainly in rural areas and small towns, while the modern economic system operates out of metropolitan centres. This has led not only to a general rural–urban imbalance in development but to the creation of regional imbalances as well. Infrastructural development has tended to have an urban bias and rural areas have been, relatively speaking, neglected. Moreover, industry has tended to concentrate in the so-called 'central corridor' of Saudi Arabia (Jeddah–Mecca–Taif–Riyadh–Hofuf–Dammam) with Jubail, Yanbu and Madinah as outposts. As a result, migration into the central corridor cities is very high. Meanwhile, the north and the south of the Kingdom risk a probable depopulation and decline.

One of the major goals of development stated in the Second Development Plan is to reduce economic dependence on the export of crude oil through the diversification of the economic base. Closely related to this is another stated goal, that of developing human resources by education, training and raising standards of health. As Saudi Arabia seeks to diversify its modern economic system it is essential that its own human resources be developed in such a way as significantly to contribute to and benefit from the development of the modern economy.[4] Although the diversification of the modern economic system may require a heavy input of foreign labour and expertise, at least in the short run, it is essential that Saudi Arabian human resources be trained and fully incorporated into the modern system. Otherwise, the Kingdom runs a very strong risk of the solidification of the dualistic division of the economy into traditional and modern systems or alternatively the replacement of the traditional productive system with a non-productive sector of the population which will have to be supported by welfare. That the emergence of a significantly large non-productive sector is a potential threat is given support by a recent manpower study by the World Bank which projects an oversupply and consequent unemployment of uneducated and unskilled Saudi Arabians (excluding nomads) amounting to eight per cent of the total Saudi Arabian labour force.

The best way, probably the only way, to achieve a well-balanced development of the modern economic system *and* guarantee the increased well-being of all groups in the society is through full incorporation of all groups in the modern economic system. This obviously implies the disappearance of the traditional system. At the same time as there will be an oversupply of unskilled and uneducated Saudi Arabian labour, there will exist, according to the World Bank, a critical shortage of skilled, professional and managerial manpower which can only partly be filled by foreigners available for employment in the Middle East after 1980.[5]

The Bedouin in Contemporary Saudi Arabia

The bedouin are singled out for special consideration in *The Second Development Plan for 1395–1400 AH : 1975–1980 AD*, a fact that shows that the government is cognisant of and concerned about the bedouin's situation. According to the plan, the life and economy of the bedouin in Saudi Arabia have the following characteristics:

1. low *per capita* income in comparison with the national average;
2. heavy reliance on raising livestock as their basic source of income while producing the major part of domestic meat supplies;
3. almost total dependence on clement weather for the survival of flocks and herds;
4. rapidly deteriorating range lands in most areas due largely to overgrazing;
5. lack of immediate access to most social, educational and other services;
6. significant migration to urban areas, resulting in an estimated net annual decrease of 2 per cent per year in the nomadic population.

The Plan goes on to explain that

> The bedouin have a complex and highly developed social, economic and legal system that has adapted to change over many hundreds of years. Nevertheless, the pace of change in the rest of the Kingdom has recently been so fast that the economic and social gap between

> the bedouin and the population is widening; consequently special programs, based on realistic appraisal of the needs and changing social and economic role of the bedouin, are required to improve the life of this segment of the population.[6]

So far, however, well past the mid-point of the period of the Second Development Plan, no specific programmes aimed at rectifying and improving the position of the bedouin have been initiated – except for one, the development of an animal subsidy programme whereby people receive a cash subsidy based on the number of animals (sheep and camels) they own. The massive King Faisal Settlement Project at Haradh, which was originally intended to be the nucleus for the settlement of 1000 bedouin families, has been abandoned as a settlement project for the bedouin and turned over to a foreign (Irish) company to run as a highly capital-intensive modern farm on a profit-sharing basis with the government. In other areas, such as the Wadi Dawasir, agricultural development is being implemented by foreign firms in collaboration with the Saudi Arabian Ministry of Agriculture and Water. These farms utilise highly capital-intensive methods, rely on a foreign labour force (often European or North American) and have essentially no interaction with the local population, although the overwhelming majority of settled, semi-settled, and nomadic bedouin in the area are interested in expanding and improving agriculture in what they consider to be their own wadi.

The substandard socio-economic conditions of the bedouin, at least in comparison with those prevailing among the rest of the Saudi Arabian population, are easily documented. In the Arabian Shield-South, an area of 202,000 square kilometres in the interior part of south-western Saudi Arabia, 72 per cent of the total employed population is engaged in traditional agriculture (including pastoralism).[7] Construction and transportation employ five per cent of the labour force. The remainder are engaged primarily in traditional retail and service activities. Professional workers account for only three per cent of the labour force, clerical workers four per cent and managerial workers only 0.2 per cent. The percentage involved in the traditional labour force is well above the national average mentioned earlier but is representative of the situation in rural areas in general.

According to the 1974 *Population Census*[8], this area has a total population of 727,432 people, approximately ten per cent of the total national population. People enumerated at waterpoints (almost all nomadic bedouin) account for 33 per cent of the total population of the Arabian Shield-South. Villagers (among whom are included a large number of sedentarised bedouin) account for 48 per cent of the population while those enumerated in emirate capitals (often no larger than villages) account for 20 per cent of the population. The area thus has a higher percentage of bedouin than the national average, which is estimated at 25 per cent.

The highest degree of illiteracy is found among those enumerated at waterpoints – 96 per cent of all people of ten years and older are illiterate as opposed to 80 per cent of all villagers of ten years and older and 54 per cent of all people in the same age category in emirate capitals. Moreover, only two per cent of children aged six to nine at waterpoints were enrolled in schools, while 50 per cent of children in the same age category from villages were in schools and 57 per cent of those in emirate capitals were in schools.

Urban areas have inevitably constituted the foci of the rapid economic change which has occurred in Saudi Arabia. Accordingly, the bedouin are migrating to the cities and are contributing a significant part of their male population to the modern and semi-modern labour force. In the Arabian Shield-South, in 1974, there were 26,286 fewer males than females present in rural areas. Since the majority of these absent males were between the ages of 20 and 39, it is obvious that they are employed in activities outside traditional herding and agriculture. These absent males represented 5.2 per cent of the population enumerated at waterpoints and 4.68 per cent of that in villages. In fact, a higher percentage of males is probably engaged in outside activities than these figures show, since many work part-time and are thus part-time residents in their tents and villages.

In a survey conducted in 1977 by Saad Eddin Ibrahim and the writer on a sample of 208 bedouin males from four major tribal groupings,[9] 33.2 per cent of the sample reported that at least one member of their household worked for the government.[10] If we add private enterprises and the self-employment of bedouin in sectors such as transportation, an even higher percentage of bedouin males could be said to work in non-pastoral activities. In view of the projected oversupply of uneducated labour, many bedouin who remain uneducated are likely to find themselves without non-pastoral job opportunities in the future. In fact, the majority of bedouin employed outside herding work are in low-level occupations. My own observations of oil camps and geological survey camps show that the majority of Saudi Arabians employed as unskilled labourers are young bedouin working to obtain money for such things as bride-wealth or to buy a motor vehicle. A large part of desert transportation is in the hands of bedouin but more sophisticated highway hauling is being done by non-bedouin, with an increasingly large number of young Europeans, Australians and New Zealanders working as drivers. Most of the soldiers in the National Guard are bedouin and some serve in the police force and army. Only a small handful have ever obtained high-level government posts – for example, there is only one deputy minister who was originally a bedouin and whose father is still a bedouin herder. There are also a few relatively well-off merchants who were originally bedouin but they form a minority among the merchant class in Saudi Arabia.

Until now, the only significant avenue which provides special training programmes and potentially leads to high-level careers in the modern sector of society is the military. The Vinnel Corporation, an American concern under contract to the Saudi Arabian government, for example, provides English language training, Arabic literacy classes and training in modern military science to members of the National Guard, all of whom are from bedouin tribes. Those who are chosen to be officers usually spend a period of up to several years in special training programmes abroad, usually in the United States. Similar programmes exist for the police, the army, the air force and the navy – although people from sedentary backgrounds as well as bedouin may be included in these programmes. The vast majority of bedouin in these programmes marry bedouin girls who remain at home in the desert with the herds – their husbands visiting them at week-ends and during vacations. Outside the military and security forces, however, very few bedouin ever receive advanced training in modern subjects, there being almost no desert-based bedouin young in universities, either within the Kingdom or abroad.[11]

Concerning health, suffice it to say that 71.7 per cent of the bedouin interviewed in the 1977 survey said they would go to a modern doctor or clinic for treatment but most (59 per cent) would have to travel a considerable distance to another community to obtain modern medical services. It is difficult for them to obtain regular medical service. If they go to a doctor or clinic in case of illness, it is only once and there is seldom any follow-up treatment. Doctors we interviewed in the field unanimously expressed the opinion that the bedouin suffer from malnutrition and anaemia and often have eye diseases. In general we found that the bedouin were quite receptive to modern medicine and one of their most emphatic requests was for conveniently located hospitals, clinics, mobile medical units and/or in-residence paramedics.[12]

Contemporary Herding Practices of the Bedouin

The herds of camels, sheep and goats which are owned and managed by bedouin households represent a significantly large element in the non-oil-based or derived wealth of Saudi Arabia.

In recent years, the government of the Kingdom has come to recognise that livestock, most of which is owned and managed by bedouin households, is a major resource of the nation and that the livestock sector of the economy should be encouraged and developed.[13] The major programme which the government has initiated in this regard is a cash subsidy programme administered by the Ministry of Agriculture and Water whereby the government annually pays 30 riyals (about $9) per sheep and 50 riyals (about $17) per camel. This programme was initiated following severe droughts which occurred during the 1960s, when there was mass starvation of animals. The subsidy programme was intended to help and to encourage the bedouin to rebuild their herds and flocks. Government loans through the Agricultural Banks are also available on extremely easy terms to individual bedouin to purchase water tankers.

The cash value of the sheep and camels owned by the bedouin is extremely high. The cash value of a one-year-old sheep is a minimum of 300 riyals (about $90) and is more likely to be in the range of about 600 riyals (about $180). The minimum price for an average full-grown milk camel is 3,000 riyals (about $900) and prices as high as 20,000 riyals (about $6,666) are quoted both for racing camels and for very fine, pure-bred milk camels. However, the bedouin do not regularly sell their animals. Instead of consuming any significant part of the meat raised on its own ranges, Saudi Arabia as a nation imports most of its meat (other than chicken). This is in spite of the fact that local mutton is the preferred meat of a majority of the increasing urban population. Thus the modern cities of the area, as described by Amin[14] and Asad[15] for earlier periods, do not consume any significant surplus production that emanates from the bedouin sector of the population. The supply of meat and other animal products to the cities seems never to have been a traditional activity of Arabian bedouin and this continues to be the case up to the present day.

For the past, it could be argued that the vagaries of weather and animal disease did not allow the bedouin the potential to produce a large enough surplus regularly to supply a large urban population. Raiding and tribal warfare, moreover, often diverted their attention from the business of herding. Today, however, increasingly large

Figure 7.1: Map of the Grazing Areas of the Principal Bedouin Tribes

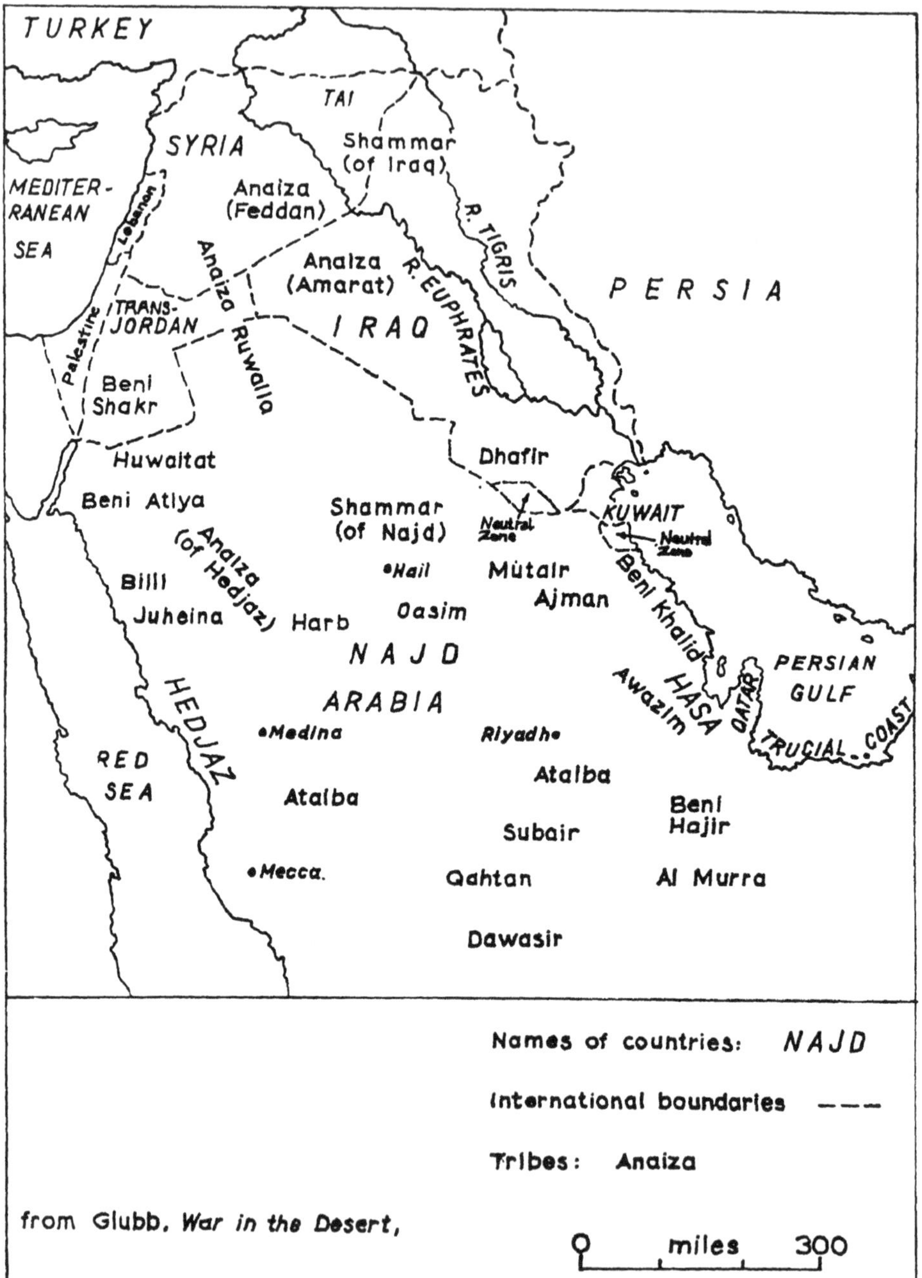

numbers of animals are being kept on the ranges by the bedouin, with consequent serious over-grazing and destruction of the rangelands.

Several major changes have occurred that are related to herding practices during the past three decades. One of the most important has been the conversion of all rangelands to Public Lands by a Royal Decree issued in 1953. This Decree made the *hema* system illegal and thus abolished the rights that tribes had traditionally (and by their own military strength) held as exclusive grazing rights to certain areas. All rangelands thus became open to any who wanted to graze them, a right which was and is upheld by the national government through its own police forces.

Another major factor that has contributed to more intensive use of the ranges has been the development of water resources – first through the modern state-owned wells which now exist throughout the desert, even in remote areas, and, more recently, through the acquisition of pick-up trucks by almost all bedouin families and water tankers by many of them. Thus, no longer are the bedouin restricted to grazing areas where they have traditional tribal rights to water resources. Finally, the generalised use of motor vehicles to transport animals and households to grazing areas has meant that the bedouin and their herds have become much more mobile than in the past.

The consequence of these modern innovations is that, as soon as rains fall in any particular area, vast numbers of bedouin, without regard to tribal origin, descend on that area with their herds and graze the area intensively until news comes of another area which has received rain, at which time they load their herds and households on Mercedes trucks (for hire usually, with a bedouin as driver) or on their own pick-ups and move on.

The only remnant of traditional herding or migration practices that still partly holds true is that most households and herds return to their tribe's traditional home territory, where their traditional tribally owned wells are located, during the summer. However, they less often cluster around wells, as in the past, but keep their animals and households dispersed on the grazing areas and truck water to them.

What appears to have happened is that unplanned, spontaneous and partial efforts at modernisation by both the government and the bedouin are leading to the potential destruction of rangelands as a result of over-grazing and vehicular traffic, without the nation having benefited from a short-term increase in its domestic meat supply.

The Royal Decree which made all rangelands Public Lands and declared *hema*s illegal was part of the government's effort to displace customary law with Islamic Sharia law throughout the nation and for all citizens. The general intention at the time was to bring to an end armed tribal conflict – for the rights which tribes claimed to specific grazing areas and reserves were usually enforced by their own military prowess, and constituted one of the major reasons underlying the endemic warfare and feuding characteristic of Arabia before the consolidation of the present nation-state of Saudi Arabia. Although it was not the intention of the law makers at the time, this Decree paved the way for open and uncontrolled use of ranges throughout the Kingdom. The development of modern water resources, furthermore, has been seen by both the bedouin and the government as a major way of improving their standard of living and giving them the benefit of modern technology. Likewise, the granting of subsidies and easy loans to purchase tankers is seen as a way of distributing some of the Kingdom's cash reserves to a segment of its population that tends to have a very low *per capita* cash income, at the same time as encouraging the bedouin to improve their herds.

What no one in the government expected, however, is that these innovations would lead mainly to an explosion in the intensity of rangeland use by the bedouin without their contributing much of their dramatically increasing surplus of animals to the national economy and for the benefit of the society at large.

Bedouin Perceptions of their Current Economic Position

The reasons for the failure of the bedouin to play the economic role expected of them can be seen from a brief overview of bedouin attitudes to their current economic role.[16]

Generally speaking, the bedouin are not happy with the present state of affairs concerning their economic activities as herdsmen. They want to improve their own level of production, they say, to be able to depend primarily on their own efforts without having to be too dependent on government bureaucracies with which they find it difficult to deal.

They are aware of, and fully agree with, the fact that there is a meat shortage in the cities. They also agree that they are the ones who own most of the animals in the Kingdom. Yet they admit that they rarely sell their animals on a regular basis or in large numbers. They say that they do not need to, as they are receiving money from the subsidy programme and from other activities (jobs, etc.) and they are not at present generally in need of extra cash. They say they often let their animals die rather than sell them. They complain, moreover, that the marketing process is difficult and that they can seldom market animals and make any money. They would not mind selling if the marketing process were easier and less haphazard and if they could be sure of maintaining a minimal core herd in spite of drought and disease. They stress the weakness and precarious nature of their position, emphasising that their survival depends on things over which they have no control – the absence of drought and disease. Their major traditional means of combating the effects of drought and disease is to keep herds as large as possible.

As a solution to the problem, the bedouin say that the government could register the animals an individual owns and then require him to sell a given proportion of the young animals each year, in an organised fashion and for a guaranteed minimum price. This requirement, they say, should be part of a larger deal for nomads to receive government aid for developing agriculture. The bedouin should grow alfalfa and other feed products for fattening their animals and to use as feed during years of drought. The over-all goal of such projects should be to make the bedouin strong and more secure, so that they do not ultimately have to depend on government aid or outside employment.

Conclusions: Incorporation of the Bedouin Socially and Economically in a Modernised Saudi Arabia

The general aim of this paper has been to draw attention to the bedouin of Saudi Arabia within the general context of the total society in which they exist. Several points remain to be made concerning their position within the changing world in which they find themselves; attention will then be focused on some avenues of directed change that might be implemented to improve their present position and to incorporate them more fully and with opportunities equal to those of other citizens in a more modernised Saudi Arabia.

The importance of the tribe as a socio-political-economic unit in Saudi Arabia has lost a great deal of its meaning given the way present national society and culture are emerging. Tribal control of grazing and migration patterns has been largely eclipsed by the 1953

Royal Decree, which legally opened all rangelands to anyone who wished to use them without regard to tribal affiliation, by the development of modern state-owned water resources and by the bedouin's almost universal acquisition of motor vehicles, which allows them much more mobility than ever existed before.

A further administrative factor lies behind the decline in political significance of the tribe: the government administers areas on the basis of localities rather than of tribal divisions. The rural areas where the bedouin live are administered by government emirs who are employees of the Ministry of Interior. Most of these men are of tribal background, but seldom do they come from shaikhly families in their own tribes. They are almost without exception from a different tribe than that which predominates in the locality they administer. Most of their duties are related to maintaining law and order and seldom have anything to do with modernisation efforts. Nowadays the traditional tribal leaders themselves mainly form a kind of social elite within their own tribes and are more actively engaged in their own economic improvement and in securing their sons positions as officers in the National Guard than in promoting general tribal politics or in leading modernisation programmes among their own fellow tribespeople.

As a result, all tribes are coming to be seen as forming a single category in Saudi Arabian society. Tribalism and bedouinism have tended to replace tribes as such in the basic fabric of Saudi Arabian social life. This phenomenon merits much more attention than can be given in this article. Essentially, however, it means that the fact of tribal origin still conditions aspects of behaviour in the emerging national society – e.g. type of work one will follow, whom one can marry – and it is a way of categorising people socially. More significant now, however, is that one is of tribal origin rather than from any one particular tribe. All people from tribes are more like each other in terms of behaviour and social identity than they are like other sectors of Saudia Arabian society – e.g. those of former slave status, those of traditional sedentary background living in villages, those who are merchants, or those who are members of the royal elite.

It should also be noted that, in the social hierarchy of Arabia, the position of people of tribal origin, essentially the bedouin, is ambivalent. Some, especially the powerful royal elite, consider the status of bedouin to be very high. Most townspeople, however, now consider them to be of low status due to their failure to achieve anything significant in modern society. They are generally seen by the more modernised urban elements as the one major group in Saudi

Arabian society which has not taken advantage of new opportunities that have developed and as a kind of pariah group in contemporary society – no matter how high their status may have been in the past.

This leads us to a consideration of what avenues might be opened up for them, if they are to be incorporated into the modern society on any kind of an equal footing with others. One avenue is through the modernisation of livestock production, whereby some bedouin may continue to practice their pastoral skills but not as subsistence-oriented producers. They would become market-oriented producers of meat for the national market. This would probably involve at least the following elements, which can only be mentioned in passing:

1. a reduction in the total number of both bedouin and animals;
2. controlled grazing practices;
3. the development of feed supplies and veterinarian services available throughout the rangeland areas to obviate the effects of drought and animal disease;
4. the development of regular markets, feed lots for fattening and finishing, and slaughter houses at appropriate locations to secure the smooth and regular distribution of meat to the wider public.

The second avenue, which should accompany the above, is the development of special programmes to train the bedouin to work and participate successfully in the modern sector of the economy. This is essential if the livestock sector is to be modernised, because it is generally believed that far fewer bedouin would need to be employed in that sector if it were developed on a more market-oriented basis and less on a household mode of production basis, as is still typical of the situation at present. The training of bedouin to participate in the modern sector is also vital to the modern sector itself, as envisaged in the Kingdom's Development Plans. The bedouin represent a sizeable proportion of the indigenous population – as much as 25 per cent – and their participation in an active way and not just as more or less passive, part-time unskilled labourers and drivers is essential if the economy is to become significantly more modernised. The bedouin and other rural groups who are increasingly subsisting on welfare and traditional low-scale productive activities must be trained and incorporated into the modern economy and society.

Many hundreds of years ago Ibn Khaldun commented that:

> *Every bedouin who is attracted to city life quickly shows himself unable [to compete] and is disgraced.* The only exceptions are such

[bedouins] as have previously accumulated property and obtained more of it than they needed and therefore achieved the amount of tranquility and luxury that is natural to civilized people. They, then, may move to a city, and their condition, as regards customs and luxury, can blend with that of its inhabitants.[17]

Ibn Khaldun's comments sound almost as if they were a description of the current situation in Saudi Arabia. It is hoped, however, that a situation will evolve whereby the accumulation of property will not be the major prerequisite for bedouin successfully to settle in the towns without being disgraced. Hopefully, a situation will emerge whereby some can go to the towns armed with modern skills which will allow them to compete and to contribute to the development of their own country, and whereby some others can make the rangelands more productive for the total society and for themselves.

Notes

1. A similar version of this paper was presented at the Third International Symposium on Man and Society in the Arab Gulf at the University of Basrah (Iraq) in March 1979. Field research on which this paper is based was conducted in 1968–70 (Cf. Donald P. Cole, *The Social and Economic Structure of the Al Murrah: A Saudi Arabian Bedouin Tribe* (Ph.D. dissertation, University of California, Berkeley, 1971); Cole, *Nomads of the Nomads: The Al Murrah Bedouin of the Empty Quarter* (Aldine, Chicago, 1975) and, more recently, under the auspices of The World Bank (in 1977) and MacLaren International Ltd (in 1977–78). The author's participation in the Inaugural Congress of the Centre for Arab Gulf Studies at the University of Exeter was partially financed by the American University in Cairo which provided funds to travel from Cairo to London. The author would like to express his gratitude to these institutions, to officials of the Saudi Arabian Ministry of Planning and their consultants from the SRI group, and to the Centre for Arab Gulf Studies at the University of Exeter for its support and co-operation. The author alone, however, is responsible for the presentation of the data and the ideas expressed here.

2. This and the following discussion of the characteristics of the contemporary economy is drawn mainly from the Kingdom of Saudi Arabia, Ministry of Planning, *The Strategies for the Third Development Plan for 1400–1405 AH – 1980–1985 AD* (manuscript, 1978).

3. The Ministry of Planning and most Saudi officials seldom consider the nomads as an element in the economy – traditional or otherwise. They are seen by them as a social phenomenon which merits little consideration when discussing the economy of Saudi Arabia.

4. Although I believe this to be a sincere desire on the part of the government, many of the best-trained Saudis opt to live and work abroad.

5. Both references to the World Bank manpower study were conveyed to me verbally.

6. Kingdom of Saudi Arabia, Ministry of Planning, *The Second Development Plan for 1395–1400 AH – 1975–1980 AD* (Riyadh, 1976), p. 422.

7. The figures given in this paragraph, and in the three which follow, are based on calculations made from information presented in the 1974 *Population Census*.

8. Kingdom of Saudi Arabia, Ministry of Finance and National Economy, *Population Census 1394 AH – 1974 AD* (Riyadh, 1974).

9. The four tribal groupings, in four different regions of the country, were the Al-Murrah in the Eastern Province, the Dawasir in southern Nejd, the Beni Zayd in the Qunfudah region of the Tihama, and the Harb near Madinah.

10. Saad Eddin Ibrahim and Donald P. Cole, 'Saudi Arabian Bedouin: An Assessment of their Needs', *Cairo Papers in Social Science*, vol. I, Monograph 5 (American University, Cairo, 1978), p. 29.

11. It should be added that occasionally some youths are sent abroad for advanced technical training relating to the oil business. An example is one youth from the Al-Murrah who was sent by ARAMCO to study in Michigan.

12. Ibrahim and Cole, 'Saudi Arabian Bedouin', pp. 84–91.

13. Cf. Nasser al-Saleh, *Problems in the Modernization of the Livestock Sector in Semi-arid Regions: A Saudi Arabian Case Study* (Ph.D. dissertation, University of Durham, 1976).

14. Samir Amin, *La nation arabe: nationalisme et luttes de classes* (Editions de Minuit, Paris, 1976).

15. Talal Asad, 'The Bedouin as a Military Force', in Cynthia Nelson (ed.), *The Desert and the Sown: Nomads in the Wider Society* (Institute of International Studies, University of California, Berkeley, 1973).

16. Evidence of the attitudes of the bedouin is taken from surveys conducted by the writer. In 1977 and 1978 the writer conducted an anthropological survey (unpublished) in the Arabian Shield-South, in the inland part of south-western Arabia, where the major bedouin tribes are the Subay, the Qahtan, the Shahran and the Beni Yam.

17. Ibn Khaldun, *The Muqaddinah: An Introduction to History* (translated from the Arabic by Franz Rosenthal) (Pantheon, New York, 1958), pp. 279–80.

Further Reading

Amin, Samir, *The Maghreb in the Modern World* (Penguin Books, Harmondsworth, 1970).

Barth, Fredrik, 'A General Perspective on Nomad–Sedentary Relations in the Middle East', in Cynthia Nelson (ed.), *The Desert and the Sown: Nomads in the Wider Society* (Institute of International Studies, University of California, Berkeley).

Cole, Donald P., 'Local Organization Among Camel Nomads and Supralocal Power Institutions in a Radically Changing Society: The Al Murrah in Saudi Arabia' (Paper presented at American Anthropological Association Meetings, San Francisco, 1975).

Ibrahim, Saad Eddin and Nicholas S. Hopkins (eds), *Arab Society in Transition: A Reader* (American University, Cairo, 1977).

Sahlins, Marshall, *Stone Age Economics* (Aldine, Chicago, 1972).

8 Changes in the Structure of Village Life in Oman

J. C. WILKINSON

The Traditional Structure

Traditionally, agriculture not only acts as the economic basis for the Oman region but its associated village life forms one of the main roots from which its socio-political organisation stems. Today this old basis has all but collapsed and with it has disappeared not just a way of life but also much of the region's stability and an essential sense of 'Omaniness' arising from the country's soil. This collapse is in part due to importing foodstuffs coupled with a fall in demand for the old products of the land (dates, camels, etc.), in part due to the availability of an alternative economy and the perceived attractions of the new centres of development, and in part due to the break-up of the organisation of the traditional social structures. It is on this last aspect that this paper will concentrate since it is here that the changes are least appreciated and the remedies most ill conceived. This is largely because of a failure to grasp the inter-connections between social, political and economic structures and to understand the mechanisms by which changes in the technology of agriculture alter the organisation of village life.

This organisation of village life may be viewed as a pyramid of socio-political institutions and cultural values built on an economic base the form of which is determined by environmental, demographic and technological constraints. None of these basal determinants can alter without affecting the others or, in turn, shifting the shape of the pyramid. Conversely, the strength of this institutional superstructure will either constrain alterations in its base, absorbing them without fundamental shifts in its organisation, or it will break apart, as is happening today. As I have shown elsewhere, this traditional structure more or less took its present form during the ninth and tenth centuries when the basic systems of institutional organisation in tribal, political and village life were established. The systems which then emerged also had a temporal dimension so that effectively there was a cyclic

Figure 8.1: Oman

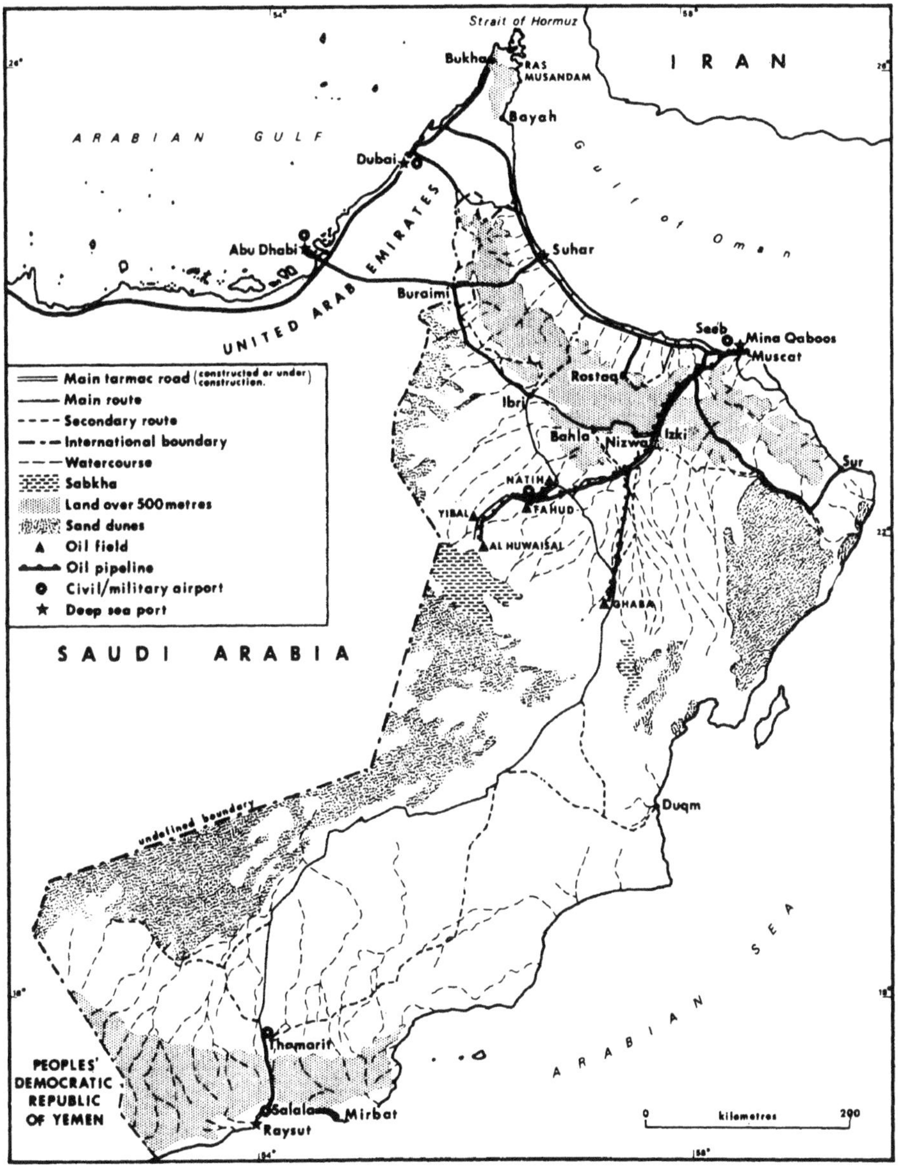

development involved in its stability, such that 'highs' of land productivity led to shifts in the pattern of land tenure which automatically triggered off reactions in the tribal system and a wave of destructiveness until a 'low' was reached: this in turn triggered off a reaction towards reunification of society and so began the move towards another 'high' in economic organisation, etc. These 'highs' and 'lows' in turn corresponded to the cycles of what I have termed the Imamate cycle. The basic condition for the continued existence of the system was isolation, or rather a boundary between outward- and inward-looking Oman, between its cosmopolitan trading society looking overseas and its inward-looking, more or less self-sufficient tribal society, with exchanges largely confined to its own members (notably between different nomadic and village groups exploiting the region's various land and marine resources). It is the breakdown of this isolation which lies at the root of the present change in the villages of the interior.

If this change is to be orderly and produce an improvement on the old way of life, then it is essential that members of the region's governments and their administrations should appreciate how the traditional system functioned, should be prepared to see if there are aspects of it which should be fostered, and should understand how their decisions interweave with those of others. This means that the decision maker must appreciate his role in that society. His starting-point should be the analysis of his own culture and history, not for self-aggrandisement or nationalistic ends, but to assess objectively the weaknesses and strengths of the past. Unfortunately, most Omanis in power today pay lip service to this past but in fact are quite ignorant about it. Nor do they really want to know anything about it because for them the old and traditional are backward while the modern is progressive. So they continue to allow the collapse of the existing systems whilst pointing to the outward veneer of modernisation as constituting development.

It is with the object of showing in part how this traditional system functioned that I have taken one of its most basic elements, the *falaj* (plural: *aflaj*), and will attempt to show how technical, demographic and environmental features are all inextricably bound into the way of life that is now being undermined through uncontrolled change.

Falaj Organisation

Briefly, a *falaj* may be described as a unified irrigation system which distributes, by means of a network of canals, a source of water to those who have established rights in it. That source of water may be a spring (rare), or a resurgence from a rock aquifer (usually a limestone), or sub-surface flows in buried gravels and pipes in wadi formations, or surface and sub-surface flows in superficial gravels (*sayl* or *ghayl*). The most reliable flows normally occur at some depth where storage is greatest: the technology used to exploit them is the *qanat*, a tunnelled, horizontal well of varying length and depth (in Oman rarely longer than 8 km or deeper than 25 m to the mother well). It is this type of *falaj* which traditionally forms the basis of village settlements of any size in the interior of the country. It is a pattern of water exploitation which is quite different from the Batina, in which the zone of almost continuous littoral settlements is based on wells.

The essential feature to note about a *qanat* is that it is an irrigation system built at 'infinite toil and expense' to exploit a scarce resource in areas of marginal settlement potential and upon which the village as a whole depends for its subsistence. In the case of Oman this original exploitation is generally of great antiquity and there are only a few traces of the original organisation left in that of the present. One trace, however, is of great importance: the layout of the *falaj* – for it is this which imposes the basic pattern of holdings. Arising from this pattern is the system each village has developed of how to deal with intra- and inter-annual variations of flow and the method by which the time units, into which the water rotation around the *falaj* network are divided, are distributed to the individual shareholders. Any attempts to alter this layout for reasons of efficiency will therefore automatically upset the existing compromise that each community has had to achieve between notions of fair dealing and efficiency in land and water allocation.

This question of fair dealing is a matter of the greatest importance in the traditional village society of interior Oman, and one in which there are a number of important regional variations. In central Oman, where Ibadi influence has been at its greatest, this aspect dominates the whole code of Islamic water and land law; in it are enshrined three basic principles that guide all *falaj* rulings. The first is that water is an essential need of the community and nothing may impede proper access to it; the second, that no alteration can be made to the *falaj* system unless it is of benefit to the community as a whole; the third, that no alterations should be made without the agreement of all the principal shareholders. Indeed, it is only when such mutual agreement breaks down that reference is made to a higher authority, the *qadi*, for arbitration. These principles can be traced back to the early part of the eighth century AD so that there exists in Ibadi *fiqh* (religious law) a corpus of some 1,200 years of recorded judgements about *aflaj* to guide the *ulama* in reaching their decisions. Recruited from a background, or educated in a culture, alien to the traditions of the interior, this legal background is something of which both the planners and local government officials are largely ignorant today. The writer has come across a number of cases recently of potential conflict in water use, ranging from too close a proximity of wells to the *falaj* off-take area, to thc capture of ground water by the installation of new settlements upstream from the old, which would never have arisen if the Islamic water code had been properly applied.

Another principle of *falaj* organisation incorporated in this law is co-operation. As al-Salimi states in the *Jawhar al-Nizām*,[1] 'Co-operation is of the essence in the organisation of agriculture and irrigation'. Yet today, when the mode is to talk about co-operatives in agriculture, one of the most highly developed co-operative systems that exist in Oman is being ignored as a result of a failure to understand how it functions, or even to appreciate its existence.

This ignorance of traditional land organisation was strikingly brought home to the present writer when investigating the old methods used for calculating time in al-Ayn (Abu Dhabi part of the Buraimi oasis). The *arif* (the man in charge of distributing the *falaj* water) was explaining the star calendar and mentioned in passing that he had been using it the night before. Upon the expression of surprise at his not having used a watch, he replied that his own was very old and did not work any more. Thinking of the generosity with which the government gave away watches to all and sundry, the writer suggested that he might obtain one from the agricultural department in the oasis. This, he said, he had tried but had been refused because the authorities could not understand what he wanted if for.

So it is that today the villagers of the interior have fewer and fewer people to whom they can turn for a balanced judgement to help them over their problems. The old administration has been broken down and replaced by a government which has little comprehension of their difficulties and the members of which grow increasingly remote from the realities of the land. Whatever its other failings, the Ibadi system of government did at least understand the workings of agriculture. Omani history is replete with examples of the intimate relationship that existed between land and government administration. To cite one example: during his thirty years as Wali of Bahla on behalf of the twentieth-century Imams (Salim b. Rashid al-Kharusi and Muhammad b. Abdullah al-Khalili), A. Zayd Abdullah b. Muhammad al-Riyami carried out major restoration work to three of Bahla's five *aflaj*, spending over £22,000 (at inter-war values!) on one of them, planted over 7,000 palms for the *bayt al-mal* (the state treasury) and tried to re-establish sugar growing; in addition he had 30 wells dug for times of drought and appointed a supervisor to see to the proper upkeep of wells in the desert region.[2] Of course, the present government can also point to considerable agricultural work, but it is minor compared to the proportion of the tiny state budget which existed in the Wali A. Zayd's time, nor is it based on knowledge of the real needs of the people. Although we can hardly expect ministers today to go out and personally help with the removal of water moss from the irrigation channels of the *bayt al-mal* property, government officials could still profitably learn from A. Zayd's example of the needs for continuous inspection, and of accessibility to those for whom he was responsible.

This is not to say that the Imamate organisation of Oman was ideal. On the contrary, one of its failings was that its taxation system, its decentralised control and its fixed order of priorities in expenditure meant that it was often unable to expend sufficient money on the upkeep of economic infrastructure and left its maintenance too much in the hands of the individual communities, who sometimes had neither the resources nor the organisational ability to deal with major maintenance work. The principle of self-help might instil a certain vigour into the rural community, but it can be carried too far, just as the welfare state principle, which is now pervading the oil-rich states of the Arabian Peninsula, is leading to an unwillingness and inability on the part of villagers to try and do something to develop and animate their own community life.

Another great failing of Imamate government from the point of view of land organisation was its perpetuation of the tribe as the effective unit of socio-political organisation. Once again, Omani history is not short of examples of the wanton destruction of irrigation works that can occur when the full forces of tribalism are unleashed in periods of government instability. But just as Imamate government could carry out considerable work on the land, so the tribal system was not as inimical to cultivation as might be thought. In central Oman agricultural workers (*bayadir*; singular: *bidar*) were assimilated, more or less as equals, into the country's tribal society so that, for example, the term *bidar* designated an occupation rather than a social structure. Part of the breakdown of traditional Arab attitudes towards those who worked the land was undoubtedly due to Ibadi influence;

this view has been reinforced by the present writer's investigations into the North African Ibadi communities of the Mzab. Yet even in those areas of Oman where the Ibadi influence has almost disappeared, tribal attitudes towards cultivating the land do not basically discourage agriculture. True, in northern Oman, for example, where there has been a more continuous history of inward migration than in central Oman, new tribal groups tend to treat the *bayadir* much more as a client class and here too there is much greater inequality, both in land holdings and in the terms of tenancy. Nevertheless, even where shaikhs exploit the villagers and fail to maintain the irrigation systems properly, the *bayadir* still retain a certain personal dignity; the villagers do not form a *daif* (subservient) class, nor in turn are the nomads ashamed to help in agricultural work at harvest time. Furthermore, since the economic interests of the *arab* (nomads) is to obtain a stake in the land and since the process of sedenterisation has absorbed generation after generation of new Arab migrants, the usual attitudes which tend to rationalise antipathy towards cultivation in terms of blood and honour are largely absent. All inhabitants of Oman get drawn, in some measure, into its traditional land exploitation system, willy nilly.

Effects of the Breakdown of the Falaj System on Village Life

It is the breakdown of the traditional social system associated with the removal of power from the interior to the coast, from people who were in close contact with their followers to a remote society that has no knowledge of these traditions, that is leading to an opening up of the gaps in society and the development of an imported snobbery towards working the land. Tribesmen and villagers previously formed part of an integrated *falaj* society, and even the famous Hinawi and Ghafiri division (based on tribal moieties), destructive as it was to so much settlement, in fact developed largely as a means for obtaining social and political equilibrium in the villages and for ensuring a degree of equality in the distribution of the benefits derived from the basic agricultural economy. Between them, the Ibadi system of government and the tribal system of social organisation sought to maintain an integrated society the members of which felt that their community was justly organised and in which they were involved as full members. The cost of maintaining this primitive 'democracy' was often great in economic terms, for the tribal system functioned by opposing rather than uniting groups, whilst the decentralised form which Ibadi government took resulted in a failure to invest sufficiently in the upkeep of the country's irrigation system. In contrast, the villager today has peace and a government with the means to better his lot. Yet there is no security, for he lives in a world in which he has lost confidence. The collapse of the old socio-political structure has left a vacuum of organisation in the villages and is a major fact contributing to the abandonment of land.

Migration from the villages, whether to the burgeoning new centres on the coast or to other prosperous parts of the Gulf region, is the main manifestation of these declining conditions. Some of the effects on the interior villages have been studied in admirable depth by various members of the Durham University research project working in the Ibri-Khabura region. The features which the present writer again wishes to emphasise are those concerning the organisation of village life.

Traditionally, the upkeep of the *falaj* system, the pattern of the agricultural calendar and the division of labour and responsibility were based on a demographic structure that now no longer exists. The result is an increasing misuse of water, a failure to react correctly to such threats as drought or flood and a general decline in agricultural standards which is particularly manifest in the present state of date palm cultivation. As a result, there is something of a shift away from the old cultivating patterns, with an increasing portion of the area under seasonal crops and a shift from the *falaj* water supply to pumps.

Several consequences are to be noted. The first is that this tendency is not evenly spread, so that the smaller, more remote and more marginal settlements are being completely abandoned: this movement becomes irreversible once the irrigation system collapses. The second is that the ability to invest in the new technology is confined to the more wealthy elements, such as the merchants or those who have gone to work in the oil-rich areas. The result is a growing class division between rich and poor and an increasing amount of absentee landlordism, a feature which was traditionally almost entirely absent in Oman (except in the Sharqiya, many of the inhabitants of which used to live or work in East Africa). More important, perhaps, than either of these consequences is the breakdown of the integrated *falaj* organisation which is the key to village unity. This breakdown occurs not really because uncontrolled use of pumps is upsetting the hydrological equilibrium of the individual drainage basins, as is the case in some places elsewhere, but rather because the new technology is bound to a tenure system based on the individual well unit, rather than a communal water supply. In contrast, on the Batina coast, where agriculture has always been based on wells, it is the hydrological factors which are more preoccupying because here the danger is that the installation of pumps inland (i.e. upstream) of the coastal settlements is leading to a shift in the delicate equilibrium at the fresh-water/salt-water interface and the salination of the old settlement; the social danger is that the wealthy, adopting the new technology, will expand at the expense of the old established settlers. But in interior Oman, where investment and labour is being drained towards the new gardens, it is the entire old settlement organisation which is being neglected. Not only is a heritage worth countless years of oil revenues being abandoned for a less efficient (in all senses) form of water exploitation, but the unifying features of its society are also being destroyed. Vigorous action is called for which is not forthcoming. On the one hand, the installation and distribution of the pumps must be carefully regulated so that their water use complements rather than competes with the *falaj* and, on the other, government-sponsored land development should be channelled through the agency of the *falaj* organisation, so that the village administration is reinforced rather than weakened, and the benefits spread more evenly through the community. At present the breakdown of the existing system and the failure to maintain the water supply is playing into the hands of the relatively wealthy and powerful who can exploit shortages and disequilibria.

This present decline of the *falaj* system is affecting not only the *falaj* institution as such but also a whole series of others dependent on it. One such example is that of *waqf* (trust). My own studies on the traditional use of *waqf* in Izki show how important this was in providing for such community interests as education, hospitality, the upkeep of religious buildings, the supply of funds for emergencies and the maintenance of the poor and orphans. In some measure these needs are being fulfilled by government organisation, in some cases more fully than under the old system. Yet it is the growth of a welfare state institution, administered by a remote central government, which is replacing self-help and the sense of communal responsibility. Once again the society is being sapped of its own energy – centuries of work are being undone without thought or even awareness of what is happening.

One other set of village institutions disappearing under the effects of modernisation, which might also be noted, is the organisation of trade.

Traditionally, virtually all sales of local produce (as also water shares belonging to the *falaj* organisation) were conducted through village auctions (*munada*). In this way price rigging was made difficult, the goods were on open display for all to inspect and bid for, and a reasonably fair price was established. Auctions also presented occasions for people to meet and formed another institution which tended to cut across the tribal *hara* (zone) divisions into which village society divided. Permanent shops existed only in the biggest centres and tended to sell specialised local produce (pottery, textiles and the work of various kinds of smiths) and imported goods. Produce destined for export (principally dates and dried fruits) was traditionally controlled by merchants who resided in regional ports and acted through a network of local agents residing in the market centres in the interior.

Today the periodic auction is being displaced by permanent shops whilst the market mechanisms are increasingly being manipulated by outsiders. Certainly the increase in demand for local produce, notably vegetables, cculd be beneficial for the cultivators, but the profits risk being siphoned off by an increasingly monosonistic merchant network aided by an unco-ordinated *laissez-faire* economy in which uncontrolled importing leads to irregular and unpredictable pricing. As a consequence, yet another village institution is breaking down, whilst the move from local exchange to a cash economy, largely stimulated by earnings arising from outside occupations, is leading to exploitation from the growing urban centres on the coast and yet further imbalance in Omani social structures.

Conclusion

So it is that the institutions of village life, on which so much of Omani society was founded and its cultural values based, are rapidly disappearing. Many of these changes are inevitable and in some respects there is not a great deal that can be done about them. What is much more concerning is the ignorance and insensitivity about this situation exhibited by the governments of the Oman region. Much is made in public relations material of rural development in Dhofar, for example, but it needed a revolution to get things moving there. In interior Oman (which has been more or less quiescent since 1963) no comparable effort has been made. For most government officials agricultural development is equated with a few experimental agricultural centres and farms, most of which are run as country estates by the wealthy. Most of these are highly inefficient in economic terms, are wasteful of water and draw off labour from villages already desperately short of manpower. In the old settlements pumps are managing to make good some of the deficit, but only at the cost of breaking down village unity and of taking an increasingly short-term view of resource exploitation. What is happening in Oman is the start of the situation which has developed in Saudi Arabia. There, for example, at al Ula in the northern Hejaz, the writer found that only a couple or so of the original 35 springs which have watered the oasis for over two millennia are now flowing, thanks to the uncontrolled exploitation by pumps, whilst the agricultural production of the oasis, despite this increased use of water, is but a shadow of the past, thanks to the emigration of its population. There too, princely estates in the desert around Riyad give an impression of agricultural development, but they are run by labourers who have had to abandon their own agricultural settlements to work them.

Whether or not Saudi Arabia can afford to abandon its traditional land resources is a debatable question: the Sultanate of Oman with its limited oil reserves most certainly cannot. More important, it cannot even afford the hiatus in present development since its water resources are exploited by one of the most delicate and capital-costly systems that has been derived for settlements in arid lands. Yet what is not often realised is that, since we can ignore these capital costs which have been written off centuries ago, the *falaj* is by far the cheapest and mechanically efficient water supply system in Oman, old and new; but only so long as it is properly maintained. Unaccountable damage has already occurred to this system due to negligence, and now the damage is accelerating. Once a *falaj* is abandoned it becomes virtually irreparable. Even more damaging to the country's development is the collapse of the social framework of village life through drawing off its population into non-productive occupations, which do nothing to better the standards of the population except for very short-term monetary gain. A major survey of one area showed that three-quarters of the male population between 14 and 40 years were absent (elsewhere in the Sultanate or abroad, mostly in Abu Dhabi). Nearly half of these were in the armed forces or the police, whilst another quarter were non-economically productive once they left home: only ten per cent were actually employed in the oil industry which basically is responsible for this change – a figure surpassed by the number of unskilled casual workers and government office messenger boys. So the stability of the land is being abandoned to marginal occupations in tertiary activities associated with a boom economy which is almost certain to be of far shorter duration than in the rest of the oil states of the Gulf region.

This process is accelerated by poor government organisation of the land exercised by remote control. Surveys are commissioned by the dozen, but the reports get lost in departmental reshuffles and remain unread. Even the basic hydrological networks which are so necessary for collecting the data for planning are ignored. Rain gauges kept by the small oil company base at Izki were found lying in the ditch when handed over to the military, whilst the one proper meteorological reporting base in the region (Sharjah) was abandoned with the reorganisation of Trucial Oman into the United Arab Emirates. Local stations set up by consultants fall into disuse the moment their surveys are finished and there is absolutely no attempt made to centralise records. With no appreciation of the basic environmental, demographic or technical variables, how can those who plan Omani society ever begin to grasp the complexities of the institutional structures to which they give rise?

One little story from the past has a moral which is still highly relevant today:

> One day while the Imam Ghassān b. 'Abdullāh (192/808–207/823) was out walking in Nizwā, he noticed that water-moss was beginning to clog one of the main irrigation channels. Realising that this was a sign of something wrong, he determined on discovering the cause. Eventually he managed to narrow it down to mismanagement by his own officials. These he therefore changed whereafter it was to be seen that the water flow in the channel increased.[4]

Notes

1. Abdullah b. Humayd al-Salimi, *Jawhar al-Nizām fi 'ilmay 'l-adyān wa'l-ahkām* (edn A. Ishaq Ibrahim Atfayyish, Cairo, 1381/1961–62).
2. Muhammad b. Abdullah al-Salimi, *Nahdat al-A'yān bi hurriyat 'Umān* (Cairo, n.d.), pp. 420ff.
3. J. S. Birks and C. A. Sinclair, *Movements of Migrant Labour from Parts of the North of the Sultanate of Oman* (International Migration Project Report, University of Durham, 1977).
4. Abdullah, b. Humayd al-Salimi, *Tuḥfat al-A'yān bi sīrat ahl 'Umān* (2 vols, Cairo, 1380/1961 edn), vol. I, pp. 125–8.

Further Reading

Birks, J. S., 'The Reaction of Rural Populations to Drought: A Case study from South East Arabia', *Erdkunde*, xxxi (1977), pp. 299–305.

—— and Letts, S. E., 'Diqal and Muqayda: Dying Oases in Arabia', *Tij. voor Ec. en. Soc. Geog. (TESG)*, lxviii (1977), pp. 145–51.

Letts, S. E., *Groundwater and its Present Day Use in Part of Northern Oman* (unpublished D.Phil. thesis, Oxford, 1979).

Townsend, J., *Oman, The Making of a Modern State* (Croom Helm, London, 1977).

Wilkinson, J. C., '*Bayāsira* and *Bayādīr*', *Arabian Studies*, i (1974), pp. 75–85.

——, *Water and Tribal Settlement in South-East Arabia: a Study of the Aflāj of Oman* (Clarendon Press, Oxford, 1977).

——, 'Islamic Water Law with Special Reference to Oasis Settlement', *J. of Arid Environments*, i (1978), pp. 87–96.

——, *Problems of Oasis Development* (School of Geography, Oxford Research Paper no. xx, 1978).

9 Economic and Social Implications of Current Development in the Arab Gulf: The Oriental Connection

J. S. BIRKS and C. A. SINCLAIR

Introduction

In 1975 there were over two-and-a-half million Arab workers and their dependants living in Arab states other than their own.[1] Since then the number of Arab workers living outside their home nation has risen by some 9 per cent; in early 1979 it is estimated that there were 1,570,000 Arab workers living abroad within the Arab world. In 1979 there were also approaching 1,000,000 non-Arab migrant workers employed within the Arab world. In total there are over 2,500,000 migrants for employment in the Arab Middle East in 1979.

The sheer volume of migration for employment, its relative importance in labour markets of the Arab world, the impact that migration for employment has upon economic development, and the mutual interdependence between nations that labour exporting and importing brings about have made migrant labour movements a leading issue of the contemporary Middle East.

The concern of Arab governments with labour migration has grown as they have perceived both advantageous and deleterious influences of migration for employment upon economic development. Consequently, international transfers of labour feature increasingly in social and economic planning within the Arab world. However, despite this contemporary concern with international migration for employment there has not yet been any regional or unified approach to what is acknowledged to be a challenging issue. Even national policies have been slow to evolve beyond a short-term and *ad hoc* basis. As a result, government action in the Arab world directed towards the movement of labour has been pragmatic, changeable, inconsistent and often contradictory. The only characteristic that policies have shared is their relatively ineffective application.

Consequently, the patterns of labour movement, which result from extraordinarily powerful labour market forces, have become deeply entrenched. The desire of the oil-exporting nations to develop rapidly has overshadowed other longer-term considerations of economic or social planning. As a result, the flows of migrant labour have become, of themselves, a major determinant of the nature of economic development in both labour-supplying and labour-importing states.

This paper focuses upon these broader issues surrounding the nature of economic development in the Arab Gulf. The Gulf states, all importers of labour, are amongst the leaders of economic and industrial development in the Arab world. For purposes of analysis, the Gulf states Kuwait, Bahrain, Qatar and the United Arab Emirates (UAE) are grouped together with the other oil-exporting states of the Arab world. Iran, which constitutes a basically separate labour market, is excluded from this assessment.

The Distribution of Wealth in the Arab World

The direction, volume and pattern of international migration for employment in the Arab world are determined essentially by the uneven distribution of oil wealth and its investment. The exploitation of oil resources, and the investment of royalties in the domestic economies of the oil-rich states, have led to wide disparities of economic development and *per capita* income between the Arab states. It is this range of *per capita* incomes which has determined the fundamentals of international labour movements.

Oil-exporting and non-oil-exporting states are here referred to as 'capital-rich' and 'capital-poor' states respectively.[2] Capital-rich and capital-poor states can best be distinguished by reference to gross national product *per capita.*

Table 9.1 shows GNP *per capita* ranging from almost $16,000 in Kuwait down to $250 for the Yemen Arab Republic.[3] This disparity, exaggerated in effect by the relatively short geographical distances over which it occurs, is the essential motivating force behind migration for employment in the Arab world. The Arab Gulf states, with the exception of Bahrain, fall firmly in the capital-rich bracket, enjoying *per capita* incomes in excess of $4,000. Bahrain, from the point of view of this analysis, behaves as a capital-rich state, despite its modest income.

Only because the national population of Saudi Arabia (at 4,593,000) is, relative to Kuwait (472,000), the UAE (200,000) and

Table 9.1: Selected Arab States: Ranked by Gross National Product *per capita*, 1976

State	GNP *per capita* US $
Kuwait	15,840
UAE	13,990
Qatar	11,400
Libyan Arab Jamahiriya	6,310
Saudi Arabia	4,480
Oman	2,680
Bahrain	2,140
Iraq	1,390
Tunisia	840
Syria	780
Jordan	610
Sudan	290
Yemen (PDRY)	280
Egypt	280
Yemen (YAR)	250

Source: World Bank, *World Development Report 1978* (1978), Table 1, pp. 76–7 and 114.

Qatar (68,000), quite large do these Gulf states rank above Saudi Arabia in terms of GNP *per capita*.

Populations and Labour Forces of the Arab States

In terms of potential economic development, it is a cruel irony that in the Arab world, generally speaking, it is the states without oil which have the larger populations.[4]

Table 9.2 shows that the range of national population sizes of the Arab states is considerable. Egypt, with 38,200,000, is followed by Morocco with 18,400,000, whilst, in contrast, tiny Qatar only comprises 68,000 nationals and the UAE 200,000 (though the wealthier Emirates of Abu Dhabi and Dubai together have less than 100,000 nationals). Of the same scale is Bahrain with 225,000 nationals. Kuwait and the Sultanate of Oman are slightly larger with national populations of 472,000 and 550,000 respectively.

Of the true capital-rich states, only Iraq has a substantial population (11,100,000). The Kingdom of Saudi Arabia and Libya, with populations of 4,600,000 and 2,100,000 respectively,[5] are already

Table 9.2: Major Arab States: Indigenous Populations Ranked by Size

State	Indigenous population	Year
Egypt	38,228,000	1976
Morocco	18,400,000	1977
Algeria	16,940,000	1977
Sudan	14,113,600	1973
Iraq	11,124,000	1975
Syria	7,335,000	1975
Tunisia	5,570,000	1975
Yemen (YAR)	5,037,000	1975
Saudi Arabia	4,592,500	1975
Jordan	2,616,700	1975
Lebanon	2,400,000	1975
Libya	2,087,900	1973
Yemen (PDRY)	1,660,000	1975
Oman	550,000	1975
Kuwait	472,100	1975
Bahrain	224,700	1976
UAE	200,000	1975
Qatar	67,900	1975
Total	131,619,400	

Sources: author's estimates from official sources; see International Migration Project, *Country Case Studies*, for details of the derivations.

finding that even these numbers do not comprise a sufficient population from which to draw a labour force to man a modern industrial sector. Nor do they amount to a substantial domestic market.

The indigenous workforces of the capital-rich states considered here average 226,000. Taken over all, the workforces of these states comprise 1,800,000. The average for the small Gulf states is less than 50,000.

The crude participation rate (percentage of the population who work) of the capital-rich states stands at less than 22 per cent, compared to almost 30 per cent in the case of the capital-poor states. Crude participation rates range from an extremely low 18.4 per cent in the case of Qatar, to 24.9 per cent in the Sultanate of Oman. Not only are workforces in the capital-rich states small; they are smaller than would be expected from total populations of this size.

Three factors account for the latter phenomenon. First, these pop-

Table 9.3: Capital-rich States: National Populations and Workforces Ranked by Size, 1975

State	Population	Workforce	Crude participation rate (%)
Saudi Arabia	4,592,500	1,026,500	22.3
Libya	2,223,700	449,200	20.2
Oman	550,000	137,000	24.9
Kuwait	472,100	91,800	19.4
Bahrain	214,000	45,800	21.3
UAE	200,000	45,000	22.3
Qatar	67,900	12,500	18.4
Total	8,320,200	1,807,800	21.7

Sources: these figures are authors' estimates, based on a large number of official and private sources; for derivation see J. S. Birks and C. A. Sinclair, International Migration Project, *Country Case Studies.*

ulations are very youthful, a larger proportion being less than 15 years of age than would be found in a more normally age-distributed population. Of Qatar's small population of 68,000, over 44 per cent are less than 15 years of age. Therefore, only a relatively small proportion falls within the age range from which the economically active are drawn. Second, the widespread expansion of secondary and university education during the 1970s[6] has held within the educational system boys, and to a lesser extent girls, who would otherwise have entered the workforce at, say, age 18. This reduces the labour force significantly, its effect being compounded by the youthful age structure of the population. Third, the labour force is reduced by women not generally working in wage employment in these states, except in a limited number of professions (teaching, nursing, etc.) and in certain women's organisations.[7] Traditional employment of women has been lost and has not been replaced by new opportunities in the modern sector.[8]

In view of the very limited size of the indigenous workforces, it is perhaps surprising that the capital-rich states have embarked upon the course of domestic economic development that they have – one of rapid industrialisation. However, the factors militating in favour of the industrialisation of the economies of the capital-rich states are now well known:[9] development on exotic levels by Third World standards went ahead despite their limited stock of indigenous human capital.

Industrialisation of the Gulf and Capital-rich States: The Demand for Labour

The shared features of the oil exporters' pattern of economic development include a large and expanding government sector, ambitious industrial development programmes based upon heavy industry and an ever-increasing standard of welfare and income. Today all Arab oil-rich states envisage industrialisation as an essential and central component of domestic development. This creation of industrial sectors has necessitated a rapid expansion in infrastructure provision, as have the burgeoning demands and aspirations of the national populations.

Before 1973, industrialisation and infrastructure provision proceeded at a relatively gentle pace. Infrastructure provision took much of the (relatively limited, compared to 1974) financial resources of the governments. Industrialisation was planned on a substantial, rather than a spectacular, scale.

The 1973 oil price rises transformed the oil exporters' ability to invest in infrastructure and even more so in industry. As a result, the pace of development in the oil-exporting states accelerated dramatically; plans for heavy industrial areas and secondary industry were effected on a new scale, almost unprecedented in the Third World. A major constraint to this economic transformation of the capital-rich states, however, was the shortage of manpower. Indeed, planners in the capital-rich states saw labour shortages as *the* major constraint to development, though patently shortcomings in the infant physical infrastructure provision of these states was also a major brake upon industrialisation.

The resulting demand for labour of virtually all skills and qualifications in the oil-exporting states, remarkable in its strength because of the financial resources of the exporters combined with their urge to develop rapidly, is the underlying essential force, expressed in terms of high rewards for labour, behind the international labour migration system.

The effect of economic development upon the region's labour market was great. Apart from the growth in employment in these capital-rich states starting from a very small base, the acceleration in the demand for labour was aggravated by the capital-rich states embarking together on their development plans' most labour-intensive stage – the construction phase.

In the capital-rich states, the government's response to this manpower shortage was to allow market forces to reign. Labour was imported with very little official constraint but for the procedure of obtaining visas. The latter procedure came to be lengthy as the government departments granting entry permits were swamped by applications, and so acted as an informal rationing process. Nevertheless, as is now well known, the result of the development of the oil-exporting states was a massive inflow of workers.[10] Most of these incoming workers originated in the capital-poor states of the Arab world.

The International Transfers of Labour

The prevalence of unemployment and underemployment amongst the relatively large workforces of the capital-poor states (which average 3.4 million workers) ensured a steady, spontaneous transfer of labour from the capital-poor to the capital-rich states within the Arab world. This began in the 1950s.[11] However, the demand for labour in the oil-exporting states reached a new peak after 1973, in terms both of the quantities and of the quality of the labour required. The scale of migration was transformed as a consequence. Migrant workers soon represented a large proportion of the workforces of the capital-rich states. In some sectors of the economy requiring specialised skills, immigrants came to comprise virtually the entire workforce.

Even in the largest economy and labour market – that of Saudi Arabia – expatriate workers now account for more than 40 per cent of the economically active (see Table 9.4). The countries with smaller economies, Kuwait and the UAE, rely on migrant labour to the extent that 69 per cent and 85 per cent respectively of their labour forces are non-national. Qatar, the smallest economy, depends upon a labour force in which more than four out of every five workers are expatriates.[12]

The large majority of migrant workers in 1975 were Arabs. In the principal countries of employment, Arabs accounted for 75 per cent of all migrants, Asians 18 per cent, Europeans 2 per cent and 'others' about 5 per cent (Table 9.5). Over all, almost half of all migrants were working in Saudi Arabia. Libya, the UAE and Kuwait together accounted for 48 per cent. Bahrain and Qatar, with their smaller economies, provided employment for 5 per cent of all migrant workers in 1975.

Most Arab migrants work in Saudi Arabia (57 per cent); this is only to be expected in view of the Kingdom's central position in the

Table 9.4: Employment by Nationality in Capital-rich States, 1975

State	Nationals' employment	% of total	Non-nationals' employment	% of total	Total employment
Saudi Arabia	1,026,500	57.0	773,400	43.0	1,799,900
Libyan Arab Jamahiriya	449,200	57.5	332,400	42.5	781,600
Kuwait	91,800	30.6	208,000	69.4	299,800
UAE	45,000	15.2	251,500	84.8	296,500
Bahrain	45,800	60.4	30,000	39.6	75,800
Qatar	12,500	18.9	53,800	81.1	66,300
Total	1,670,800	50.3	1,649,100	49.7	3,319,900

Source: J. S. Birks and C. A. Sinclair, International Migration Project, *Country Case Studies.*

Table 9.5: Migrant Workers by Ethnic Origin and Country of Employment, 1975

	Ethnic origin									
	Arab		Asian		European		Iranian, Turkish, migrant workforce African and other		Total	
State	No.	% of state total	No.	% of state total	No.	% of state total	No.	% of state total	No.	% of total column
Bahrain	6,200	20.7	16,600	55.3	4,400	14.7	2,800	9.3	30,000	1.8
Kuwait	143,300	68.9	33,600	16.1	2,000	1.0	29,100	14.0	208,000	12.6
Libyan Arab Jamahiriya	310,400	93.4	5,500	1.7	7,000	2.1	9,500	2.9	332,400	20.2
Qatar	15,000	27.9	34,000	63.2	800	1.5	4,000	7.4	53,800	3.3
Saudi Arabia	699,900	90.5	38,000	4.9	15,000	1.9	20,500	2.6	773,400	46.9
UAE	62,000	24.6	163,500	65.0	5,000	2.0	21,000	8.4	251,500	15.2
Total	1,236,800	75.0	291,200	17.6	34,200	2.1	86,900	5.3	1,649,100	100.0

Source: as for Table 9.4.

Table 9.6: Arab Migrant Workers in the Arab Region, 1975

Countries of Employment (% from country of origin)	Countries of Origin (% Distribution between Countries of Employment)					
	Egypt	Yemen (YAR)	Jordan and Palestine	Yemen (PDRY)	Syria	Lebanon
	(%)	(%)	(%)	(%)	(%)	(%)
Saudi Arabia	95,000 (23.9)	280,400 (96.6)	175,000 (66.1)	55,000 (77.9)	15,000 (21.3)	20,000 (40.3)
(%)	(13.6)	(40.1)	(25.0)	(7.9)	(2.1)	(2.9)
Libya	229,500 (57.8)	–	14,150 (5.3)	–	13,000 (19.5)	5,700 (11.5)
(%)	(73.9)		(4.6)		(4.2)	(1.8)
Kuwait	37,558 (9.4)	2,757 (1.0)	47,653 (18.0)	8,658 (12.2)	16,547 (23.4)	7,232 (14.6)
(%)	(26.2)	(1.9)	(33.3)	(6.0)	(11.5)	(5.0)
UAE	12,500 (3.1)	4,500 (1.6)	14,500 (5.5)	4,500 (6.4)	4,500 (6.4)	4,500 (9.0)
(%)	(20.2)	(7.3)	(23.4)	(7.3)	(7.3)	(7.3)
Jordan (East Bank)	5,300 (1.3)	–	–	–	20,000 (28.4)	7,500 (15.1)
(%)	(16.2)				(61.0)	(22.8)
Iraq	7,000 (1.8)	–	5,000 (1.9)	–	–	3,000 (6.0)
(%)	(46.1)		(32.9)			(19.7)
Qatar	2,850 (0.7)	11,250 (0.4)	6,000 (2.3)	1,250 (1.8)	750 (1.1)	500 (1.0)
(%)	(19.2)	(8.4)	(40.3)	(8.4)	(5.0)	(3.4)
Oman	4,600 (1.2)	100 (0.0)	1,600 (0.6)	100 (0.1)	400 (0.6)	1,100 (2.2)
(%)	(52.3)	(1.1)	(18.2)	(1.1)	(4.5)	(12.5)
Bahrain	1,237 (0.3)	1,121 (0.4)	614 (0.2)	1,122 (1.6)	68 (0.1)	129 (0.3)
(%)	(20.0)	(18.1)	(9.9)	(18.1)	(1.1)	(2.1)
Yemen (YAR)	2,000 (0.5)	–	200 (0.1)	–	150 (0.2)	–
(%)	(85.1)		(8.5)		(6.4)	
Total	397,545 (100.0)	290,128 (100.0)	264,717 (100.0)	70,820 (100.0)	70,415 (100.0)	49,651 (100.0)
(%)	(30.7)	(22.4)	(20.4)	(5.5)	(5.4)	(3.8)

Note: – indicates no migrants for this nationality recorded.

Table 9.6: (Continued)

Countries of Employment (% from country of origin	Countries of Origin (% Distribution between Countries of Employment)						
	Sudan	Tunisia	Oman	Iraq	Somalia	Morocco and Algeria	Total
	(%)	(%)	(%)	(%)	(%)	(%)	(%)
Saudi Arabia	35,000 (76.3)	–	17,500 (45.6)	2,000 (9.7)	5,000 (76.4)	–	699,900 (54.0)
(%)	(5.0)		(2.5)	(0.3)	(0.6)		(100.0)
Libya	7,000 (15.3)	38,500 (99.6)	–	–	–	2,500 (98.2)	310,350 (24.0)
(%)	(2.3)	(12.4)				(0.8)	(100.0)
Kuwait	873 (1.9)	49 (0.1)	3,660 (9.5)	17,999 (87.3)	247 (3.8)	47 (0.8)	143,280 (11.1)
(%)	(0.6)	(0.0)	(2.6)	(12.7)	(0.2)	(0.0)	(100.0)
UAE	1,500 (3.2)	–	14,000 (36.4)	500 (2.4)	1,000 (15.2)	–	62,000 (4.8
(%)	(2.3)		(22.5)	(0.8)	(1.6)		(100.0)
Jordan (East Bank)	–	–	–	–	–	–	32,800 (2.4)
(%)							(100.0)
Iraq	200 (0.4)	–	–	–	–	–	15,200 (1.2)
(%)	(1.3)						(100.0)
Qatar	400 (0.9)	–	1,870 (4.9)	–	–	–	14,870 (1.1)
(%)	(2.7)		(12.6)				(100.0)
Oman	500 (1.1)	100 (0.3)	–	–	300 (4.6)	–	8,800 (0.7)
(%)	(5.7)	(1.1)			(3.5)		(100.0)
Bahrain	400 (0.9)	–	1,383 (3.6)	126 (0.6)	–	–	6,200 (0.5)
(%)	(6.5)		(22.2)	(2.0)			(100.0)
Yemen (YAR)	–	–	–	–	–	–	2,350 (0.2)
(%)							(100.0)
Total	45,873 (100.0)	38,649 (100.0)	38,413 (100.0)	20,625 (100.0)	6,547 (100.0)	2,547 (100.0)	1,295,750 (100.0)
(%)	(3.5)	(3.0)	(3.0)	(1.6)	(0.5)	(0.2)	(100.0)

Note: – indicates no migrants for this nationality recorded.
Sources: Figures based on J. S. Birks and C. A. Sinclair, *Country Case Studies, Saudi Arabia, Kuwait, Bahrain, Qatar, United Arab Emirates, Libya, Jordan, Egypt, Sudan, Yemen Arab Republic, Oman, Syria, Morocco, Algeria, Tunisia*, International Migration Project (Department of Economics, Durham University, 1977/78), and Current Estimates of International Migration Project Staff.

region, physical size, enormous oil revenues, commensurate objectives and political inclinations. Closer inspection of the characteristics of Arab migrants reveals that, in 1975, Egypt, Jordan and the Yemen Arab Republic together accounted for 74 per cent of the total migrant workforce (Table 9.6). Most Egyptian migrants in 1975 were working in Libya, though 95,000 (24 per cent) were in Saudi Arabia. Egypt's proximity to Libya is the chief explanation for their substantial presence there. Almost all Yemeni migrants were working in Saudi Arabia: the attraction of the high wages offered in the neighbouring country evidently accounted for this. Jordanian and Palestinian migrants were working mainly in Saudi Arabia, but also in Kuwait, Libya and the UAE.

By 1975, some Asian labour was being used in the Arab world, but on a small scale. Only in the UAE and the Sultanate of Oman did Asian labour make a substantial contribution to the labour force in 1975, when the majority (57 per cent) of Asian workers in the Arab world worked in the UAE (Table 9.5).

Indians and Pakistanis have long been involved in economic development in the Middle East. As traders and entrepreneurs they had existed, in small numbers, under the traditional economic order in the peninsula. In World War II they were introduced in substantial numbers as part of the British war effort in the region. Subsequently, Indians and Pakistanis continued to make a contribution to the labour market, becoming associated with certain tasks and esablished in particular countries, such as Kuwait, Saudi Arabia and Bahrain. Until 1973, though, the numbers of workers in the Arab world from the Asian sub-continent were small, and their participation informal and spontaneous.

The New Scale of Economic Development in 1975 Transforms Migrant Labour Patterns

In 1975 several aspects of the Middle Eastern labour market were changing. The volume of demand for labour soared as development plans, redrawn on a new scale after the 1973 oil price increase, were implemented. Targets embodied in them were exceeded. The increased labour demand engendered by this rapid development of the capital-rich states occurred just when Iranian and Iraqi migrant workers in the Gulf states were returning home. Iran and Iraq, which had previously supplied a significant amount of labour to Saudi Arabia and the Gulf states, began to develop their own economies, attracting home large numbers of their nationals.

The expansion in labour demand and the contemporaneous withdrawal of part of the supply increased markedly the pressure upon the capital-poor Arab states to supply yet more manpower. However, by 1975, a relatively high proportion of all potential migrants in the Arab labour-exporting countries was already working abroad.

Indeed, the proportion of the national labour forces of Jordan (East Bank), the Sultanate of Oman and the Yemen Arab Republic which was employed abroad was close to one-third in 1975 (Table 9.7). In

Table 9.7: Migrant Workers and Domestic Workforces of Labour-sending Countries, 1975

Country	Size of workforce	Number of workers abroad	Proportion of workforce abroad
Jordan (East Bank)	532,800[a]	150,000[a]	28.1
Oman	137,000[b]	38,413[b]	28.0
N. Yemen	1,070,000[c]	290,128[d]	27.1
Syria	1,838,948[e]	70,415[f]	3.8
Egypt	10,756,000[g]	397,545[h]	3.7
Sudan	3,700,000[i]	45,873[j]	1.2
Total	18,034,748	992,374	5.5

Sources:

(a) based on J. S. Birks and C. A. Sinclair, *Country Case Study: Hashemite Kingdom of Jordan*, International Migration Project (Department of Economics, Durham University, October 1978).

(b) J. S. Birks and C. A. Sinclair, *The Sultanate of Oman: Economic Development, the Domestic Labour Market and International Migration*, Migration for Employment Project, World Employment Programme Research, Working Paper no. 27 (ILO, Geneva, May 1978), Table 23, p. 84.

(c) Central Planning Organisation, *Population Statistics in the Yemen Arab Republic* (Sana'a, 1976), Table 1 (Arabic).

(d) J. Socknat and C. A. Sinclair, *Migration Abroad for Employment and Its Impact on the Yemen Arab Republic*, Topic Paper, International Migration Project (July 1978), Table 23, p. 37.

(e) Central Bureau of Statistics, Damascus, *Statistical Abstract, 1977*, Table 11/3, p. 144.

(f) M. E. Sales, *Country Case Study: Syrian Arab Republic*, International Migration Project (Economics Department, October 1978).

(g) Ministry of Planning, Egypt, *Five Year Plan*, 1978–82, vol. I, Table 4, p. 31 (Arabic).

(h) J. S. Birks and C. A. Sinclair, *Country Case Study: Arab Republic of Egypt*, International Migration Project (March 1978), Table 19, p. 38.

(i) Estimate based on Department of Statistics, Khartoum, *Preliminary Results of the 1973 Population Census* (1977), Table 16 (Arabic).

(j) J. S. Birks and C. A. Sinclair, *Country Case Study: The Republic of the Sudan*, International Migration Project (March 1978), Table 34, p. 58.

Syria, Egypt and the Sudan the number of migrants abroad, though forming a smaller proportion of their domestic workforces, was also close to the potential number of workers who were prepared or able to migrate.[13]

Nevertheless, during 1975 and 1976, when the opportunities for migrant workers in oil-rich states became even more attractive, yet more workers departed from the capital-poor states. However, the rather limited number of extra workers drawn from the Arab supplying states in 1975/76 fell well short of the burgeoning demands of the oil-rich states. As a result, the rapidly industrialising wealthy states had to turn elsewhere for additional supplies of labour.

The Changing Perspective of the Migrant-receiving Countries of the Gulf: The Employment of Indians and Pakistanis

The shortage of Arab labour in the region meant that the oil exporters had to broaden their areas of labour recruitment. They turned, in their search for more manpower, to Asia, in particular to the Indian subcontinent and the countries of the south-east of the continent.

The four Gulf states of Kuwait, Bahrain, Qatar and the UAE had already experienced a marked shift in the composition of the labour market before 1975. Between 1970 and 1975, the proportion of jobs occupied by expatriate Arabs fell by 17 per cent. The Asians' share of the workforce rose from a quarter to a half of the total, their number

Table 9.8: Workforces of Kuwait, Bahrain, Qatar and the United Arab Emirates, by Ethnic Origin, 1970 and 1975

	1970		1975	
	Number	%	Number	%
Non-national Arabs	165,934	51.0	226,350	41.7
Asians	83,869	25.8	247,720	45.7
Iranians, Europeans and others	75,295	23.2	68,432	12.6
Total	325,098	100.0	542,502	100.0
Nationals	147,560	31.2[a]	195,115	26.5[a]
Grand Total	472,658	100.0	737,617	100.0

Note: (a) percentage of all employment.
Source: J. S. Birks and C. A. Sinclair, International Migration Project, *Country Case Studies*.

rising from 83,900 to 247,700. These Asians were mainly Indians and Pakistanis. The increased participation of Indians and Pakistanis was both a cause and a consequence of the formalisation of labour supplies from the sub-continent through a series of recruitment and manpower-supplying agencies.

The recruiting agents, private sector entrepreneurs from Asia, drew profit from the migration of so many for employment. Representatives of agents, living in the Gulf states, identified employers' labour requirements and specified the skill levels, trades and numbers needed. The requirements could be met quickly as the agents in India, Pakistan and Sri Lanka had ready lists of would-be migrants according to qualifications and availability. These applicants would be trade-tested before being despatched to the country of employment.

Therefore, in the mid-1970s, just when Arab labour was becoming short in supply, expensive and of less predictable quality (as the potential maximum level of Arab exports was neared), Indian and Pakistani labour of known skill and capability became available quickly and easily. This regularisation of the Asian–Arabian labour flow by agents, who could above all supply labour speedily, encouraged the rapid increase in utilisation of Indian and Pakistani labour in the capital-rich states during the period of their most frenetic development.

In 1977 and 1978, however, both Indian and Pakistani governments intervened in this system of labour recruitment. Intervention stemmed mainly from the abuse of human rights suffered by employees recruited through labour agencies. It is also of note, though, that some concern had been expressed in Pakistan about shortages of certain types of labour, ostensibly brought about by the scale of labour exporting.

The constraint upon the supply of Indian and Pakistani labour resulting from government intervention has added strength to the Oriental connection, to which this paper now turns.

The Perspective of the Gulf States and Saudi Arabia Continues to Evolve: The Oriental Connection

Formalisation of labour supplies to the capital-rich states has been taken to a new extreme by countries which have recently become, and now feature large in the Arab region as, suppliers of labour. The countries of South-East Asia – referred to here as the Orient, and including Indonesia, Korea, Malaya, Nepal, the Philippines, Taiwan and Thailand – have, since 1973/74, come to account for a rapidly increasing share of the labour market. In 1970 very few migrants of Oriental origin were working in the capital-rich states of the Arab Gulf; by 1975 they numbered some 15,000 workers. In 1979, the number of workers from the Far East in the capital-rich states exceeded 160,000.

The utilisation of Oriental labour is the result of the coincidence of the varied social and economic programmes pursued by the governments of the Gulf states. Disenchantment with the wider cultural and social implications of hosting large migrant populations in these Gulf states is growing. The indigenes of the Gulf states are becoming concerned at the possibility of being 'swamped' by the immigrant communities associated with the migrant labour forces. The implications of, for example, Qatari nationals comprising so small a proportion of the total population of their own country are great, and little evaluated. Apart from fears of numerical domination, there is concern amongst Arab policy makers in the Gulf states over the considerable cultural impact which expatriates have on the Arab indigenes and their customs. Shaikh Sultan Bin-Mohammed al Qasimi, Ruler of Sharjah, observed: 'they [migrant workers] have caused problems, and have had an effect on life, on traditions, on everything.'[14] In Kuwait, the rights of various classes of 'national' are openly debated. Although less overt in the other capital-rich states, these considerations feature increasingly in decision making, and are assuming significance in the shaping of future economic development and the labour markets.

These concerns are separate from (though related to) the economic costs of supporting growing expatriate communities. The establishment of nuclear family groups amongst the immigrant communities is a major aspect of their growing political motivation and strength. As immigrant families become established permanently, so their household heads become concerned to secure rights similar to those of nationals.

This growing disenchantment in the Gulf states with hosting such large numbers of migrants appears to present planners with a conflicting aim to the underlying thrust of economic and social policy in the capital-rich states of the Middle East – rapid economic growth based upon industrialisation. How, given the limited human capital in the capital-rich states, can rapid economic development continue without their populations becoming totally outnumbered in their own country?

Enclave Development in the Capital-rich States

The compromise chosen by the rulers of the oil-exporting states has been to separate physically new industrial areas (upon which future growth and development will be based) from existing urban areas. In this way, it is hoped that what are perceived to be the undesirable aspects of labour importing (the close and prolonged contact between indigenes and immigrants and the economic cost of supporting expatriates within the country of employment) will be minimised. Examples of such 'enclave' industrial areas are becoming numerous in the capital-rich countries of the Arab world: Shuaiba (Kuwait), Umm Said (Qatar), Jebel Ali (Dubai), Ruwais (Abu Dhabi), Yenbo and Jubail (Saudi Arabia) were all built on 'desert' sites away from major centres of population.

In order to limit the costs of infrastructure provision and to facilitate the 'containment' of the immigrant populations at these large industrial sites, there is a clear trend toward the recruitment of single, unaccompanied males to build and subsequently also to run the plants. This enables the industrial areas to be operated on a 'work camp' basis, with only a minimum amount of services provided for the all-male population and labour force. Thus social and infrastructural overheads are minimised, and the growth of the expatriate population is kept to a minimum by the exclusion of the migrant labourers' families, who remain at home in the country of origin of labour. Such work camps, in which the men who operate these enclaves live, resemble the normal camps associated with the construction industry. However, the camps associated with enclaves are to be operated on a long-term, rather than just a temporary, basis. Workers in enclaves mingle little with the indigenes and the established communities in the major urban centres. The cultural impact of the large expatriate labour forces is therefore minimised.

The countries providing the labour for this enclave form of development have been, almost without exception, Oriental. These South-East Asian companies have taken on large-scale contracts and supplied workforces of all skill levels prepared to live and operate in these work camp conditions. The camps are provided by the contractors themselves as part of the project. The Arab capital-rich governments have therefore discharged their responsibility for the provision of infrastructure for these immigrant workforces.[15]

One of the earliest major enclave contracts which set the pattern was the dry dock in Bahrain.[16] South Koreans provided the labour force and expertise for the $30 million contract. The Koreans were entirely self-sufficient in housing, which they built themselves. Food and recreational facilities were flown direct from Korea. After completion of the dock on time, the Koreans all left Bahrain. In their departure, the Koreans appeased one of the major fears of the governments of the capital-rich countries – the dallying of workers after the completion of the contract for which they were brought in. It is this process by which the more permanent communities of immigrants are built up. The departure of the Koreans contrasted very favourably, in the minds of the Bahrainis, with the aftermath of the construction of the aluminium plant for ALBA, when large numbers of migrants who had been employed building the plant remained. The aluminium plant was not constructed as an enclave.

A similar policy of enclave containment of labour forces has been adopted for the industrial development of Jebel Ali, Dubai. Isolation is achieved by siting the development away from Dubai city. The chief reason militating in favour of enclave development here is the sheer volume of labour required for Jebel Ali. Figures of estimated project employment in 1985 (Table 9.9) are equivalent to the entire population of Dubai Emirate in 1977. If this scale of demand for labour were to be met in the open market of the Emirates, it would be disruptive of the whole economy and would make arrivals of labour hard to monitor and control. In short, the UAE's economy and labour market would be severely distorted if developments on the scale of Jebel Ali were not isolated from the labour market at large.

Oriental companies are supplying the self-contained workforce to construct the large-scale plant and infrastructure of Jebel Ali. The site

Table 9.9: Dubai: Employment Estimates for Jebel Ali by Major Occupational Group, 1981–85

Occupational Group	1981	1985
Management, professional and technical workers	4,800	10,550
Supervisors, skilled manual workers, foremen and office workers	14,250	29,200
Semi-skilled manual and office workers	24,450	53,850
Total	43,500	93,600
Associated Population	67,600	160,100

Source: Dubai, 1977.

will continue to be run as an enclave after the completion of construction, being operated by contracts similar to those issued for its construction phase. It will probably never be thought desirable to integrate the Jebel Ali developments into the wide economy of Dubai or the Emirates as a whole.[17]

Although less advanced at the present, the Ruwais development (Abu Dhabi) will be built and operated on a similar basis. The Yenbo and Jubail enclaves in Saudi Arabia are also being built by Orientals with enclave-type contracts. Saudi Arabian manpower will not be available to operate these industrial areas (let alone construct them, a task which is almost entirely in the hands of the Orientals), so Yenbo and Jubail will continue as enclaves, operated by Far Eastern labour which will not integrate with the Saudi national populations.

Yet Orientals are employed within the Arab world not only as enclave labour forces. Companies from South-East Asia have tendered successfully and are meeting deadlines on non-enclave contracts; the provision of infrastructure in Riyadh, for example, is being effected by Oriental firms, as are major hotel and office building contracts in other capital-rich states.

Orientals will probably continue to be employed in the capital-rich countries by choice instead of Arab labour. Not only is Oriental labour more cost-effective; not only do Oriental companies offer very attractive 'enclave packages' to capital-rich countries, minimising difficulties for indigenous planners; the Orientals, by virtue of their preparedness to live in enclave developments, and return home after contracts are complete, offer overriding social advantages as a labour supply for which knowledge of Arabic is not essential.

It is with the probability of increased substitution of Oriental for Arab labour supplies that the paper turns to projections of the labour markets in the Gulf and other capital-rich states up to 1985. These projections quantify present market trends to demonstrate their future significance for the Gulf states, Saudi Arabia and Libya.[18]

The Projected Demand for Labour in the Capital-rich States 1975–85

The projections deal with labour demand in the capital-rich states only, since, from the present perspective, this is the significant international demand. The projection of labour demand for each capital-rich state is based upon the growth of total employment from 1970 to 1975, amended in view of development plans, major projects, stated objectives and success in meeting past deadlines. Employment in 1975

Table 9.10: Major Capital-rich States: Total Employment Projected to 1985

	1975	%	1980	%	1985
Saudi Arabia	1,799,900	5.0	2,297,200	3.5	2,728,400
Libya	781,600	5.8	1,036,000	4.5	1,291,000
Kuwait	299,800	4.7	377,100	3.2	441,400
UAE	296,500	5.4	386,500	5.4	502,700
Bahrain	75,800	4.1	92,700	3.5	110,100
Qatar	66,300	9.9	106,300	5.5	138,900
Total	3,319,900	5.3	4,295,800	3.9	5,212,500

and 1985 is shown in Table 9.10 for each capital-rich state. Over-all employment increases by 4.6 per cent per annum between 1975 and 1985. This amounts to some 1.9 million extra workers.

The Projected Domestic Supply of Labour in the Capital-rich States, 1975–85

To estimate the proportion of total labour demand which could be met by indigenous labour supplies, indigenous workforces have been projected forwards at a rate consistent with growth between 1970 and 1975. However, this rate has been adjusted to take into account likely changes in relevant economic or social variables (naturalisations, and the participation of women in the economy). The national workforces of the six capital-rich states are projected to rise in total from 1,670,000 persons in 1975, to 2,200,000 in 1985, at an annual rate of 2.6 per cent (Table 9.11).

Table 9.11: Major Capital-rich States: Employment of Nationals Projected to 1985

	1975	%	1980	%	1985
Saudi Arabia	1,026,500	2.0	1,133,300	2.2	1,263,600
Libyan Arab Jamahiriya	449,200	3.2	525,800	3.0	609,500
Kuwait	91,800	5.0	117,200	3.2	137,200
Bahrain	45,800	4.5	57,100	3.2	66,800
UAE	45,000	3.2	52,700	3.0	61,100
Qatar	12,500	4.5	15,600	3.2	18,300
Total	1,670,800	2.6	1,901,700	2.5	2,156,500

The difference, therefore, between demand and supply in Tables 9.10 and 9.11 gives an estimate of the required number of migrant workers. The number of migrants, it is known, was 1,700,000 in 1975 (in these six capital-rich states above) and so becomes 3,100,000 in 1985.

The Projected International Supply of Labour to these Capital-rich States, 1975–85

In 1975, three-quarters of all migrant workers in the capital-rich states were Arabs (Table 9.12). The estimation of the future supply of Arab labour is based on a key assumption: by 1975 the majority of Arabs from the countries of origin who were able and willing to migrate, and whose skills were employable in the capital-rich states, were already abroad. It is therefore presumed that large extra reserves of Arab migrant labour did not exist after 1975. However, the high real wages in the capital-rich states did attract an additional number of Arab migrants after 1975. They are shown in Table 9.12 under the heading 'once and for all increase'. This number is added to those already

Table 9.12: Number of Arab Migrants Abroad in 1975 and Projected Number for 1985 by Country of Origin

Country of origin	1975 no. of migrants	Once and for all increase	Annual growth of migrants abroad	No. available in 1985
Egypt	397,545	50,000	3.0	601,600
Yemen (YAR)	290,128	15,000	3.0	409,200
Jordan and Palestine	264,717	20,000	3.0	382,500
Yemen (PDRY)	70,630	–	3.0	95,000
Syria	70,415	–	3.0	95,000
Lebanon	49,661	5,000	3.0	73,000
Sudan	45,873	10,000	3.0	75,000
Tunisia	38,649	40,000	3.0	115,000
Oman	38,413	–	3.0	51,000
Iraq	20,625	–	–3.0	11,000
Somalia	6,547	5,000	3.0	15,000
Morocco	2,529	–	3.0	3,300
Algeria	18	–	–	–
Total	1,295,750	–		1,926,600

Sources: Table 9.4 and authors' estimates.

recorded as abroad in 1975. Apart from this increase, extra Arab migrants in the market are projected to increase by, in most cases, 3 per cent per annum from 1975 to 1985. Thus, in Table 9.12, 1,300,000 Arab migrants abroad in 1975 are shown, and just over 1,900,000 'able and willing' Arab migrants are predicted by 1985.[19]

The Resolution of Demand for and Supply of Labour in 1985

At this point, where demand for labour is reconciled with the supply, the nature of the assumptions made becomes critical to the resulting picture.

Two scenarios are presented (see Tables 9.13 and 9.14). The first is one in which every able and willing Arab migrant finds employment in one of the capital-rich states. This demonstrates the maximum possible contribution of Arabs to the development of the capital-rich states.

Scenario One: Maximum Penetration of Capital-Rich Labour Markets in 1985 by Arab Migrant Workers

Here, it is presumed that the entire number of 1.9 million 'able and willing' Arab migrants (derived from Table 9.12) are employed in the capital-rich states. It is also assumed that the demand for the services of Europeans rises to a stable level of 70,000. It is predicted that the number of 'Iranians and others' will fall, from 86,100 in 1975 to 70,000 in 1985, as they are increasingly drawn back to Iran as development proceeds there. (Recent developments in Iran do not, it is felt, call this presumption into question.) The number of Asians (Indians and Pakistanis) employed increases from 277,500 to 500,000 from 1975 to 1985 (Table 9.13).

Table 9.13: Resolution of Labour Demand and Supply: Maximum Arab Penetration of Capital-rich Labour Markets (Scenario One)

	1975	%	1985	%
Total labour demand	3,319,900	100.0	5,212,500	100.0
of which nationals	1,670,800	50.3	2,156,500	41.4
residual demand for migrants	1,649,100	100.0	3,056,000	100.0
of which Arabs	1,236,600	75.0	1,926,600	63.0
Asians (Indians and Pakistanis)	277,500	16.8	500,000	16.4
Orientals	14,600	0.9	489,400	16.0
Europeans and Americans	34,300	2.1	70,000	2.3
Iranians and others	86,100	5.2	70,000	2.3

This leaves a deficit of some 489,400. This, it is postulated, would be met by Orientals. Therefore, the relative market shares of each group in 1985, if the capital-rich states' labour markets are presumed to be receptive of Arab migrant labour to the extent that Arab countries of origin are able to supply migrant labour, is as follows: Arab migrants, 63 per cent (1975, 75 per cent); Asian migrants 16.4 per cent (1975, 16.8 per cent); Oriental migrants 16.0 per cent (1975, 0.9 per cent); European migrants 2.3 per cent (1975, 2.1 per cent); Iranians and others 2.3 per cent (1975, 5.2 per cent).

Two aspects of this pattern are important. First, the labour markets of the capital-rich states would continue to rely on non-Arab labour to an increasing extent. Even if every available Arab migrant were accepted in 1985, there would remain a shortfall of employment. Therefore, even if all available Arabs are employed in the capital-rich states, their proportional contribution to the labour market falls. Second, this shortfall in the supply of labour would be met from Asian sources, and increasingly from the Orient, in particular.

Scenario Two: A Selective Labour Market in the Capital-rich States, Less Open to Arab Labour

The analysis of the labour markets of capital-rich states shows that they are becoming increasingly selective over the nationalities employed on account of wider issues associated with hosting large numbers of migrants.

In scenario two it is assumed that, as a result of these market trends, the number of Arabs working in capital-rich states remains constant and does not rise between 1975 and 1985. Arabs remain in employment; each one who retires or who returns home is replaced by another Arab migrant. However, every new job is given to an Asian or an Oriental migrant. In the light of the preceding pages this is postulated by the authors to be the scenario closer to reality. In this more likely scenario, the Arab migrants' share of the capital-rich states' labour market falls from 75 per cent in 1975 to 41 per cent in 1985 (Table 9.14). Together, Asian and Oriental migrants increase in number from 292,000 (17.5 per cent) in 1975 to 1,679,400 (55 per cent) in 1985.

Thus, by 1985, the labour market of the Arab world would have dramatically different characteristics from those which it had in 1975. Such is the pace of change in the Middle East that this should come as no surprise.

Table 9.14: Resolution of Labour Demand and Supply: A More Selective Labour Market in the Capital-rich States, Less Open to Arab Labour (Scenario Two)

	1975	%	1985	%
Total labour demand	3,319,900		5,212,500	100.0
of which nationals	1,670,800	50.3	2,156,500	41.4
residual demand for migrants	1,649,100		3,056,000	100.0
of which Arabs	1,236,600		1,236,600	40.5
Asians	277,500		500,000	16.3
Orientals	14,600		1,179,400	38.6
Europeans and Americans	34,300		70,000	2.3
Iranians	86,100		70,000	2.3

Conclusions

In the projections the consequences of the inability of Arab countries to meet the labour demands of the capital-rich states is made clear: the Asian and Oriental presence inevitably increases substantially. This picture has been drawn on the basis of clearly perceived market trends. Today (1979) monitoring of labour market trends suggests that scenario two is fast developing.

Despite the evidence on which these projections are based, it might be thought remarkable that Asians and Orientals will come to dominate the labour markets of the capital-rich states when widespread unemployment exists in Egypt and Morocco. Considerations of equity and Arab solidarity should militate in favour of using this unemployed Arab labour before that of other regions. Indeed, this view is embodied in the labour law of the capital-rich states.

Yet in reality these considerations are of little relevance: whatever the overt desire of governments, development is executed through private contractors and establishments. These executors of development are concerned primarily with market factors. In the labour market, Asian and Oriental manpower is more cost-effective in the majority of cases than is Arab labour. Thus the former is preferred. Employment of Orientals in enclaves – where a large part of the future labour demand is found – falls within the overt (and now declared) policy aims of the governments of the Gulf states.

The evidence suggests that the Gulf states have little intention of abandoning their development aims; indeed, they have only a limited capacity to restrain the rate of growth. Their dependence on migrant workers is pervasive and extensive, and will inevitably increase.

In 1975 indigenous labour accounted for 50 per cent of employment in the capital-rich states; by 1985 this will have fallen to 41 per cent. In 1975 Arabs (indigenes and expatriates) absorbed 88 per cent of all jobs. By 1985, under scenario two, the Arab share would fall to 65 per cent. It is the implications of the Arab share of the market falling and of nationals becoming an ever-smaller minority in the capital-rich states, especially the Gulf states, that cause intermittent attempts to restrain development.

The fear is that, as nationals become a smaller minority, their national identity and culture will be lost. These concerns have some empirical basis: by 1985 the number of Asian and Oriental workers could have risen to as many as 1,600,000 from their 1975 total of 292,000. These figures relate to migrant workers: the settling of even a proportion of these workers with their families will create yet another challenge to the social fabric of the Gulf and other capital-rich Arab states.

Notes

1. Throughout this paper, only migrants for employment are considered. Refugees, those migrating for educational purposes, tourists, and those crossing borders for other reasons such as pilgrimage are excluded. Normally, figures quoted refer to migrant workers, excluding dependants. Where dependants are included, they are mentioned specifically.
2. This division was first made in the early 1970s (R. E. Mabro, 'Employment, Choice of Technology, Sectoral Priorities', *Manpower and Employment in Arab Countries, Some Critical Issues* (ILO, Geneva, 1975), pp. 16–31). It has remained valid and, indeed, become of increasing signficance since then.
3. $250 *per capita* is the figure given in the World Bank source quoted. If remittances were fully added into this figure, it is likely that the GNP figure would rise. The figure quoted here serves, however, to illustrate the groupings made.
4. Egypt, the most populous state in the Middle East with 38,228,000 inhabitants, does have oil, producing over 400,000 barrels of oil per day. This is an amount equivalent to Qatar's production. All of Egypt's oil, however, is used domestically, and the fact that her population is 630 times as large as Qatar's means that Egypt ranks firmly near the foot of the league table of *per capita* incomes.
5. For details of the derivations of the populations of these states see J. S. Birks and C. A. Sinclair, *The Kingdom of Saudi Arabia and the Libyan Arab Jamahiriya: Key Countries of Employment*, World Employment Programme Research Working Papers, WEP 2–26/WP 35 (ILO, Geneva, 1979).
6. See C. A. Sinclair, *Education in Kuwait, Bahrain and Qatar: An Economic Assessment* (unpublished Ph.D. thesis, Durham University, 1977).
7. J. S. Birks and S. E. Letts, 'Women in Rural Arab Society: Old Roles and New in the Sultanate of Oman', *Journal of Gulf and Arabian Peninsula Studies*, 3, 10 (Kuwait, April 1977), pp. 49–65 (in Arabic); C. Makhlouf-Obermeyer, *Changing Veils: A Study of Women in South Arabia* (Croom Helm, London, 1978).

8. In contrast, in two majo: capital-rich states, Saudi Arabia and Libya, the agricultural sector has survived, largely in traditional form. Its survival depends on female labour and, in some respects, women now take a larger role in agriculture in these two states than they did under the traditional order.

9. See also J. E. Hazelton, 'Gold Rush Economics: Development Planning in the Persian/Arabian Gulf,' *Studies in Comparative International Development*, 13, 2 (New York, 1978), pp. 3–22; J. S. Birks and C. A. Sinclair, *A Preliminary Assessment of International Labour Migration in the Arab World: Background, Perspectives and Prospects*, World Employment Programme Research Working Paper, WEP 2–26/WP (ILO, Geneva, 1978).

10. J. S. Birks and C. A. Sinclair, *The Nature and Process of Labour Importing: The Arab Gulf States of Kuwait, Bahrain, Qatar and the United Arab Emirates*, World Employment Programme Research Working Paper, WEP 2–26/WP (ILO, Geneva, 1978).

11. For an introduction to this, see J. S. Birks and C. A. Sinclair, 'The International Migration Project: An Enquiry into the Middle East Labour Market', *International Migration Review* (New York, Spring 1979) (forthcoming).

12. J. S. Birks and C. A. Sinclair, *Nature and Process of Labour Importing: The Arabian Gulf States of Kuwait, Bahrain, Qatar and the United Arab Emirates*, mimeographed World Employment Programme Working Paper, WEP 2–26/WP 30 (ILO, Geneva, August 1978).

13. J. S. Birks and C. A. Sinclair, *Human Capital on the Nile, Development and Migration in the Arab Republic of Egypt and the Republic of the Sudan*, World Employment Programme Research Working Paper, WEP 2–26/WP 29 (ILO, Geneva, 1978).

14. *Middle East Economic Digest* (15 December 1978), p. 43.

15. J. S. Birks and C. A. Sinclair, *Saudi Arabia and the Libyan Arab Jamahiriya, Key Countries of Employment*, mimeographed World Employment Programme Working Paper, WEP 2–26/WP 35 (ILO, Geneva, Summer 1979).

16. J. S. Birks and C. A. Sinclair, *The State of Bahrain, Country Case Study*, International Migration Project (Durham, 1978).

17. J. S. Birks and C. A. Sinclair, *The United Arab Emirates, Country Case Study*, International Migration Project (Durham, 1978).

18. The projection is highly aggregated: labour is assumed to be homogenous, which it is not, and patterns of development are assumed to remain from 1979 until 1985 very much as they presently appear. However, they are unlikely to change dramatically. By examining the aggregate over-all pattern, inadequacies in specification are of a diminished significance. Also reduced, though, is the utility of this projection in planning terms to any one country.

19. A net increase of the stock of migrants for employment abroad of 3 per cent in gross terms represents an actual flow of new migrants which is considerably higher than 3 per cent. Most migrants return home after a few years abroad; a typical migrant workforce would be one in which about 25 per cent return home each year. In addition to these 25 per cent, each year a proportion die or retire permanently, say one per cent. Thus, to increase the stock of migrants abroad by 3 per cent per annum requires the departure from home of about 29 per cent of the stock abroad. Therefore, while a net increase of 3 per cent per annum is not a dramatic increase, it implies a continuing migrant traffic of large proportions.

10 Political Participation and the Constitutional Experiments in the Arab Gulf: Bahrain and Qatar

EMILE A. NAKHLEH

1. Perspective

The pivotal question which faces the societies of the Arab Gulf today is: will change be gradual and peaceful or will it produce instability and violence? The basic thesis of this article is that:

1. Evolutionary change in Gulf societies, particularly the family-ruled emirates, can come about peacefully only through a process of internal political reform. Such a process would involve the establishment of a system which would invite, encourage and guarantee popular participation in the governing of the country.

2. To function effectively and to endure peacefully, such participation would have to be institutionalised, both by decree and by legisation.

3. While the relationship of the ruler to his people through the daily *majlis* may be described as 'democratic', in contemporary society the people must have a systematic method, clearly defined, to reach the ruler and his government and to influence decision making. It will not be long before the 'ways of the desert' will be antiquated by the rising level of education of the populace.

The events in Iran have indicated to neighbouring rulers that military might is not the most fundamental source of legitimacy and that, honed as it may be, a military machine can bring about neither popular support of the regime nor voluntary compliance on the part of the citizenry. The Iranian revolution also made clear the difference which exists between government by force and government by consent – under the former authority flows from the top, under the latter government is shared with the people.

Before proceeding to examine the experience which the Arab Gulf states have had with constitutionalism, it may be valuable to outline the main characteristics which these states (specifically Saudi Arabia, Kuwait, Bahrain, Qatar, Oman and the United Arab Emirates with its component states) share:

1. They are ruled by powerful families which form a modern extension of an old tribal tradition.

2. The reins of government are tightly held in the hands of the ruling family which usually makes decisions on every major issue with minimal popular input into the decision-making process.

3. In most of these tribal states the ruling families have set afoot a cautious process of inviting some form of popular participation in government. However, the ruling families have generally made it known to their peoples that this form of popular participation is basically an extension of the Islamic concept of *shura*. Translated into reality, this means that the ruler is not bound by any decision of, or resolutions passed by, the consultative bodies.

4. The moves which the ruling families in these states have initiated toward popular participation have focused on the preparation of a constitutional document, first approved by the ruling family and then (specifically in the case of Kuwait and Bahrain) submitted to some type of representative body, generally known as a constitutional assembly.

5. Territorially, demographically and administratively, the new states of the Gulf are closer in form and political structure to classical city-states than to the modern version of the nation-state. However, in almost every one of these states, the ruling family has displayed a certain flexibility and a desire to transform its littoral city-state into a modern entity aspiring to the title of nation-state.

6. Economically, the new Gulf states are engaged in a vigorous process of development. The wealth from oil has helped these countries to forge ahead with the physical transformation of their tribal societies, thereby preparing the ground for the sociological, psychological and organisational modernity to follow.[1]

The Path to Constitutionalism

In their attempt to establish a functionally modern form of government, the ruling families in these states have had to rely on one or two theoretical bases for legitimacy: either on Islamic tenets of government (*Sharia*) as expressed in the *Quran* and the *Hadith*, or on a somewhat more secular constitutional document. Even in the latter case, however, Islam has continued to constitute a major source of legislation. All six states have established a cabinet system of government (Council of Ministers), but the ruler retains almost absolute power. Of the six states involved, two (Saudi Arabia and Oman) have no written constitutions. Saudi Arabia maintains that its ultimate law is derived from the *Quran* and the *Hadith* and that sovereignty resides in the King.[2] In Oman, the Sultan is the ultimate authority and absolute ruler. Ministers and other high government officials are appointed directly by the Sultan.[3]

Of the other four states, two (the United Arab Emirates and Qatar) still operate under provisional constitutions which have not been fully implemented, particularly in the area of popular representation. No elections have been held in either country. The remaining two (Kuwait and Bahrain) have promulgated constitutions (Kuwait in 1962 and Bahrain in 1973) which called for popularly elected national assemblies or parliaments.[4] Elections were actually held in both countries, and national assemblies did function for fourteen years in Kuwait and one-and-a-half years in Bahrain. Serious constitutional crises erupted in both countries, involving a complete breakdown of co-operation between the ruling family and the assembly. As a result, the Emir of Bahrain dissolved the Bahraini National Assembly in June 1975, and this act was followed by the dissolution of the Kuwaiti National Assembly in August 1976.[5] The constitutional provisions which call for elections after a period of time following such a dissolution were suspended by emiri decrees in both countries, and this situation continues at the time of writing. Before any specific analysis is attempted, several general observations may be useful:

1. Although relative progress has been achieved in the building of modern structures of government, authority has remained strongly vested in the person of the ruler and in his family. In a significant way, the move toward constitutional monarchy has not eliminated the tribal source of legitimacy.

2. Even in the two countries in which popular elections have been held, the ruler is hereditary and the ruler's accession to power is not a matter of popular decision. Usually the inner councils of the ruling family decide who the heir apparent should be and ultimately who should rule. Members of the ruling family in each state also occupy the most important cabinet posts and other government positions. Table 10.1 indicates that fifty per cent of cabinet posts in 1978 in both Bahrain and Qatar were held by members of the ruling family.

3. Although the four Constitutions, provisional and otherwise, describe the new process of government as being democratic, one must be careful not to compare this peculiarly Gulf venture into democracy to any specific democratic form of government in the West. The process of transformation from classical tribalism into an urban and affluent form of tribalism must be examined in the context of the traditionally Muslim Gulf. The transformation from tribal rule to a limited form of popular government has, at best, been extremely slow.

4. Under the four Constitutions, family rule continues on a hereditary basis. While theoretically government in the four states is divided into the executive, legislative and judicial branches, the emir is the chief executive and remains the source of legitimacy and authority.

5. While the theoretical orientation of the new Constitutions is secularist, the body politic is solidly based on Islam. Islam is the official religion of the state and Islamic law is a primary source of legislation.

In the case of the United Arab Emirates, the Provisional Constitution adopted in 1971 is a federal document defining the powers and authority of major government offices and branches of the federal government as well as of the individual emirates within the union.[6] Article 45 of the Constitution establishes five major federal branches ('authorities') of government: the Supreme Council of the Union, the President of the Union and his Deputy, the Union's Council of Ministers, the Federal National Council and the Federal Judicature. Article 68 states that membership in the Federal National Council shall consist of forty, with the seats distributed among the member emirates as follows: eight each from Abu Dhabi and Dubai, six from Sharjah and Ras al-Khaimah, and four each from Ajman, Umm al-

Table 10.1: Ministerial Posts: Bahrain and Qatar (1978)

Ministry	Bahrain	Qatar
Ruler	Sh. Isa bin Sulman al-Khalifa	Sh. Khalifa bin Hamad al-Thani
Prime Minister	Sh. Khalifa bin Sulman al-Khalifa[a]	Sh. Khalifa bin Hamad al-Thani[c]
Defence	Sh. Hamad bin Isa al-Khalifa[b]	Sh. Hamad bin Khalifa al-Thani[b]
Foreign Affairs	Sh. Muhammad bin Mubarak al-Khalifa	Sh. Suhaym bin Hamad al-Thani[a]
Interior	Sh. Muhammad bin Khalifa bin Hamad al-Khalifa	Sh. Khalid bin Hamad al-Thani[a]
Education	Sh. Abd al-Aziz bin Muhammad al-Khalifa	e
Justice and Islamic Affairs	Sh. Abdalla bin Khalid al-Khalifa	e
Labour and Social Affairs	Sh. Isa bin Muhammad al-Khalifa	Mr Ali bin Ahmad al-Ansari
Finance	Mr Ibrahim Abd al-Karim	Sh. Abd al-Aziz bin Khalifa al-Thani[b]
Development and Industry	Mr Yusif Ahmad al-Shirawi	d
Municipal Affairs	d	Sh. Muhammad bin Jabir al-Thani
Housing	Sh. Khalid bin Abdullah al-Khalifa	d
Cabinet Affairs	Mr Jawad Salim al-Urayyid	d
Legal Affairs	Dr Husayn Muhammad al-Baharna	d
Health	Dr Ali Fakhru	Mr Khalid Muhammad al-Manai
Information	Mr Tariq Abd al-Rahman al-Muayyid	Mr Isa Ghanim al-Kawari
Economy and Commerce	d	Sh. Nasir bin Khalid al-Thani
Electricity and Water	d	Sh. Jasim bin Muhammad al-Thani
Public Works	Mr Majid al-Jishi	Mr Khalid bin Abdalla al-Atiyya
Transportation	Mr Ibrahim Muhammad Hasan Humaydan	Mr Abdalla bin Nasir al-Suwaydi
National Economy and Agriculture[f]	Mr Habib Qasim	Sh. Faysal bin Thani al-Thani

Notes:
(a) Ruler's brother.
(b) Ruler's son.
(c) The ruler also holds the title of Prime Minister.
(d) Blank space indicates this cabinet post non-existent.
(e) Post is vacant.
(f) In Qatar this post is called Industry and Agriculture.

Qaywayn, and Fujayrah.[7] Article 69 gives individual emirates the power to select their own representatives to the Federal National Council in the manner in which they see fit. None of the member emirates has opted for an election method, and no elections have ever been held.

In the remainder of this paper we will concentrate upon the experience of two states in seeking to move towards constitutionalism: Bahrain and Qatar. Bahrain and Qatar are the two lower Gulf emirates which in 1971 went separate ways from the rest of the Trucial Coast emirates and declared their independence. Despite their participation in the federation talks between 1968 and 1971, which led to the seven other emirates forming the United Arab Emirates, they opted for independence.[8] Since independence, the rulers of both countries have expressed the desire for a constitutional form of government. In Bahrain, a constitutional experiment was attempted and failed. In Qatar, the Provisional Constitution has so far not even been implemented. The following discussion will focus on the two constitutions separately and will attempt to delineate the common characteristics of both constitutions and the common problems in both countries.

The Bahraini Experience

In his 1971 National Day speech the Emir of Bahrain explicitly recognised the need for a constitution. Bahrain's modern polity, he stated, should be based on a constitution the functions of which would be (a) to protect the unity of the country and the cohesion of Bahraini society; (b) to define and guarantee such basic individual freedoms as education, health, work and expression; and (c) to establish a framework in which the people would by right participate in the governing of their country.[9] Bahraini elites reacted very favourably to the Emir's statement and, regardless of their different ideologies, unanimously supported the proposal.[10] On 20 June 1972, the Emir decreed (Law No. 12, 1972) that a Constitutional Assembly (*majlis tasisi*) be established for the purpose of discussing and ratifying a constitution. What is interesting for the purposes of this discussion is the Emir's perception of the entire constitutional process. He did not view the Constitution as a popular document based on popular sovereignty. On the contrary, much like the ruler of Qatar and other neighbouring shaikhs, he viewed the Constitution as a gift from him to the people – an expression of royal benevolence. Secondly, the ruler believed that the Constitution was neither a response to any popular demand nor an admission that the people had any legitimate right to participate in government. Popular participation would occur only at the invitation of the ruler. Put differently, 'the ruling family as a symbol of sovereignty was never questioned'.[11] Moreover, in his speech convening the Constitutional Assembly, the ruler referred to the principle of *shura*, implying that, regardless of any constitutional prescription, the ruler was to remain the ultimate sovereign.[12] Nevertheless, in the summer of 1972 the ruler did initiate the first steps towards a constitution.

Bahrain's first election ever, which was held on 1 December 1972, produced a Constitutional Assembly which was charged with approving a draft constitution submitted by the Council of Ministers. The election to the Constitutional Assembly, the composition of the Assembly itself and the resulting Constitution reflected two diametrically opposed attitudes within the al-Khalifa family:

1. a sincere desire for democracy on the part of some members of the family, involving a genuine commitment to transform Bahrain's classical tribalism into a modern representative nation-state;

2. a calculated, conscious desire of other members of the family to retain as much power in the hands of the ruling family as possible.

Some factions within the family supported the election; others feared it. One old-guard Khalifa minister was quoted as having said on the eve of the election: 'Three disasters befell Bahrain in November – the cholera outbreak, the Bapco refinery fire, and the election to the Constitutional Assembly.' The Bahraini government was obviously caught in the clash between the rhetoric of democracy and the expectations that rhetoric had created. None the less, in December 1972 Bahrain elected its first Constitutional Assembly and, a year later, the first National Assembly was elected as specified in the constitution.[13]

On 7 December 1973, about 27,000 Bahraini male citizens went to the polls to elect the thirty members of the first National Assembly (*al-Majlis al-Watani*) in the history of Bahrain. That election had special significance because of the timing, the national and regional context and some unexpected voting patterns which emerged. Bahrain was the first of the lower Arab Gulf states to have a constitution, a popular election and a representative body. In fact, of all the Arab Gulf states, only Bahrain and Kuwait even attempted to operate under a functional constitution of any kind.

More importantly, Bahrain's National Assembly election was the first such election in any Gulf or Arab country after the October War. Secondly, the election was held within the context of the oil embargo with which the Arab Gulf states levered themselves into the centre of international politics. The singularity of the election was further enhanced when one considered the strong participation of Bahrain's leftist forces in the election and the seemingly surprising victory of at least eight candidates from that bloc. Another interesting aspect of this first brush with democracy was the relatively open atmosphere surrounding the election. The al-Khalifa ruling family had decided to allow a free atmosphere to prevail during the period immediately preceding the election; the people responded by overwhelmingly electing candidates from the leftist/nationalist/reformist bloc.

Because of the preceding factors the National Assembly election was not only a domestic event; it was closely watched by every state in the region. States outside the region, specifically the United States and the United Kingdom, and less directly Japan, the Soviet Union and China, must also have closely weighed the election trends. Such interest must also have been shared by major international corporations involved in the Gulf. Late in 1973 it seemed evident that patterns emerging from the Bahraini election would indicate what influences would affect future political structures in the Gulf, both traditional and reformist. The advent of twentieth-century institutions in the region would certainly be shaped by developments in Bahrain, as would the future orientation and the possibilities of success of Gulf revolutionary movements.

Neighbouring emirs carefully studied the election results. To most ruling families, the Bahraini election brought certain discomforts because a successful institutionalisation of constitutionalism in Bahrain was perceived by these rulers as a pacesetter and as a signal that participatory government was imminent. The implication was that, if the ruling families were to survive, the regimes must somehow be opened up to popular involvement. Most rulers in the area felt with apprehension the liberalising winds that seemed to blow across the Gulf from the tiny island country of Bahrain.

Contrary to the expectations of many in late 1973 and early 1974, the constitutional experiment in Bahrain did not endure. The entire experiment may be divided into two major periods: the Constitutional

Assembly (16 December 1972–9 June 1973) and the National Assembly (16 December 1973–30 June, 1975). The Constitutional Assembly functioned relatively smoothly. It was composed of forty-two members: 22 elected, 8 appointed by the Emir, and 12 ministers. The Assembly's primary function was to discuss the draft Constitution which had been prepared by the al-Khalifa family, based largely on the Kuwaiti model. The Assembly met twice a week for 46 sessions. Of those, 38 sessions were public and 8 were executive sessions. The executive sessions dealt with such major topics as the by-laws of the Assembly, the Islamic nature of the state and the Emir's personal income.

At the conclusion of these sessions and after interesting and often lively debate that totalled over 150 hours, the Assembly approved a draft constitution consisting of 109 articles and presented it to the Emir for ratification and promulgation, which duly took place on 6 December 1973. The Constitution consisted of five major chapters: The State; Basic Principles of Society; General Rights and Duties; Branches (the Emir, the Legislative, the Executive, the Judiciary); and General Rules and Procedures.

The Constitution called for the creation of a National Assembly (Article 43) the members of which were to be elected directly by the people by secret ballot. The ministers would be *ex officio* members of the National Assembly. The Assembly would constitute, under the Emir, the sole legislative body in the country. Article 65 gave the Emir the right to dissolve the National Assembly by decree (with reasons). According to Section 2 of the same Article, however, if the National Assembly were dissolved, elections for a new Assembly should be held not later than two months from the date of dissolution. If no such elections were held (Section 3), the dissolved Assembly would regain all of its constitutional authority and would convene as if it had not been dissolved.

The first session of the National Assembly was convened by the Emir under the Constitution on 16 December 1973. That legislative session ended on 30 June 1974, after 54 meetings, mostly on Wednesdays and Sundays. The session was not exceptionally eventful; several meetings were spent on procedural matters pertaining to the by-laws of the Assembly. The second and last legislative session of the National Assembly was opened on 23 October 1974 and continued through approximately 50 meetings up to June 1975. During that legislative session meetings were characterised by rancour and open hostility between the government/ruling family and some members, particularly those belonging to the leftist–reformist bloc. Rational debate gave way to hostile confrontations, attitudes hardened and ideological positions polarised. Among the major issues that occupied the Assembly in late spring 1975 were inflation, housing, the national budget, government expenditures, internal security, Gulf security and the American naval presence at the facility at Jufair, just outside Manama.

For all intents and purposes, the processes of the National Assembly had come to a halt by May 1975. Accusations and allegations filled the air. The government claimed that the leftists or 'communists' in the National Assembly were bent on destroying the entire democratic experiment; this bloc in turn claimed that the government, particularly the Prime Minister, was no longer interested in continuing the democratic experiment and was determined to torpedo the entire process of popular participation. It was also alleged, particularly by leftist elements in the Assembly, that the ruling family was under foreign pressure (Saudi, Iranian and American) to end the whole experiment. They alleged that the public security bill, which was sponsored by the government and which was the focus of heated debate in the Assembly, was an indication that the ruling family was seriously considering the curtailment of the freedom of expression, which was the cornerstone of the democratic experiment. The government replied that it was only seeking to restrain communist elements.

The confrontation between the government and the Assembly led the government to boycott the last few sessions of the Assembly. The Prime Minister maintained that it was impossible for him or his ministers to work with the Assembly. Accordingly, he submitted his resignation to his brother the Emir and proposed that the National Assembly be dissolved and be restructured under a new election law. The Emir accepted the government's resignation and asked the Prime Minister to form a new government. On 26 August 1975, the Emir duly dissolved the National Assembly (Decree No. 14, 1975) under Article 65, Section 1, of the Constitution. At the same time, he ordered (Order No. 4, 1975) that Section 2 of the same Article, which called for a new election within two months, be suspended. Thus the entire democratic experiment in Bahrain came to an end.[14]

The Qatari Experience

Qatar has experienced neither the euphoria of drafting, ratifying and promulgating a constitution, nor the trauma of the failure of such a constitution. Generally speaking, the al-Thani ruling family in Qatar has not supported the more liberal trends of its al-Khalifa counterpart in Bahrain. Furthermore, compared to Bahrain, Qatar has had a smaller population, a more limited level of education and a much more recent labour tradition. Being part of the Arabian desert mainland, Qatar has not experienced as much interaction with other cultures as has the island country of Bahrain. In addition, Qatar has not had a politically conscious class of urban intelligentsia, as is the case in Bahrain. Accordingly, Qatar has had a very different constitutional experience from that of Bahrain.

Like Bahrain, however, Qatar is ruled by an Emir who is the source of authority in the country. It is a tribal society which adheres to a conservative interpretation of Islam (*wahhabism*) and in which the relationship between the ruler and his subjects is based on the principles of *shura*. The first Constitution in Qatar was promulgated on 2 April 1970 by the former ruler, Shaikh Ahmad bin Ali al-Thani, before Qatar became an independent state. It was called *al-Nizam al-Asasi al-Muaqqat li al-Hukum fi Qatar* (Provisional Constitution of Qatar).[15]

This Provisional Constitution was promulgated in the belief that Qatar would be a member of the Federation of Arab Emirates and as a response to the suggestion by the Supreme Council of the Federation that each emirate develop its own constitutional system.[16]

In addition to defining the Arab and Islamic nature of Qatar, the Provisional Constitution also establishes hereditary rule residing in the al-Thani family. Under Article 23, the ruler is the chief executive, the supreme ruler, the commander-in-chief, the head of state and the source of legitimacy. In law making, the ruler is assisted by a *Majlis Shura* (Advisory Council) (Article 43). The Advisory Council is convened and adjourned by the ruler (Article 59), who also has the power to dissolve the Council if need be (Article 68). As in the Bahraini Constitution, if the Council is dissolved, a new Council must be formed within two months of the date of dissolution. The Advisory Council was to consist of 20 members appointed by the ruler and 40 candidates elected by the people (Article 45). The ministers were also to be members *ex officio* of the Advisory Council (Article 44). No election was ever held.

The Provisional Constitution, which was to remain in effect until a permanent constitution was adopted (Article 28), was itself amended two years later by the present ruler, Shaikh Khalifa bin Hamad al-Thani. After Shaikh Khalifa deposed the former ruler on 22 February

1972, he amended the Provisional Constitution in what came to be known as *al-haraka al-Tashihiyya* (the corrective movement). It was replaced by what is known as the 'Amended Provisional Constitution for Qatar'.[17]

Between April 1970 and April 1972, three major developments occurred in Qatar: the emirate withdrew from the Federation of Arab Emirates; it declared its independence in September 1971; and in February 1972 a peaceful *coup d'état* occurred which resulted in Shaikh Khalifa's coming to power.

The principal amendment deals with the composition and membership of the Advisory Council. Whereas, under the previous system, Council members were to be elected, the Amended Provisional Constitution specified that the first Advisory Council was to be appointed by the Emir (Article 41). Shaikh Khalifa believed that, during the transitional period, elections were neither necessary nor useful. In a magazine interview he stated that the people 'needed time to learn to play the game of democracy and practice it'.[18] This was in 1973. So far, it seems, the transitional period has not ended, the Advisory Council continues to be appointed and no elections are anticipated in the near future.

Common Characteristics of the Bahraini and Qatari Constitutions

For purposes of comparison between the two Constitutions it would be useful to examine three specific indicators: how the sources of legitimacy are defined; to what degree popular participation is permitted; and how authority is shared among the divisions of government. Admittedly this comparison is only theoretical, for in one country the Constitution has been suspended and in the other it has yet to be implemented. Yet both states have clearly stated their commitment to their respective Constitutions, and laws and decrees in both countries continue to be made in the name of the Constitution.

On legitimacy, the Bahraini Constitution establishes several fundamental principles. First, 'Bahrain is a sovereign independent Islamic Arab state' (Article 1) and, second, 'Bahrain's rule is hereditary, vested in the person and descendants of Shaikh Isa bin Sulman al-Khalifa, from father to his eldest son' (Article 1). Third, 'Islam is the official religion of the state, and Islamic law (*sharia*) is a primary source of legislation' (Article 2). Fourth, the 'Emir is the head of state, and his person is protected and above reproach' (Article 33). The

Qatari Constitution establishes similar sources of legitimacy. First, 'Qatar is a sovereign independent Arab state' (Article 1) and, second, 'Islam is the official religion, and Islamic law is the primary source of legislation' (Article 1). Third, 'the system is democratic' (Article 1) and fourth, 'the Emir is the head of state, and his person is protected and above reproach' (Article 20). Fifth, 'the rule in the state is hereditary, vested in the family of al-Thani' (Article 21).

On the question of popular participation, the Bahraini Constitution makes several explicit statements. First, as was pointed out above, the people are considered the source of authority and members of the National Assembly are popularly elected by secret ballot according to law (Article 43). The freedoms of conscience, speech, press, correspondence and organisation are protected by law (Articles 22, 23, 24, 26 and 27) and 'members of the National Assembly represent the whole people' (Article 63). The Qatari Constitution refers to popular participation in government, but only obliquely. The people's role in government is discussed only in future terms, to be realised once the 'transitional stage' (Preamble), presently served by the Provisional Constitution, comes to an end. At this stage even the Advisory Council (a semi-parliament) is appointed by the ruler and participates only indirectly in legislation; Council members usually represent the prominent families in the community (Articles 40–43). Once the transitional stage comes to an end, at a time to be decided later by an emiri decree, and once a permanent constitution is promulgated, the Advisory Council would be popularly elected by secret ballot (Article 46).

Although both Constitutions call for the division of government into three branches, the Bahraini Constitution is again more explicit on the sharing and distribution of authority among the branches. The system of government is based on the separation of powers among the legislative, executive and judicial branches (Article 32). However, unlike the separation of powers in the United States, the legislative branch in Bahrain is headed jointly by the ruler and the National Assembly; the ruler also heads the executive branch and judicial decisions are always rendered in his name (Article 32). Legislative bills become law once they pass the National Assembly and are ratified by the ruler (Article 42). The judiciary is independent and autonomous (Article 101), and judges should not be subjected to undue influence from any source (Article 101).

The Qatari Constitution also divides the government into branches, but only two are named separately and explicitly: the executive, headed by the ruler in co-operation with the Council of Ministers (Article 18), and the judiciary, in which court decisions are rendered in the name of the ruler (Article 19). The only reference to the legislative branch under this section of the Constitution is that the ruler promulgates laws upon the suggestion of the Council of Ministers and after consulting the Advisory Council (Article 17).

The above political indicators seem to reveal at least two points:

1. As an evolutionary process of reform, the political development which has been planned in the Gulf seems to be a synthesis of traditional tribalism and modern democracy.

2. The Bahraini political system seems to be at a more advanced stage than the Qatari system in terms of popular participation in government, government accountability and popular sovereignty.

Concluding Comments

In the light of the above discussion, an immediate question comes to mind: why did the constitutional experiment in the Arab Gulf emirates fail? While this is a difficult question to answer, it is possible to make several observations:

1. 'Going democratic' required more than just an intent on the part of the ruler and the ruling family to open up the regime.

2. Participatory government and continued authoritarian family rule are by definition contradictory. Sharing in government requires both rights and responsibilities as well as a sincere commitment to the spirit of compromise.

3. Because of education, communications and, above all, the oil wealth, the ruling families could not keep foreign ideas from invading their own societies. Consequently, the traditional family-type communal relationship between the ruler and his people began to face tremendous social strains. Traditionalism needed to yield to new social demands.

4. The whole constitutional experiment seems to have started on the wrong foot. The rhetoric of democracy could not measure up to the reality of authoritarian government and, when a conflict erupted

between the people and the ruling family over the source of authority, the so-called 'game of democracy' came to a halt, with individual liberty on the losing end.

5. Perhaps the whole attempt to become democratic was premature. A successful democratic process requires more than instant wealth to translate the people's goodwill and traditional loyalty and support into a functional system of participatory government. What might be needed first is a commitment to create a more rational economy in those societies.

6. For democracy to function effectively at least three basic conditions must be fulfilled: the relationship between the government and the governed must be clearly defined; democracy must be recognised as a right that belongs to the people, rather than being a gift from the ruler; and the process must become institutionalised and not subject to the whim of any one ruler or any one ruling family. These conditions were absent.

7. Other factors aiding the establishment and functioning of a democratic system are: a reasonable level of education and literacy, a healthy economy, a reasonably large middle class, a fairly self-reliant indigenous population and, of course, an effective government based on a tradition of voluntary compliance with the law. These elements were only partially present.

In conclusion, if Arab Gulf societies are to enjoy long-term stability, internal political reform must be a top priority. The ruling families must realise that, if popular participation is channelled properly, it can be a great asset to the regime and a stabilising force in society. If an evolutionary process of political reform is not encouraged and maintained, revolution becomes the only alternative. Iran is just around the corner!

Notes

1. Emile A. Nakhleh, *Bahrain: Political Development in a Modernizing Society* (D. C. Heath, Lexington, Mass., 1976), pp. 166–7.
2. Emile A. Nakhleh, *Arab–American Relations in the Persian Gulf* (American Enterprise Institute for Public Policy Research, Washington, DC, 1975) and *The United States and Saudi Arabia: A Policy Analysis* (American Enterprise Institute for Public Policy Research, Washington, DC, 1975).

3. John Duke Anthony, *Arab States of the Lower Gulf: People, Politics, Petroleum* (The Middle East Institute, Washington, DC, 1975).

4. See Yahya al-Jamal, *al-Nizam al-Dasturi fi al-Kuwait* [*Constitutional System in Kuwait*] (Kuwait University Press, Kuwait, 1971); Government of Kuwait, *Dastur Dawlat al-Kuwait wa Qanun al-Intikhab* [*Kuwait's Constitution and the Election Law*] (Kuwait Government Press, Kuwait, 1962); State of Bahrain, *Dastur Dawlat al-Bahrain* [*Constitution of the State of Bahrain*] (*Official Gazette*, Bahrain, 6 December 1973).

5 For an analysis of the dissolution, see *al-Adwa'* (Bahrain, May–August 1975); *Sada al-'Usbu'* (Bahrain, May–July 1975); *al-Tali'a* (Kuwait, May–August 1975); *al-Bahrain al-Yom* (Bahrain, May/August 1975); *al-Tali'a* (Kuwait, 31 August 1976).

6. 'The Provisional Constitution of the United Arab Amirates', *The Middle East Journal*, vol. 26, no. 3 (Summer 1972), pp. 307–25. For a discussion of the union itself see John Duke Anthony, 'The Union of Arab Amirates', *The Middle East Journal*, vol. 26, no. 3 (Summer 1972), pp. 271–87.

7. Ras al-Khaimah, which joined the union in February 1972, was allotted six seats on the Council.

8. For an excellent treatment of the background of the federation, see Riyad Nijib al-Rayyis, *Sira' al-Wahat wa al-Naft: Humum al-Khalij al-'Arabi Bayna 1968–1971* [*Struggle of Oases and Oil: Troubles of the Arabian Gulf, 1968–1971*] (al-Nahar Press, Beirut, 1973).

9. State of Bahrain, Ministry of Information, *Huna al-Bahrain* (December 1971), p. 3.

10. See a series of newspaper interviews conducted with Bahraini elites entitled 'What do the People Want in a Constitution?', *al-Adwa'* (February–April 1972).

11. Nakhleh, *Bahrain: Political Development in a Modernizing Society*, p. 125.

12. For the full text of the speech, see *Akhbar al-Bahrain* (18 December 1972), pp. 1–3.

13. For a detailed examination of the activities of the Constitutional Assembly and an analysis of the constitutional debate in the Assembly, see *Minutes of the Constitution Assembly* (16 December 1972–9 June 1973). Special supplements to Bahrain's *Official Gazette*.

14. For further details, see *al-Bahrain al-Yom* (27 August 1975), pp. 1–17 and *al-Adwa'* (28 August 1975), pp. 2–5.

15. Government of Qatar, *Official Gazette* (2 April 1970), pp. 1–8.

16. Ibid., p. 9.

17. State of Qatar, *Official Gazette* (22 April 1972), pp. 1–9.

18. *al-Hawadith* (Beirut, February 1973), p. 11.

11 Federalism in the United Arab Emirates: Prospects and Regional Implications*

NAOMI SAKR

Introduction

The first half of 1979 saw perhaps the most critical phase yet in the short history of the federation of the United Arab Emirates. International and domestic factors combined to raise basic questions regarding the future of the federation. Internationally, the principal problems followed from the demise of the Shah of Iran, as this led, on the one hand, to the United States apparently thinking seriously about intensifying the US military presence in the Indian Ocean and the Gulf and, on the other, to federal government concern about the allegiance of the approximately 100,000 UAE inhabitants of Iranian origin – heightened by a fear that the new Iranian regime would pursue irredentist claims on the Arab side of the Gulf. The policy issues raised by developments of such fundamental importance to the UAE constituted potential for bitter disagreement among the rulers of the seven constituent emirates.

The effects of developments at the international level could have been much less significant had they not come at a critical moment in the evolution of the UAE's own federal institutions. The Supreme Council of the federation (consisting of the rulers of the seven emirates) was already split by differences over the relative powers of the federal and emirate governments – with Shaikh Rashid of Dubai taking a strong stand against what he saw as the tendency of the federal authorities to expand their powers. These differences made it impossible for a meeting of the Supreme Council to be convened in the early part of 1979 and the subordinate cabinet and Federal National Council (consisting of delegates from the constituent emirates) also retreated into a state of suspended animation. Attempts by the Federal National Council to solve problems by proposing a greater degree of integration among the constituent emirates simply made matters worse by further antagonising Shaikh Rashid.

The immediate crisis in the federal machinery was overcome by the appointment of Shaikh Rashid as federal Prime Minister, with a new cabinet taking office on 1 July. Whether the new arrangement would make it any easier for the federal institutions to deal effectively with the problems facing the UAE, however, remained to be seen. It could be contended that a more fundamental challenge to the federation's institutions than that posed by disagreements among the seven rulers was the upsurge of political consciousness and questioning among the population. The latter, which was both the natural outcome of improved educational opportunities and the result of events inside and outside the UAE, came to focus upon certain key demands: that the Federal National Council be directly elected; that industrialisation plans be reviewed so as to reduce the reliance on an immigrant labour force; and that measures be taken to eliminate the bureaucratic formalities which were making contact, communication and mobility difficult among the different emirates.

In view of the recent problems, the object of this article is to assess the federation's ability to survive, and to suggest the lines along which current difficulties could be resolved.

The Evolution of Federal Machinery

There are certain features of the history of the UAE which may help in gauging the federation's ability to withstand inter-emirate crises. The federation agreement signed by six of the emirates in 1971 and adhered to shortly afterwards by Ras al-Khaimah was not a surprise move nor a reversal of any previous trend. It was the logical conclusion to a series of steps dating back as far as the middle of the nineteenth century. In 1835 the chiefs of Abu Dhabi, Dubai, Sharjah and Ajman signed a one-year truce, intended by Britain to prevent inter-tribal warfare at sea, in which they undertook to report any aggression to the British authorities rather than retaliate themselves. This truce was renewed at intervals until, in 1853, a Perpetual Maritime Truce was signed, calling a halt to all hostilities at sea. The ending of this so-called 'piracy' allowed the Bani Yas tribe, dominant in both Abu Dhabi and Dubai, to gain ascendancy over the Qawasim, who were located principally in Sharjah and Ras al-Khaimah. Concepts of tribal territory, however, were generally vague. When oil discoveries in the Gulf area prompted the first attempt by Britain to define individual rulers' territorial claims in 1937, it became clear that, apart from the inhabitants of Dubai and Umm al-Qaywayn, no one was really sure where their boundaries lay. A glance at the present-day map of the northern emirates demonstrates the extent of the confusion. The map reveals a veritable jigsaw puzzle of territories in which both Ras al-Khaimah and Fujayrah are divided into two portions, Ajman is divided into three and Sharjah into no less than five. The emirates, then, have never been wholly discrete units. They have always formed part of a larger area, the rulers of which had together established a *modus vivendi* at sea as well as on land. Meetings between these rulers were institutionalised in 1952 with the formation of the Trucial States Council which, although it could not enforce action, could promote discussion. The first concrete step towards federation came in February 1968 when Abu Dhabi and Dubai agreed on a form of union. Ten days later the leaders of the remaining five Trucial States, together with the rulers of Bahrain and Qatar, agreed to join. Bahrain and Qatar subsequently changed their minds and Ras al-Khaimah equivocated. But, exactly four years later, the formation of the UAE was complete.

The evolution of the UAE since those first steps were taken in 1968 can be divided into three stages, each one marked by the identification of certain sectors as key areas of co-operation. In their initial agreement in 1968 Abu Dhabi and Dubai showed themselves to be primarily interested in co-ordination on foreign affairs, security, defence, social services and immigration.[1] The rulers of the nine states originally interested in federation likewise set up committees to look into social services, communications, currency and labour laws, but not, significantly, defence. The UAE's Provisional Constitution of 1971 – stage two – followed much the same lines. It extended federal responsibility initially to foreign affairs, education, health and essential public works, justice and communications, but this time not to immigration or defence. Under that Constitution, each emirate was to contribute 10 per cent of its income to the federal budget. The start of the third stage came with the expiry of the temporary Constitution and of Shaikh Zayed's five-year term as President at the end of 1976. By this time Shaikh Zayed's concern had focused on extending federal control over the armed forces and immigation and on raising individual contributions to the federal budget to 50 per cent of each emirate's revenues. Shaikh Zayed felt so strongly about these issues that he threatened not to accept re-election unless agreement could be reached. In the face of this threat a compromise was worked out to merge the armed forces, bring arms purchases under federal control and raise individual emirates' budget contributions to 25 per cent.[2] Immigration was to be brought under the aegis of the federal Interior Ministry and the Provisional Constitution, with these amendments, was extended for a further five years.

Issues of Contention: Defence, Immigration and Finance

Developments over the past decade, therefore, help to isolate the issues – defence, immigration and finance – that have been contentious from the outset. An analysis of how contentious they remain may help to indicate the direction in which the federation is moving.

Quite clearly, a unified defence policy is crucial to any attempt at nation building. It must also be crucial to any federation formed as a result of the member states' desire to preserve their joint sovereignty against the threat of absorption by neighbouring powers. Prior to the armed forces merger which followed the constitutional crisis of 1976, the four biggest emirates each had their own armies and bought their own arms. The attempt at merger, far from ending competition among the emirates, brought matters to a head. For a while a balance of power was established between Abu Dhabi and Dubai through the appointment of Shaikh Zayed's son and heir, Shaikh Khalifa, as Deputy Commander-in-Chief and Shaikh Rashid's son, Shaikh Mohammad, as Defence Minister. But in February 1978 Shaikh Zayed tipped the balance by appointing his other son, Shaikh Sultan, to the post of Commander-in-Chief. Shaikh Rashid went on record as questioning this choice[3] and that same year ordered Scorpion tanks of his own from Britain. Dubai has also omitted to participate in the sending of UAE forces to Beirut. A continuing lack of cohesion within an army of the size and composition of that of the UAE could be critical. Altogether, out of a total population now estimated at 877,000, the army, navy and air force together number 30,000 men, while internal security personnel number another 20,000. The over-all total is said by some observers to comprise as many as 28 different nationalities,[4] with Omanis accounting for a large proportion of the expatriates. Inevitably there have been fears of subversion. In March 1973, 37 suspected members of the People's Front for the Liberation of Oman and the Arab Gulf were arrested in Abu Dhabi, some of them members of the Abu Dhabi Defence Force.

Linked with the question of security is that of immigration, which in turn is related to the extent and intensity of the industrialisation programme. Disagreements on immigration policy are no new phenomena for the UAE. Fear of an influx of foreigners has existed in Abu Dhabi since the first oil was struck; Shaikh Shakhbut is known to have objected to the possibility that 'his people' might become a minority in their own country as had already happened in Kuwait. In its three-year Development Plan for 1977–79, Abu Dhabi outlined its strategy on immigration as following 'a clear and wise policy regarding immigration and naturalisation which should be coherent with the special circumstances of the country'. The Plan fixed allocations for importing additional manpower over the three-year period at between 191,000 and 244,000, giving an over-all population target of 457,000–503,000 by 1979.[5] Dubai, on the other hand, as a cosmopolitan trading centre, has always adopted a *laissez-faire* attitude to immigration. It is calculated that Jebel Ali industrial zone, when consisting of the full complement of plants (aluminium smelter, steel mill, liquefied petroleum gas plant, power generation and desalination plants, 74-berth port complex and airport) will require a workforce and contingent population of 400,000 by 1985.[6] This compares with a projected requirement of 80,000–100,000 for the industrial zone at Ruwais in Abu Dhabi, if this project goes ahead in its most ambitious form. Immigration problems have, theoretically, been a federal preserve since 1977. But, as in the case of the army merger, the attempted centralisation of immigration regulations and procedures brought underlying tensions to the fore. The ministry concerned clamped down on transit visas, which made life very difficult for businessmen and gave Dubai cause for alarm. In May 1978 the new regulations had to be relaxed; the attempt to create a unified immigration policy was postponed.

At the time of writing, however, the issue of immigration remains a highly urgent one: it may not be possible to shelve the issue, for projections on the availability of migrant labour are basic to any coherent attempt at managing the economy. Unless the federation as a whole pursues a consistent policy in this sphere, neither public corporations nor private businesses will be able to plan realistically for the future. The Planning Ministry is waiting anxiously for guidance.[7] Staff at this ministry point out that even a continuation of the present *laissez-faire* attitude represents a policy option which could form a basis for economic projection. Indeed, they view this as one of the options open for the period from 1980 to 1985. Alternatively, the government could decide to fix the population at, say, one million by

1985, but this would have repercussions for growth since it represents an increase of only 123,000 on the figure for 1979. Vital to any decision on immigration would be clear indications as to the source of additional labour. The UAE news agency announced recently that the government was aiming for a point where 90–95 per cent of oil sector employees would be of Arab origin.[8] In their case study of immigration into the UAE, however, Birks and Sinclair[9] provide a breakdown of work permit applications by nationality which shows that, in 1976, 68.6 per cent of all economically active immigrants applying for visas were Asian, against only 20.2 per cent Arabs. They also predict that labour supplies still to be tapped from Arab sources are relatively limited and that Jebel Ali and Ruwais will have to be implemented using labourers from Asia and the Far East who are prepared to tolerate a work-camp existence and make minimal demands on local services.

Following on from the question of immigration and industrialisation comes that of finance and budget contributions. In fact these questions are so closely interrelated that it is reasonable to argue that the budget issue is not separate at all but is merely a restatement of the other issues in different terms. If this is the case, then it reduces and simplifies the causes of inter-emirate tension.

There are several reasons for viewing arguments over the budget as academic. Not least is the fact that the income of the emirates other than Abu Dhabi and Dubai is so small as to make very little real difference to federal spending power. Sharjah, for example, has said it will pay 50 per cent of its revenues to the federal treasury. But, although it is an oil producer, its output declined from 22,100 barrels a day in 1978 to 16,500 barrels a day in mid-1979. Moreover, revenue from this production has to be split with Iran and Umm al-Qaywayn. Over all, Sharjah's current annual oil takings may amount to around $33 million[10] and, since there are at present plans for the drilling of only one more well, this is not likely to change much in the near future. The outlook for Ras al-Khaimah is much the same. Its hopes of an oil find are fading fast, leaving quarries and taxes as the principal sources of income, estimated at around $33.5 million a year.[11] Fujayrah, like Sharjah, is willing to pay the required 50 per cent, but its resources are limited to fisheries and agriculture, with perhaps some income from tourism coming in the future. A mineral survey has located what may be commercially exploitable deposits of copper and chrome in Fujayrah but development of these could take at least five years. This leaves Ajman and Umm al-Qaywayn, both of which rely on federal funding for the industrial projects they have under way. Umm al-Qaywayn is hoping to develop its gas reserves but this will be an expensive process and earlier optimism on these reserves now looks premature. At any rate, the respective incomes of the five smaller emirates are dwarfed by federal budget expenditure, which reached a peak of Dh13,150 million ($1 equals approximately Dh3.74) in 1977. As for the two remaining members of the UAE, Abu Dhabi is known to have contributed 90 per cent of all federal funds in recent years. This leaves Dubai, which is believed to have annual revenues amounting to perhaps $3,000–3,500 million but which is now understood to have agreed to contribute $1,750 million of that to the federal budget (following from the Kuwaiti mediation which helped resolve the crisis in the early part of 1979). Altogether, local observers estimate that, if each emirate pledged half its income, this would give the federation some Dh18,000 million to spend in 1979. This figure, however, merely serves to underline the academic nature of the budget dispute. For, despite the additional aid commitments assumed by the UAE at the Arab summit meeting in Baghdad in October 1978, it is virtually certain that a budget allocation of Dh18,000 million could not be spent. Over-all expenditure had to be cut from its 1977 peak to a level of only Dh10,500 million in 1978 and even then achievement rates for development spending are reported to have fallen to 31 per cent against 53 per cent for the previous year.[12] It should also be remembered that, despite its proclaimed reluctance to continue to foot federal bills, Abu Dhabi runs no risk of running short of cash. Not only have oil prices risen dramatically in 1979, but Abu Dhabi is one of the few oil producers that can expect to increase production in coming years. Its crude oil output, which last year ran at an average rate of 1.45 million barrels a day, should be up to around 2 million barrels a day by the early 1980s. This increase will result from the development of the Upper Zakum offshore field which, according to the General Manager of the Abu Dhabi National Oil Company, Mahmoud Hamra-Krouha, could produce at rates of between 0.5 million and 1 million barrels a day for 60–70 years.[13] In addition, Abu Dhabi has recently announced the discovery of what could be one of the world's biggest gas reserves, lying under the Umm Shaif offshore fields. Abu Dhabi's earnings from hydrocarbons, therefore, seem to be assured for a long time to come.

Thus, when Shaikh Zayed complains in public about financial commitments to the federation (as he did complain to a Kuwaiti newspaper in October 1977) there are grounds for believing that he has other reasons for complaining than questions of finance as such. Several possible reasons come to mind. The first of these arises from the imbalance between expenditure in Abu Dhabi and Dubai. A study presented by a UAE delegation to a recent conference on Industrial Development in the Gulf stated that the total cost of projects under way in the UAE was Dh10,352 million.[14] Of this, the report said, Dh8,405 million was being spent in Dubai. That imbalance may be attributed to the growing recognition in Abu Dhabi that industrialisation in fields other than petrochemicals has to be very carefully thought out. Mohammad Habroush, Managing Director of the Abu Dhabi Investment Authority and Chairman of Abu Dhabi's Department of Finance, is among those known to feel strongly about the need for selectivity. He has been quoted as saying that 'industrialisation for its own sake was a slogan widely but sometimes mistakenly adopted in the developing world'.[15] Sources close to Shaikh Zayed, keenly aware of the human problems posed by massive immigration and of the need to provide economic and political outlets for the immigrant population, have pointed out to this writer that, in the long run, the only solution to these problems is to minimise industrialisation at home. One way to do this, they say, is to invest abroad – in India or Sudan. UAE investment in Sudan, in fact, is already a reality, as is shown by the existence of the Emirates–Sudan Investment Company and its five newly established subsidiaries, each with substantial capital and a detailed list of worthy projects. If the sophisticated reappraisal of industrialisation now in train in Abu Dhabi were to spread to Dubai, much of the friction now existing between the two emirates could disappear. In fact, Shaikh Rashid may already have started to rethink his emirate's ambitious plans. Early in 1978 British banking sources described him as being reluctant to get involved in any major new project and at one point during the year he refused to allow the Dubai Aluminium Company to raise a loan on his personal guarantee. UAE residents are highly conscious of the heavy burden of debt servicing awaiting Dubai in the 1980s; combined repayments in 1979–80 are not expected to fall far short of $800 million. Shaikh Rashid himself, meanwhile, may well have come to question the vast programme of industrial expansion drawn up for him by Western consultants who are singularly keen to justify *their* advice by according *him* a reputation for 'shrewd business sense'.

Two other possible explanations for Shaikh Zayed's complaints about inequitable contributions to the federal budget lie in the enormous debts incurred by two of the smaller emirates – Sharjah and

Ras al-Khaimah – and by the failure of all the emirates, except for Abu Dhabi, to declare their revenues. Sharjah and Ras al-Khaimah are both thought to have debt-servicing ratios of 100 per cent or more and Abu Dhabi has found itself obliged, on occasion, to allocate funds for these emirates' debts to be repaid. Ideally, in Abu Dhabi's view, such funds would only be made available in return for greater federal control.

A fourth and final factor affecting the budget debate is that of ownership of natural resources. It was predicted early in 1978 that the next proposed amendment to the Constitution would curtail individual emirates' rights to develop their resources independently. Theoretically, such an amendment would entail a considerable loss of freedom for the individual emirates. In practice, however, it is questionable whether the smaller emirates have sufficient resources to warrant concern over separate ownership, and the experience of Dubai suggests that individual states (apart from Abu Dhabi) may simply not be able to develop their resources independently. The Jebel Ali zone, for instance, will be partially supplied with gas from Dubai itself but will also rely on 60–120 million cubic feet of gas a day from outside sources. Dubai tried to obtain this gas from various sources including Oman and Umm al-Qaywayn before finally entering into a supply agreement making it dependent on Abu Dhabi. Meanwhile, the hope of finding oil in Ras al-Khaimah and more gas in Umm al-Qaywayn is encouraging these emirates to hold out for separate ownership. While they struggle to retain their independence and while Abu Dhabi seeks ways to persuade them to toe the federal line, what is really at stake, however, are not questions of centralisation *versus* decentralisation but of better planning *versus* the dissipation of resources. In fact, the majority of points of conflict between Abu Dhabi and the other emirates need not be viewed – as they normally are – in terms of arguments for or against centralisation of authority. In essence they are arguments about planning.

There is a growing feeling throughout the UAE that co-ordinated planning cannot be put off any longer. Planning Minister Said Ghobash told an international audience at the start of 1979 that 'capital alone cannot pave the road for development'. 'There is a general awareness and appreciation', he said, 'of the need to define a comprehensive development strategy'.[16] The Planning Ministry says it could be ready to launch a federal plan by December 1980. What it needs is the impetus that can only come from a political agreement. That agreement is more likely to be achieved if the parties involved are able to distinguish between a tendency to centralisation and economic dominance by a single emirate, on the one hand, and a rationally planned use of resources, on the other. It may be that the latter can be achieved without the former.

Notes

*This is a heavily abridged version of the paper originally presented in the conference mentioned in the preface, the concluding part of which listed reasons for believing that the UAE could function satisfactorily as a federation and suggested, with reference to developments in the Gulf as a whole, that it should seek to do so and not attempt to become a unitary state.

1. K. G. Fenelon, *The United Arab Emirates* (Longman, 1973), pp. 22–3.
2. This figure was quoted to the author by Shaikh Zayed's Press Secretary, Mr Zaki Nuseibeh, during an interview in Abu Dhabi in March 1979. Some other sources give a figure of 20 per cent.
3. *Al-Hawadess* (16 June 1978).
4. Michael Tingay, 'Legions Galore', *UAE Survey, Financial Times* (25 June 1979).
5. Abu Dhabi Department of Planning, *Basic Indicators for the Socio-Economic Development Plan* (1977–79), p. 2.
6. J. S. Birks and C. A. Sinclair, *International Migration Project – Country Case Study: the United Arab Emirates* (University of Durham, 1978), p. 15.
7. The information which follows is taken from interviews with Ministry personnel carried out by the writer in March 1979.
8. *Wampress* (28 June 1979).
9. Birks and Sinclair, *United Arab Emirates*, p. 26. See also their contribution to this book.
10. Kathleen Bishtawi, 'Sharjah, Out of the Gloom', *UAE Survey, Financial Times* (25 June 1979).
11. Tewfik Mishlawi, 'Belt-tightening in the UAE: Bankers Grow Anxious about Loans to Smaller Shaikhdoms', *The Middle East* (September 1978).
12. Ann Fyfe, 'UAE Unity Problem Resolved', *The Middle East* (June 1979).
13. Interview with K. Done, *The Financial Times* (11 May 1979).
14. *Wampress* (4 June 1979).
15. Ann Fyfe, 'UAE soul-search on industry role', *The Middle East* (February 1979).
16. Said Ghobash, *Development Planning in the UAE* (paper delivered at Stanford Research Institute Symposium on Planning, 21 January 1979).

12 The Prospects for Integration in the Arab Gulf

TIM NIBLOCK

Introduction

The most basic need for integration[1] among the states of the Arab Gulf is clearly to serve the long-term economic and social interests of the population. While the benefits of oil may raise current standards of income and create an infrastructural basis which helps to satisfy current needs, the economic survival of the smaller Gulf states would clearly be impossible without oil – at least if the populations were to continue to enjoy a reasonable standard of living. Economic strategy, therefore, needs to be geared towards establishing economic structures which can provide the populations of the area with a satisfactory economic life after the depletion of oil, and these structures inevitably involve the existence of an integrated unit covering at least some of the existing states.

This article will contend that the vast array of agreements on co-operation and co-ordination which have been made among Arab Gulf countries in recent years (especially since 1972) have not substantially advanced the above-mentioned goal; that these forms of co-operation and co-ordination are not currently helping to create an integrated economic unit the structures of which will satisfy the needs of the population after the depletion of oil; that an indication of the failure of existing co-operation and co-ordination is reflected in the declining proportion which intra-regional trade constitutes even in the non-oil global trade of the states of the area; that what is currently required is not simply more co-operation and co-ordination within the existing economic structure, but the creation of a radically different economic structure; and that the creation of such an economic structure (and hence the establishment of a coherently integrated unit) may depend upon political changes within the states themselves – changes which would give greater responsibility and representation to those social elements whose interests may be most closely tied to an enhanced level of integration and whose awareness of the long-term problems facing their societies is most acute.

Current patterns of co-operation and co-ordination may, of course, be beneficial in other respects – or from the point of view of other interests. External interests, whose concern is with the 'stability' of the area and the protection of their own interests there, may find in current patterns a satisfactory basis for the pursuit of their objectives. Local rulers, intent on protecting their regimes against internal and external threats and seeking to gain for their states whatever benefit is available from regional co-operation within existing economic structures, may also find current patterns satisfactory. Our concern here, however, is with a different objective.

The focus of this paper is on the position of the smaller Arab Gulf states – Bahrain, Kuwait, Oman, Qatar and the UAE. The long-term necessity for integration among units the populations of which barely exceed one million is particularly evident. An integrated unit comprising the above five states, however, would still have a population of less than four million (on current figures); hence the value of the integrative process covering Saudi Arabia and also Iraq. Even this seven-state unit would have a population of less than 24 million and could perhaps best function as a 'regional island' within a more loosely integrated or co-ordinated Arab world. Whether there are 'systemic' factors which make it unlikely for the states concerned to come together within this pattern of integration will not be considered here.[2]

In the sections which follow, the development of the links of co-operation and co-ordination among the Arab Gulf states over recent years will be documented. Space does not permit a consideration of the effectiveness of each agreement made; rather, consideration will later be given to the effectiveness and value of the whole network of agreements made and organisations established.

Co-operation and Co-ordination before 1968

The principal characteristics of the development of co-operative links among the states of the Arab Gulf in this early period were: the co-ordination under the British protectorate of policy in those states which were not yet fully sovereign (Bahrain, Qatar and the seven Trucial States); the activities of Kuwait and, to a lesser extent, Saudi Arabia, Bahrain and Qatar in extending aid to those states which were not yet producing oil (the Trucial States); and the initiation of co-operative economic arrangements between Kuwait and Iraq and between Kuwait and Saudi Arabia.

Co-ordination Under the British Protectorate

The main organs of co-ordination in the Trucial States were: the Trucial States Council, of which the 30 meetings between 1952 and 1968 brought the rulers together to discuss matters of mutual concern; the Trucial States Development Fund, established in 1965 to approve and monitor development projects in the area; and the Trucial Oman Scouts, responsible for the security of the area, under the British protectorate.

The existence of the British protectorate covering Bahrain and Qatar as well as the Trucial States ensured the uniformity of economic practice among these states, such that the area constituted a free trade area with common external tariffs. The Gulf rupee, managed by the Bank of India, was the currency used by all states up to 1966. In the latter year, following the devaluation of the Indian rupee, the area split into two currency groupings – that of the Qatar–Dubai riyal and that of the Bahrain dinar (used in Abu Dhabi and some of the smaller states, as well as Bahrain).

It may be significant that the motive force which brought the Trucial States Development Fund into existence was not a direct response to internal pressures for development, but rather the desire to counter an external influence. The Arab League had been planning a similar fund for the development of the Trucial States.

Gulf State Aid to the Trucial States

By 1968 Kuwait had become deeply involved in the development process within the Trucial States.[3] This involvement dates from 1952, but the main programme was initiated in 1962 when a Gulf Permanent Assistance Committee (GUPAC) was established in Kuwait to recommend and administer aid to those states. By 1968 Kuwait was operating some 32 schools, two hospitals and seven clinics in the area, at no cost to the local population. GUPAC also financed the construction, although not the operation, of four general hospitals, two sanatoria and 12 schools. A number of resource surveys were also carried out. After 1966, GUPAC was replaced by the General Authority for South Arabian and Gulf States.

Other aid for the Trucial States came from Saudi Arabia, Bahrain and Qatar, although none of this was as substantial as that from

Kuwait. Saudi Arabia financed the construction of the Abu Dhabi–Dubai road (as also its extension to Ras al-Khaimah after 1968); Qatar and Bahrain both provided small numbers of teachers to the schools in the Trucial States, on a grant basis, and both also made grants to the Trucial States Development Fund at its inception (BD 333,250 from Qatar, BD 53,298 from Bahrain).[4]

Co-operative Arrangements Among the Independent Gulf States

As with Gulf state aid to the Trucial States, Kuwait appears to have played the most active role in pioneering co-operative arrangements with its two neighbours. Following the earlier tension between Kuwait and Iraq after Kuwaiti independence in 1961, the Kuwait government extended a KD 25 million grant to Iraq in 1963 and an Economic Co-ordination Agreement was signed in 1964. Under the terms of this agreement a further protocol was signed in February 1967 allowing free trade between the two states and encouraging barter deals so as to promote trade.[5] Although the latter agreement was never fully implemented, trade between the two states was fostered.

Following the visit of the Emir of Kuwait to Iraq in June 1966, joint committees were established to examine the thorny question of the border and to promote Kuwait capital investment in Iraqi development projects. Discussions were also under way in 1966–68 for the provision of fresh water supplies from the Shatt al-Arab to Kuwait by pipeline, although these discussions were ultimately abortive. A further measure of Kuwaiti–Iraqi co-operation was the support given by Kuwait to Iraq in the course of Iraq's dispute with the Iraq Petroleum Company, in 1967–68.

Relations between Kuwait and Saudi Arabia involved considerable co-operation and co-ordination in oil production and international oil policy. The fact that the two countries shared control of the Neutral Zone, and that the Neutral Zone was an oil-production area, made such contact and co-ordination necessary. In March 1967, moreover, the two countries established a joint committee to co-ordinate their international oil policies, with the consultations of this committee reaching a climax after the 1967 Arab–Israeli war and the subsequent temporary oil boycott of the United States and Britain.

Contact between Saudi Arabia and Iraq was limited and the general relationship was characterised by hostility – due, in part, to their support of different sides in the Yemen conflict.

The Years of Federative Effort, 1968–72

Over these years, the trend towards developing co-operative relations among the states of the Arab Gulf was dominated by attempts to create a nine-state federation (the Trucial States, Bahrain and Qatar), culminating in the failure of the original scheme but in the establishment, in 1971, of the United Arab Emirates, linking the seven Trucial States. Other prominent aspects of this period were: the conclusion of a further set of economic and cultural co-operation agreements among the states of the area; the expansion of the physical communications infrastructure connecting the various states; the attempts to settle and define the frontiers between the states; the increase of aid from the richer states to the poorer; and the role played by chambers of commerce in pressing for greater co-operation and co-ordination.

Co-operation and Co-ordination Associated with the Federal Project

Although there had previously been intimations (e.g. a report in *Al-Rai al-Aam* of Kuwait, 12 May 1966) that the Arab Gulf states under British protection might seek some form of mutual association as an independent state, it was clearly the British government's decision in January 1968 to withdraw its forces from the area which set in motion the attempts to federate. Within one month of the British government statement, the announcement was made that Abu Dhabi and Dubai would federate (18 February 1968), and on 28 February it was announced that a nine-state federation had been agreed. The impulse to integrate clearly came from the desire (shared by the regimes themselves and by external forces with interests in the area) to protect the states and regimes from any instability which might arise after the withdrawal, not from a conviction that the economic needs of the population could be catered for more effectively within a unitary framework.[6]

The course of the negotiations which spread through 1968, 1969, 1970 and 1971 on the creation of a federation will not be covered here, nor will the federal structure which emerged in the United Arab Emirates be examined. Both are covered by Naomi Sakr's article in this book. The focus, rather, will be on those aspects of the attempt at creating a federation which laid the basis for the further development of co-operation and co-ordination among the Arab Gulf states (i.e. considering the United Arab Emirates now as one state).

There are two main ways in which the federal project created a basis for enhanced co-operation between the United Arab Emirates and other Arab Gulf states in the years which followed 1971. First, the network of joint committees which were established to examine aspects of integration, and the intensive meetings which took place at different levels, opened up contacts between the rulers of Bahrain, Qatar and the Trucial States,[7] and between administrative departments in the different states bearing responsibility for similar fields. The fact of discussing their common problems and seeking common solutions to them created channels for pursuing schemes of co-operation and co-ordination after 1971, even though the nine-state federation itself had failed to materialise.

The joint committees established at this time, and which continued to operate until 1971, covered a wide variety of fields. In July 1968 the provisional Federal Supreme Council established joint committees to study and examine the means by which currencies, postal services, educational systems, labour and social security laws and the laws relating to ownership of property could be unified. In January 1969 a committee was established to consider ways in which communications systems could be more closely linked, and in the same month a committee to unify the health systems was established. A further committee concerned with the creation of a customs union among the nine states was set up in August 1970. In addition to the detailed lower-level work within the joint committees there were also, of course, the higher-level meetings: the meetings of the nine rulers formalised as the Federal Supreme Council (five meetings held from 1968 to 1971); the meetings of the deputy rulers, intended to clarify the issues upon which the FSC needed to decide (six meetings held from 1968 to 1971); and the frequent bilateral talks between individual rulers seeking to find solutions to the problems in the federative process.

The other way in which the federal project enhanced co-operation in a wider regional setting is through the involvement of Kuwait and, to a lesser extent, Saudi Arabia in attempting to bring the federation into existence. The Kuwait government played an active diplomatic role in this process, mediating among the states when difficulties arose and emphasising the vital interests which were at stake in the creation of a federation. The principal Kuwaiti initiatives took place in June 1968 and December 1969, when the Kuwait Foreign Minister undertook tours of all the states involved in the federation in an attempt to mediate over the differences which had arisen, and in

August 1970, when the Kuwait Foreign Minister and the adviser to the Saudi Arabian monarch on Gulf affairs toured the Gulf states in one last attempt to resolve differences. Kuwait was to continue to play this role of mediator and conciliator after the independence of the United Arab Emirates, on those occasions when differences arose between the component parts of the federal entity.[8]

Economic and Cultural Co-operation

The main agreements signed over this period on increased economic and cultural co-operation in the area were all between Kuwait and Iraq. Within the framework of the Economic Co-operation Agreement of 1964, a joint committee was established in January 1968 to study and promote co-operation in iron and steel and in the petrochemical and sulphur industries. One result of the deliberations of this committee was the establishment in March 1968 of a joint Iraqi–Kuwaiti company to exploit sulphur deposits in Mishrak, Iraq. In September 1968 the two countries concluded an agreement to co-ordinate their information media (exchange of radio and television programmes, etc.) as part of a programme to 'preserve the Arab character of the Gulf'. Lastly, in March 1971, an agreement was signed which exempted all animal, agricultural and industrial products traded between the two countries from tax and which envisaged the trade between them rising in value to ID 5 million in each direction.

The activities of the joint committee and the operation of the agreement on tax-free trade, however, were both to be disrupted in 1972 and the years which followed by the intensification of the border dispute between the two countries.

Expansion of the Communications Infrastructure

A number of schemes were undertaken which brought the states of the Arab Gulf closer to one another, in terms of the time taken to travel or communicate between them. In February 1970 the Hofuf–Salwa road linking Saudi Arabia and Qatar was completed, and in the same year work was pressed ahead on the link road between Kuwait and Saudi Arabia. The Abu Dhabi–Qatar, Abu Dhabi–Dubai, Dubai–Sharjah and Sharjah–Ras al-Khaimah roads were all undertaken and mostly completed over the 1968–1971 period.

Arrangements were made over the same period, and most of the work completed, for the establishment of modern telecommunications links between the Arab Gulf states and, under an agreement made in

March 1969, Saudi Arabia and Kuwait facilitated use of each other's telecommunications systems.

Border Settlement

The process of seeking to delineate the land and offshore borders between the Arab Gulf states was pushed ahead over the period in question, although many of the most difficult issues remained unsettled at the end of the period. Among the Trucial States, the offshore boundary between Abu Dhabi and Dubai was agreed in February 1968 and the land boundary between the two states was formally delineated in February 1969. The land boundary between Abu Dhabi and Ras al-Khaimah was also formally delineated in February 1969. Severe differences, reaching their climax in July 1970, existed between Sharjah and Umm al-Qaywayn as to their offshore boundary (in oil-rich waters), and differences continued between Dubai and Sharjah on their land boundary.

Saudi Arabia and Kuwait concluded negotiations in December 1969 for the division of the Neutral Zone (which thereafter became the Partitioned Zone) between them, and the division proceeded forthwith under the supervision of a joint committee. The oil resources of the area were to continue to be shared on a 50–50 basis, with the joint committee co-ordinating control of the oil operations. A similar agreement on oil sharing was concluded between Qatar and Abu Dhabi with respect to the offshore Bunduq field in November 1969, following the delineation of the offshore border between the two states. The border issue between Kuwait and Iraq, however, remained unsolved despite talks on the issue in February 1970, as also did the border issue between Saudi Arabia and Abu Dhabi – with Saudi Arabia restating its claim to the Buraimi oasis and to access to the Gulf in the area of Khor al-Udaid at the base of the Qatar peninsula in July 1970. Differences between Qatar and Bahrain over Hawar island remained.

Gulf State Aid to Other Gulf States

After 1968 the pattern of aid giving from one Arab Gulf state to another became more diverse than it had previously been. Abu Dhabi entered the field as an aid giver, contributing virtually the whole of the £2,500,000 budget of the Trucial States Development Fund for 1971 and helping to fund (together with Britain) the establishment and operation of the Bahrain Technical College. Saudi Arabia began to offer substantial numbers of scholarships for Gulf students to pursue their studies in Saudi educational institutions – 70 were offered in August 1968 and a further 60 in July 1969 – and also financed the establishment of an Islamic court in Fujayrah (agreed upon in August 1969). In May 1969 an agreement was concluded whereby Iraqi judges would serve, at the expense of the Iraqi government, in the Trucial States, and around the same time scholarships for students from other Gulf states were made available in Iraqi educational institutions. Kuwait continued to maintain the educational and medical services previously established, embarking in December 1969 on a programme to expand the medical services (both sets of services were taken over by the United Arab Emirates government in 1972). The Kuwait Fund for Arab Economic Development provided a KD 1 million loan to Bahrain for the aluminium smelter project, and loans of KD 3 million and KD 3.8 million were extended in 1970 to Iraq for electricity and cement projects. In 1970 the Kuwait government donated to Dubai equipment for the establishment of Dubai's television station.

Chambers of Commerce Role in Promoting Co-operation

The trend towards inter-governmental co-operation in the Arab Gulf was mirrored by private business interests seeking co-operative arrangements. Businessmen from the nine states involved in the projected federation met in Bahrain in April 1969 to lay the basis for a Gulf Chamber of Commerce; they resolved to press collectively for the liberalisation of customs regulations and the introduction of free transit and trade in the Arab Gulf area as a whole. Following a visit to Bahrain by the Kuwaiti Chamber of Commerce in February 1970, the Chambers of Commerce of the two states signed an agreement envisaging extensive co-operation between the private sectors – involving, among other items, the establishment of a Kuwait–Bahrain bank (set up in 1971) and Kuwaiti private sector participation in the Bahrain flour-milling industry (implemented in 1970). Similar arrangements on co-operation, but with less specific projects mentioned, were reached between the Qatari and Kuwaiti Chambers of Commerce in the same month, and between the Iraqi and Qatari Chambers of Commerce in August 1970.

Economic and Social Interchange and Co-ordination, 1972–79

The level of co-operation and co-ordination among the Arab Gulf states since 1972 has shown a marked advance over that which existed previously. Most notable has been the host of economic and social co-operation and co-ordination agreements concluded among the states. The attempts at enhancing co-operation and co-ordination in these spheres may be divided into the following categories:

1. broad agreements laying down general principles for co-operation and co-ordination;
2. agreements to pursue specific policies of co-operation and co-ordination;
3. establishment of joint committees for considering or implementing schemes of co-operation and co-ordination;
4. co-ordination of currencies;
5. cultural and social co-operation and co-ordination;
6. joint projects;
7. functional organisations established by a number of Arab Gulf states to serve their collective needs;
8. Intra-Gulf aid giving.

The concern here is with agreements made, not with whether or how the agreements were implemented. The latter dimension will be covered, in broad perspective, later. One aspect which emerges clearly, however, will be mentioned at this stage: while the myriads of joint committees and economic co-operation agreements have often failed to have much effect, activities in the field of functional organisation have often been more productive.

Broad Agreements Laying Down General Principles for Co-operation and Co-ordination

Two sets of agreements on such general principles have been reached, both within the past two years. The first was in October 1977 and was the product of the first general conference of Arab Gulf Trade Ministers. All seven Arab Gulf states (Bahrain, Iraq, Kuwait, Oman, Qatar, Saudi Arabia and the United Arab Emirates) were parties to the agreement, which sought to lay down a framework within which co-operation among the Arab Gulf states should proceed. The main elements of the framework were: that the states would endeavour to make progress towards 'some form of co-operation such as a common market'; that maximum security should be given to funds invested in one state by organisations of another; that joint industrial, agricultural and commercial projects should be undertaken where possible; and that co-operation should be pursued in the fields of educational and scientific research.

The second set of agreements consisted of those concluded between Kuwait and Bahrain, Qatar, the United Arab Emirates and Oman in December 1978, following the visits of the Kuwaiti Prime Minister to these states. Each of the agreements envisaged the unification of policies on customs and tariffs, the unification of legislation relating to the protection of local industries, and the encouragement of joint projects between Kuwait and the country concerned.

Agreements to Pursue Specific Policies of Co-operation and Co-ordination

A series of agreements between Kuwait and Bahrain, Qatar and the United Arab Emirates, all signed in June 1973, guaranteed the free movement of capital, labour and produce between Kuwait and each of these countries – in effect creating a free trade area, as Bahrain, Qatar and the United Arab Emirates were already linked by free trade. A further advance towards creating a unified market covering these four states was made in May 1975, when they agreed on measures to unify their import policies relating to foodstuffs.

A measure of free trade was introduced between Saudi Arabia and Bahrain in April 1975, when these states agreed that most of the major products traded between them should be exempt from customs duties, and in October 1978 Kuwait and Iraq agreed to exempt all goods traded between them from customs duties (an agreement which followed the pattern of the February 1971 free trade agreement between the same two countries, the implementation of which was disrupted by the border dispute).

Establishment of Joint Committees for Considering or Implementing Schemes of Co-operation and Co-ordination

By the end of the period under consideration, joint committees were in operation covering the development of co-operative relations between most of the Arab Gulf states. Most of these joint committees were responsible for considering and recommending to their respective governments broad measures of co-operation and co-ordination – measures which could be taken to encourage trade, areas of economic activity where joint projects could be undertaken, etc. Such joint committees, covering broad measures of co-operation and co-ordination, were established between Bahrain and Qatar in November 1972, between Kuwait and Bahrain, Qatar and the United Arab Emirates in June 1973, and between Saudi Arabia and Bahrain, Kuwait, Qatar and the United Arab Emirates in the early months of 1978.

There were also joint committees established to consider particular schemes of co-operation. In April 1977, Kuwait and Saudi Arabia established a joint committee on industrial co-ordination, with specific authority to recommend and encourage joint enterprises in the fields of cement, glass and car tyre production and to recommend means whereby Saudi Arabia, in creating its own iron and steel industry, could consider the needs of Kuwait. An agreement in November 1977 between Iraq and Kuwait established a number of joint technical committees to consider specific projects: the supply to Kuwait of water from the Shatt al-Arab, the supply to southern Iraq of electrical power from Kuwait, and the construction of a railway linking Kuwait with Basra.

Co-ordination of Currencies

The moves aimed at co-ordinating currencies in the Arab Gulf have now been proceeding for more than four years, but with only limited success. Kuwait, Bahrain, Qatar and the United Arab Emirates originally agreed in May 1975 to seek means of unifying their currencies. It proved difficult to include the strong Kuwaiti dinar in the scheme, with the result that the other three states pressed ahead on their own. In August 1976 the United Arab Emirates and Qatar agreed to retain their currencies at a fixed parity with relation to one another and, in September of that year, Bahrain entered the arrangement. The currency of any one of the states was to be accepted as legal tender in the remaining two. In spite of the agreement, however, the currencies were allowed to diverge in the course of 1976–77 before being brought back into alignment when all three of the states revalued their currencies against the dollar and temporarily re-established a fixed parity with relation to one another in January 1978. Since then, however, a further divergence has occurred.

Cultural and Social Co-operation and Co-ordination

Cultural co-operation, especially among the smaller Arab Gulf states, has proceeded within the framework of co-operation agreements, covering the exchange of scholarships, television programmes and technical information. The co-operation agreements (mentioned earlier in the context of economic co-operation) between Kuwait and Bahrain, Qatar and the United Arab Emirates in June 1973 all laid down a framework for such exchanges, as did a cultural and educational co-operation agreement signed between Saudi Arabia and the United Arab Emirates in April 1975. Even without the existence of such agreements, the provision of scholarships by one Gulf state for students from another has proceeded and expanded – as in the case of the substantial number of Gulf students at all levels who have pursued their education in Iraq, at the expense of the Iraqi government. The fact that all of the institutions of higher education in the Gulf, together with many of the lower-level institutions, contain such large numbers of students from Gulf states other than the one in which they are situated is evidence of the extent of the exchange. In the case of the Bahrain technical college, the institution was established specifically to serve the technical training needs of the Arab Gulf states as a whole.

Other measures of cultural co-ordination have been the attempts to co-ordinate goals and curricula. The conference of Arab Gulf Education Ministers, held in April 1978, ended in agreement that such goals and curricula should be standardised, and committees were established to recommend the means by which this standardisation could be achieved, and hopefully later to follow through the implementation. All seven Arab Gulf states were involved in this agreement.

Joint Projects

Although most of the joint committees on economic co-operation were instructed to examine the possibility of joint projects in different fields, the number of joint projects actually undertaken, on a government-to-government basis, has been limited. One area in which joint projects have been carried through, moreover, has been outside the scope of the activities of these committees – namely the oil industry. In the latter industry states have co-operated in the development of oilfields which straddle borders – such as the Bunduq field between the United Arab Emirates and Qatar, the Abu Sarafa field between Bahrain and Saudi Arabia, and the oilfields of the Partitioned Zone between Kuwait and Saudi Arabia.

Outside the oil sector, the main projects have been the joint cement venture between Saudi Arabia and Bahrain (first announced in April 1975, formally agreed in August 1977), being set up in Hofuf with a 25 per cent Bahraini contribution, and the joint Kuwaiti–Saudi Arabian project for the production of cement and clinker (agreement signed in June 1976). Currently projected are the schemes to construct a petrochemical complex in Oman with Kuwaiti participation and an oil refinery in Ras al-Khaimah, also with Kuwaiti participation.

Functional organisations

There have so far been six organisations created jointly by Arab Gulf states for the running of some service or facility needed by Arab Gulf states generally. A further three organisations have been established with Arab Gulf states as the major participants but with an added element from outside the area.

The first functional organisation to be established was Gulf Air, set up in March 1973 (on the basis of the previously existing Gulf Aviation Company) and owned jointly by Bahrain, Oman, Qatar and the United Arab Emirates. At a meeting in January 1976, the Arab Gulf Finance and Transport Ministers decided upon the establishment of a further two functional organisations – a shipping company and an international bank. The former was formally initiated as the United Arab Shipping Company in May 1976, with the participation of Bahrain, Iraq, Kuwait, Qatar, Saudi Arabia and the United Arab Emirates; the latter was set up in Bahrain with the participation of the same group of states, in November 1976, as the Gulf International Bank. The shipping company started trading on the basis of the 40 ships taken over from the former Kuwait Shipping Company, enjoying a nominal capital of $200 million, while the Gulf International Bank was granted a nominal capital of BD 40 million.

A meeting of Arab Gulf Ministers of Information, also in January 1976, accepted a proposal from Kuwait for the establishment of an Arab Gulf News Agency under the joint over-all authority of Bahrain, Iraq, Kuwait, Oman, Qatar, Saudi Arabia and the United Arab Emirates. After some complaints from Iran as to its nomenclature, the agency was eventually founded as the Gulf News Agency – beginning transmissions in March 1978. A further meeting of Arab Gulf ministers – in this case Industry Ministers, in March 1976 – led to the creation of a further functional organisation: the Gulf Industries Consultancy Organisation, which held its first meeting in Doha, in February 1977. The Consultancy Organisation was given responsibility for preparing studies of the possibilities of industrial co-ordination among Arab Gulf states, providing technical assistance in the preparation and evaluation of development projects, and reducing dependency on foreign consultancy groups.

The remaining functional organisation, the Gulf Ports Union, was established in October 1976 to co-ordinate handlings between the ports of the seven Arab Gulf states.

The functional organisations within which Arab Gulf states play the dominant role (and provide all of the finance), yet which also involve an element external to the Gulf, are the Arab Petroleum Investment Company (established in January 1975 and jointly financed by Kuwait, Saudi Arabia and the United Arab Emirates to promote hydrocarbons development, but coming under the over-all authority of OAPEC), the Gulf Oragnisation for the Development of Egypt (which began operation early in 1977, under the joint authority of Kuwait, Qatar, Saudi Arabia, the United Arab Emirates and Egypt but the activities of which have been suspended since the Camp David agreements) and the Arab Organisation for Industrialisation (also beginning operation early in 1977, under the joint authority of Qatar, Saudi Arabia, the United Arab Emirates and Egypt, and currently suspended). The Gulf States also, of course, constitute the main part of the membership of OAPEC, but Libya too is a member.

Intra-Gulf Aid

The pattern of intra-Gulf aid which has emerged since 1972 is of a flow of grants and loans from the larger oil producers to the smaller ones, Bahrain and Oman, whose receipts from oil have not been sufficient to cover the costs of their development projects. The major disbursements to Bahrain have been a £34 million loan from Abu Dhabi (November 1974) for projects in housing, hospitals and electricity; a KD 10 million loan from Kuwait (October 1976) for power projects; a $50 million grant from Saudi Arabia (March 1977) for a sports complex; and a joint loan of BD 33 million (1 Bahrain Dinar equals approximately $1) from Kuwait, Saudi Arabia and Abu Dhabi (November 1977) for power projects. The loans from Kuwait were from the Kuwait Fund for Arab Economic Development, those from Abu Dhabi were from the Abu Dhabi Fund for Economic and Social Development, and that from Saudi Arabia was from the Saudi Arabian Development Fund.

Major disbursements to Oman have been a $26 million loan from Kuwait (November 1976) for natural gas projects; a loan of $100 million from Saudi Arabia (July 1977) for copper mining; and a further $96.2 million loan from Saudi Arabia (July 1977) for the construction of administrative and social centres in Dhofar. The Kuwait Fund for Arab Economic Development and the Saudi Arabian Development Fund were involved.

Further Aspects of Co-ordination, 1972–79

Planning and Discussion of More Advanced Integration

The measures of co-operation and co-ordination mentioned above have been carried through within a context of continuing discussion regarding a more far-reaching integration. This discussion has taken three forms. The first, limited mainly to the three years which followed the establishment of the United Arab Emirates, has been discussion of the possibility of resurrecting the nine-state federation idea – i.e. bringing Qatar and Bahrain into the existing federation. Initiatives to bring this about were undertaken by the United Arab Emirates Foreign Minister in March 1973, June 1973 and November 1974, but with little apparent progress towards resolving the differences which had caused the failure of the original scheme.

The second form was the discussion of a 'single political and economic plan' for the Arab Gulf states – the idea that through continuous bilateral and multilateral discussion, co-ordinated policies both in domestic development and in international politics could be pursued by the Arab Gulf states. This matter was discussed in talks between the Foreign Ministers of Bahrain, Qatar and the United Arab Emirates in July 1973, and between those Foreign Ministers and that of Oman in April 1974. The elements of co-operation and co-ordination which were in fact brought about over these years (as mentioned above) could be considered part of the process of creating the 'single plan'. The co-ordination envisaged in discussion of the plan, however, seems to be greater than what was actually achieved.

The third form has been discussion of the creation of a Gulf common market (an idea which seems also to have been an element in the 'single plan' proposition). Following a proposal made by the ruler of Qatar, the Foreign Minister of Kuwait undertook discussions among other Arab Gulf governments on this subject in January 1973; more extensive discussions were held in the course of February 1976, when a Kuwaiti economic delegation toured the other Arab Gulf states with a view to examining the problems in the creation of a common market. Further discussions on the subject took place during the meeting of the Arab Gulf Trade Ministers in October 1977, and during the meeting of the Kuwaiti–Saudi Joint Co-operation Committee in January 1978.

Although there has been no formal establishment of a common market organisation in the Arab Gulf, some of the aspects of common market practice have been in existence there for some years. The area already enjoys virtually free trade, and the bilateral arrangements co-ordinating rates of tariff on imported goods have gone some way towards creating common external tariffs.

The Co-ordination of International Policies

The trends towards social and economic integration are inevitably affected by elements of co-operation and divergence within the political sphere. The continuous exchange of ministerial visits, together with the basic similarity of the problems facing the regimes, has enabled the states (especially the smaller Gulf states) to pursue broadly similar policies with regard to the outside world – whether on matters relating to the Arab–Israeli dispute (Camp David agreement, etc.), on negotiating positions with the oil companies over pricing and supply (usually discussed and co-ordinated among Arab Gulf states before the wider meetings within OPEC), on attitudes towards Iran and towards great power activities in the Gulf region, or on defence. The latter field has seen attempts to standardise weaponry (in a series of bilaterial talks in 1976–77), statements of mutual defence in case of aggression (e.g. Saudi Arabia–UAE, April 1975) and the frequent exchange of military delegations.

The 'co-ordination' of international policy has, on occasions, appeared more as pressure by one of the larger states on one of the smaller – as in November/December 1971 when the newly formed government of the United Arab Emirates announced its intention to establish diplomatic relations with the Soviet Union, only to withdraw from this standpoint following 'talks' with the government of Saudi Arabia.

Success in co-ordinating policy towards the outside world has been accompanied by continuing intra-regional border disputes, with the differences between Kuwait and Iraq becoming pronounced in November/December 1976 (followed, in July 1977, by agreement on a framework within which to solve future differences), the re-emergence of tension between Bahrain and Qatar over Hawar Island in April 1976, and the differences between Oman and the United Arab Emirates over the location of the Omani–Ras al-Khaimah border in 1977/78.

Intra-regional Trade: A Standard for Evaluating Progress Towards a Coherent Structure for Long-term Needs

The information presented above indicates that co-operation and co-ordination among Arab Gulf states has advanced on many levels over recent years. The measure of the value of these forms of co-operation and co-ordination, as laid down at the outset of this paper, is whether they are helping to create an economic structure which will satisfy the needs of the populations after the depletion of oil resources; and the only precise measure of whether the area is indeed advancing towards a pattern of economy which could be self-supporting without oil, on the assumption that existing units are too small to achieve such an objective, is the level of intra-regional trade.

Intra-regional trade as a proportion of total non-oil trade has in recent years been higher in the case of Kuwait than in that of other Arab Gulf states.[9] Tracing the pattern of trade development in the 'best case' state will help towards an understanding of the over-all trends in the area. The period taken is that between 1970 and 1976; 1976 is the latest year for which figures detailing the breakdown of Kuwaiti trade with the Arab Gulf are available. The total of Kuwaiti imports over this period grew from KD 223,267,000 to KD 971,992,000; imports from Arab Gulf countries grew from KD 4,171,000 to KD 4,466,000 – such that the percentage of intra-regional trade to total imports fell from 2 per cent to less than .5 per cent. The total of Kuwaiti non-oil exports came to KD 26,384,000 in 1970, rising to KD 215,636,000 in 1976; non-oil exports to other Arab Gulf states rose from KD 11,313,000 in 1970 to KD 61,910,000 in 1976. The percentage of total non-oil exports constituted by this intra-regional trade fell from 43 per cent to 30 per cent. While the latter percentages are high, it should be borne in mind that the total value of non-oil exports was limited. Taking non-oil imports and exports together, Kuwait's intra-regional trade declined as a percentage of total trade from 6 per cent to 3 per cent. If oil were taken into account, the percentage of intra-Gulf trade to total trade falls from 0.5 per cent in 1970 to 0.2 per cent in 1976.

For other Arab Gulf states the percentage share of intra-regional trade has consistently been smaller than in the case of Kuwait – substantially smaller in all cases except that of Bahrain. The many agreements on economic co-operation and co-ordination among the Arab Gulf states, therefore, have not succeeded in creating a greater measure of mutual economic dependence but have, rather, been accompanied by decreasing mutual economic dependence. No doubt there may be some more positive aspects to the situation: many of the agreements mentioned earlier will not yet have had time to affect the flows of trade, and high imports from outside of the Gulf area are partly caused by the need to import capital equipment – which may ultimately play a valuable role in furthering Gulf trade. There is little indication, however, that the decrease in mutual economic dependence is about to be reversed; on the contrary current development plans show a marked similarity to each other in terms of priorities for productive investment, with each state investing in a similar range of light industries as also in building materials, petrochemicals, fertilisers, etc. The comparison may be unfair at this stage, but the extent of the undertaking which lies ahead for the Arab Gulf countries in creating an integrated economic unit can be assessed with reference to the experience of the European Economic Community – where the member states accounted for about 35 per cent of each other's trade before the Community's inception, rising to about 50 per cent within five years of the inception.[10]

Political Dynamics of the Process of Integration

Existing patterns of co-operation and co-ordination, thus, have failed to increase the degree of mutual economic dependence, and have thereby failed to progress towards one aspect of the economic structure which will be necessary to provide the populations of the Arab Gulf with a reasonable standard of living after the depletion of oil. A radically different approach would seem necessary to redirect existing channels of economic development into a direction where the region might enjoy a measure of self-sufficiency without oil. The transition from being oil-rentier states to a situation where domestic agriculture and industry provide the mainsprings for the satisfaction of popular needs in the region will require more than sporadic co-operation and co-ordination within existing economic structures.

It seems unlikely that existing political structures within the smaller Gulf states could provide the dynamic towards an integrated entity planned to satisfy goals of long-term economic self-sufficiency. Patriarchal elites, while they may favour some increased co-ordination among the Gulf states, would correctly recognise that far-reaching integration would threaten their authority and freedom of action. Moreover, the planning and direction of the economic system which would be necessary to bring about the transition would be impossible without some re-distribution of economic power, which would again go against the interests of the existing patriarchal elites.

Two aspects of the progression towards creating an integrated unit in the Arab Gulf, enjoying a measure of self-sufficiency, will be examined here at greater length. The first takes its theme from the writings of theorists of regional integration. A common theme in such writing (whether functionalist, transactionalist or other[11]) has been the stress that for successful integration all participating units need to stand to gain from the process of integration – both in the short term and in the long term. The initiative and impetus towards integration is seen as constituted by crises in nation-states, the solution of which can be found by organisation at a higher level. The higher-level organisation overcomes the short-term problems, while ensuring that in the longer term such problems will not arise again.

The long-term advantages of integration in the Gulf are clear (as outlined earlier) but the short-term advantages which could provide the vital stimulus for successful integration are not so evident. The immense gains from oil production and export have enabled existing governments to solve many of the most pressing social and economic needs; there exists no immediate and urgent economic crisis the solution of which depends on a higher form of organisation. The problem of integration in the Gulf would appear to be that the major gains are all in the long term – after oil has been depleted – and that governments seldom respond to problems the solution of which could be left to a future generation.

There is, however, one short-term problem the critical nature of which could yet provide a substantial impetus towards integration. Existing patterns of development, with each state responsible for the whole range of social and economic developments within its own territory, are not only wasteful of resources – which in view of the scale of resources available may not be significant – but are also wasteful of labour supply. The wastage occurs through the separate administration of industries and services the activities of which could be operated on a regional basis with a much reduced over-all labour force; through the establishment in each state of industries the small-scale production of which requires more over-all labour than an industrial enterprise producing for the whole area; and through the establishment of projects (airports, dry docks, etc.) which would simply be unnecessary (on a multiple basis) in an integrated unit. The absence of an integrated development strategy, therefore, is a factor which intensifies the shortage of local labour, helping to turn the inhabitants of the Arab Gulf into a minority within their own countries. It is possible that growing concern at the social and political implications of the demographic change which is occurring,[12] especially the heavy involvement of non-Arab labour and expertise, could provide a short-term stimulus towards integration.

The second aspect of the progression towards integration to be examined here is the nature of the social forces which could be expected to play a positive role in such a progression. The improbability of current patriarchal leaderships playing a positive role has already been contended. Business elements may play a more positive role, but are unlikely to occupy the position which such elements occupied in European integration. The pragmatic interests of European businessmen were served by integration, for the dominant elements consisted of industrialists who required larger markets within which to reap the economies of scale made possible by modern technology. While there are such elements in Gulf business also, a large part of the business community consists of importers and those who engage in stable and riskless deals in land and housing. The latter type of businessman does not have the same pragmatic need for integration as the industrialist; indeed, the agent of a foreign company may have an interest in opposing integration, so as to maintain his monopoly. The most crucial interests of many Gulf businessmen, moreover, now appear to be held outside the Gulf.

The possibility of labour constituting a force for integration is also questionable, due to the composition of the labour force. While labour stands to gain most from an integration which makes possible coherent long-term industrialisation, the heavy reliance upon imported labour diminishes the likelihood of effective pressure-group activity. Labourers who regard their stay in the Gulf as temporary are unlikely to be active in pressing for integration. The role of labour as a force for integration, therefore, may depend on the proportion of native inhabitants in the labour force – the labour force in Bahrain, consequently, is capable of playing a more significant role than those in the other small states.

Rural elements, whether peasant or nomad, have seldom in modern times played notably positive roles in processes of national or regional integration. They are as unlikely to play a positive role in the Gulf as they are elsewhere. Traditional loyalties, illiteracy and the highly localised focus of their economic concerns militate against rural involvement in the integration process.

The social elements which seem most likely to favour integration are the educated and socially conscious personnel in the professions, civil service and corporations, with schools and universities constituting the breeding-grounds for the emergence of new movements favouring integration. These elements would combine an appreciation of the long-term necessity of integration for the vitality of their societies with an awareness that the security of their own positions is dependent upon the existence of a coherent economic structure. The possibility of such elements helping to promote integration, however, requires there to be a political framework which makes possible widespread political participation.

Notes

1. The term 'integration' rather than 'co-operation' or 'co-ordination' is used here when referring to future prospects, as it is assumed that the size of the tasks ahead will require a strongly centralised regional leadership. We will not, however, seek to determine the point at which co-operation becomes co-ordination, or co-ordination becomes integration.

2. The 'systemic' factor in integration relates to the influences inherent in the international system which may affect the desire of a state to enter into a particular integrative scheme. A state may be drawn to a different grouping, on grounds of ideology, security, economic interest, etc. The most obvious example of such a systemic difficulty at present would be the case of Iraq, with the possible development of an Iraqi–Syrian union.

3. Information from R. Mallakh, *Kuwait: Economic Development and Regional Cooperation* (University of Chicago Press, 1968), pp. 208–10.

4. See M. Sadik and W. Snavely, *Bahrain, Qatar and the United Arab Emirates* (Lexington Books, Mass., 1972), p. 189.

5. Except where otherwise mentioned, all information on agreements signed, discussions held, etc. in what follows is taken from *Arab Report and Record* for the period in question.

6. A further indication of the factors motivating the attempt to create a federation is the case of Bahrain. For as long as Iran maintained its irredentist claims to the island, the Bahrain government played an active and conciliatory role in the attempt to form a federation. After Iran dropped its claims in May 1970, the Bahrain government seemed to lose much of its original enthusiasm for the scheme – taking a tougher line in defence of its own positions in federal discussions. Bahrain duly became independent in August 1971.

7. The first ever exchange of official visits between the rulers of Bahrain and Qatar, for example, occurred in May 1969 and was undertaken with a view to discussing the federal project. Traditional rivalries between the ruling families of the two states had previously prevented such visits.

8. The most recent example of this occurred in March–April 1979 when the initiative taken by the Kuwait Foreign Minister seems to have succeeded in settling the differences which had arisen between the rulers of Abu Dhabi and Dubai.

9. The figures given in this paragraph are taken from the *Kuwait Annual Statistical Abstract, 1978*.

10. See J. Williamson and A. Bottrill, 'The Impact of Customs Unions on Trade in Manufactures', in B. M. Krauss (ed.), *The Economics of Integration* (George Allen and Unwin, London, 1973), pp. 118–39.

11. See, for example, K. Deutsch, *Political Community and the North Atlantic Area* (Alfred Knopf, 1968), and E. Haas, *The Uniting of Europe* (Stanford Univ. Press, 1958).

12. The nature of this demographic change is well documented in the article by J. Birks and C. Sinclair in this book.

Further Reading

Mohamed Hisham Khawajikia, '*Al-Takamal al-Iqtisādi fī al-Khalīj al-Arabi*' ('Economic Co-ordination in the Arab Gulf'), publications of the *Journal of Gulf and Arabian Peninsula Studies* (Kuwait, 1978).

Abdalla Abu Ayash, '*Afāq al-Tanmia al-Sana'ia fī al-Khalīj al-Arabi*' ('Horizons of Industrial Development in the Arab Gulf'), publications of the *Journal of Gulf and Arabian Peninsula Studies* (Kuwait, 1978).

Burhan Al-Dajani, *Al-Suq al-Khalīji al-Mashtarakah* (*The Gulf Common Market*) (Kuwait Chamber of Commerce, 1975).

Mohamed Hisham Khawajikia, '*Al-Kuwait wa al-Takamal al-Iqtisādi al-Khalīji*' ('Kuwait and Economic Co-ordination in the Gulf'), *Journal of Gulf and Arabian Peninsula Studies* (Kuwait, January 1977).

13 The Gulf Between Two Revolutions: 1958–1979

FRED HALLIDAY

Perspective

After an interval of some years, the political situation in the region surrounding the Gulf – including in this region Iran and Iraq, as well as the Arabian Peninsula – appears once again to be entering a period of considerable uncertainty. The two most evident aspects of this new situation are the revolution in Iran and the break between Egypt and the majority of Arab states in the Gulf after Camp David; but, even within the realm of politics, there are other developments of a more local character which both interrelate with these regional developments and spring from causes specific to the countries in question. Among these other phenomena we can include: the uncertain 'stop–go' policies of the rulers of Kuwait and Bahrain towards elected parliaments; the persistent divisions within the United Arab Emirates; the re-emergence of unrest in North Oman and the strained relations between Muscat and other Arab capitals; and the muffled conflicts within Saudi society. The old focus of Peninsula politics, North Yemen, has once more become a centre of regional conflict, with the February 1979 war between the Yemen Arab Republic (YAR) and the People's Democratic Republic of Yemen (PDRY) and the apparent weakness of the former's government; meanwhile, on the margins of the region, developments in Ethiopia and in Afghanistan have confirmed the sense of many of the Gulf's rulers that hostile forces are gaining strength just over the horizon.

Somewhat separate from these events is a more diffuse and yet more palpable set of issues concerning the pattern of social and economic development in the oil-producing states and the related problem of the links between the Gulf and the major oil-importing countries. Whilst the volumes of oil revenue have continued to rise, the post-1973 boom in the Gulf has slowed down; new social tensions created by the oil-based changes and by the short-sightedness of Gulf rulers themselves are becoming more prominent inside these states, at the very moment that the international economic situation on which the Gulf so relies is becoming even less favourable. For, if the producer states are encountering new obstacles in their social and economic development, the oil-importing countries are going through a protracted recession, the particular form of which – stagnation plus inflation – has eroded the terms of trade of the OPEC countries and simultaneously cut back the attractiveness for the oil states of investment in the industrialised world. The disputes over oil output and posted prices, apparently becalmed in the mid-1970s, have now revived and have been joined to another area of disagreement between the oil exporters and oil consumers over longer-run energy policy; again something temporarily soothed in the post-1973 period. Whilst this dissension has encouraged conflicts between the major oil-consumer countries (e.g. Europe/USA, Japan/the rest), it has at the same time led them to be more willing, in public declamations for their own potentially anti-Arab publics, to place the blame for their problems on the OPEC countries, as they did in 1973. A substantial rift between producers and consumers has therefore emerged under the impact of the recession. In this way, the full circle of economic and political factors has been drawn, with the issues surrounding oil now more than ever intertwined with the foreign policy dispute in the Arab and industrialised worlds over Egypt's relations with Israel and, in particular, the USA's role in encouraging a negotiated peace. This nexus of socio-economic problems, strategic and local, which is now becoming clearer, therefore underlies and reinforces the more immediate, more strictly political, tensions evident in the states surrounding the Gulf.

It is in many ways premature to evaluate the import and likely outcome of this new situation, and the following analysis is a *preliminary* attempt to place it within the context of recent Gulf history and to examine some prominent features of the present balance of forces in the Gulf. This article argues that, whilst some problems are the same and whilst others may appear the same as a decade or two ago, the novelty of the present tensions is as important as their continuity with previous ones. First of all, the countries of the region are now interlocked with each other and with the rest of the Middle East and the international economy in a quite new way – a linkage that is a two-way street. The changes of the past two decades have integrated the Gulf into a broader set of political and economic structures; whilst, as a result of oil, this certainly gives the Gulf states a more influential place in the Middle East, it has also meant that the Gulf states are exposed to new destabilising factors to which they were not so vulnerable in the past. Indeed, the price of the new international role which Riyadh, Kuwait and Abu Dhabi can now play is their new vulnerability to events outside the Gulf – whether in connection with Palestine or with the vagaries of the Dow–Jones industrial average. Secondly, as the following analysis tries to show, the Gulf has, over the past two decades, gone through a period of reorganisation which has altered many of the internal, especially the political, characteristics of the countries involved. This reorganisation came to an end in the mid-1970s with the formation of a new regional political system. What the present situation represents is therefore a fresh, rather distinct, period of political instability. This instability is not so much a continuation of the previous conflicts as a product of the solutions, counter-revolutionary in the main, which have been found to these conflicts. The present tensions therefore reflect this new situation – both the new regional vulnerability of the Gulf states and the transient character of the internal restabilisation which was effected earlier in the decade.

This recent integration of the Gulf into the broader pattern of Middle Eastern politics has brought into closer contact two groups of countries – the Gulf/Peninsula and the Mashreq/Egypt area – which were previously rather separate, and it has also forged a link between two issues which dominated these two areas but were in the past conveniently separated – oil and Palestine. The 1973 war, with the accompanying oil embargo, dramatically showed how these separations no longer held: how the divisions that had subsisted over some decades but had, for the West, been conveniently disjoined were now being bridged. The history of the Gulf's transformation over the past two decades is therefore to a marked degree also the history of the growth of this two-way influence, of the manner in which the Palestinian question and Arab nationalism generally have more and more affected the Gulf, and of how the Gulf itself has, through the power of the oil producers, begun to affect the evolution of the Palestinian issue.

Simultaneous Formation, Separate Development

The relative separation of the Gulf from events in Egypt and the Mashreq throughout most of this century is something that occurred in spite of the fact that both areas shared a common moment of historical formation. It was World War I and the collapse of two of the three main regional powers – Russia and Turkey – which led to the establishment of the contemporary state system in the Middle East. In the newly liberated Ottoman territories of the Mashreq new state entities appeared through colonial delimitation – in Palestine, Jordan, Syria and Lebanon. Egypt had already been occupied by Britain in 1882 and was therefore separate from this post-1918 process; yet here too the war had a decisive political impact, leading as it did to the emergence of the first nationalist movement of a mass character around the Wafd Party. In the Gulf and Peninsula, the war had equally important consequences. In Iraq, freed from the Turks, the British installed the Hashimite monarch Faisal in 1920. In North Yemen, where Ottoman power had also held until the war, a new independent and unified state emerged under the control of the Hamid ad-Din Imams. In Saudi Arabia the aftermath of the war saw the rise of the Saudi family's power in Nejd, and by 1926 the Saudis had unified the Arabian deserts into a single state for the first time in centuries. Across the Gulf in Iran, World War I finally swept away the remnants of the Qajar dynasty and provided the vacuum in which Reza Khan seized power in 1921; five years later, in 1926, he established the new Pahlavi dynasty. Within eight years of the end of World War I, therefore, new royal families had come into power in the four most populous states of the region: between them the Saudi, Hamid ad-Din, Hashimite and Pahlavi regimes formed the basis for a stable and conservative regional system – a strategic bloc running from Khorasan in the north-east to Bab al-Mandeb in the south-west. Britain was the dominant military power in the Gulf area as a whole but, with the exception of Iraq up to 1932, it held formal colonial power only in the small coastal states of the Peninsula which it had occupied during the nineteenth century in order to protect the route to India. It was the post-1918 royal families, backed by imperialist influence, who bore the main burdens of political consolidation.[1]

However, if both the Mashreq and the Gulf acquired new monarchical systems and their current boundaries in the aftermath of World War I, this was more for reasons of international politics than because there existed an internal political homogeneity or unity between these different states. The two regions were markedly different in economic and political structures: the Arab nationalist upsurge during World War I under the leadership of Sherif Hussain of Mecca was, in retrospect, an interlude which suggested a degree of unified Arab politics far greater than that which in fact existed. This disunity is nowhere clearer than in the dislocated manner in which the 1918 settlement broke down. In the Mashreq it was the Palestine war of 1948–49 which led to successive military coups in Syria (1949) and Egypt (1952) and which laid the basis for the Arab nationalist movement of the 1950s and 1960s. Palestine was the most prominent issue and the symbol around which politics in the Mashreq and Egypt revolved, and it was the Mashreq and Egypt which set the dominant tone in Arab politics in this era.

If there was turmoil elsewhere in the Arab world, this was to be found not in the Gulf but in the Maghreb, where the liberation struggle in Algeria after 1954 and the independence movements in Morocco and Tunisia were terminating French domination in the region. Iran was the one exception, given the economic and political conflicts that lasted until Mosadeq's overthrow in 1953; but this reflected its different situation following upon the occupation of 1941, for, as in Palestine, World War II had disrupted the pre-existing situation. Iran's turmoil had little effect on the rest of the area. In the Arab Gulf region there was, throughout the 1950s, no decolonisation nor sustained political opposition nor did the Palestine issue play as significant a role as it had elsewhere. There were nationalist demonstrations in favour of Egypt in 1956 in Aden, Kuwait and Bahrain, and failed uprisings in North Yemen (1948) and Oman (1957–59), but these manifestations of opposition were contained and the governments of the region were, for their part, unwilling or unable to act decisively against Israel and its British and French allies. Politically, many states were under strong British influence and in no position to challenge it: Iraq, Kuwait, Bahrain and Qatar were all oil producers falling into this category, even though Iraq had formally been an independent state since 1932. Saudi Arabia was, for its part, lacking in the capacity to influence events and was under US protection. Moreover, Arab oil represented a far smaller percentage of world output than it did later, and the oil that was blocked from reaching Europe by the closure of the Suez Canal in 1956–57 was compensated for by increased Venezuelan output; hence, even had they wanted to, these states would have been in a weaker position to influence Western policy then than they later were. But there were other factors internal to these Arab countries which also played a role. The regimes were alarmed by the kind of nationalism being advocated by Nasser's Egypt and opposition political groups favouring one or other kind of Arab nationalism had only just begun to develop. Compared to either the Mashreq or the Maghreb, the Gulf was politically isolated, anaesthetised from the effects of the Palestinian question and of the rise of Arab nationalism. Here the dissolution of the post-1918 system was to come later than in the Mashreq and Maghreb; yet, when it did come, it happened in a remarkably synchronic form.

The Dissolution

The breakdown of the post-1918 system in the Gulf began in the late 1950s. It led to a decade and a half of turmoil which ended in the mid-1970s when a new restabilised Gulf order came temporarily into existence. Throughout this period, it is possible to chart how the early isolation of the Gulf from the rest of Arab politics was gradually being broken down and how the new order that structured the Gulf's role in the Middle East generally was being built out of the dissolution of the old. At the risk of some compression, one can identify six distinct processes involved in this period of change; each began around 1960 and reached a certain point of completion or transition in the mid-1970s, specifically in 1975. Hence, looking backwards from that year, it is possible to reconstruct the manner in which the Gulf, internally and internationally, was transformed over roughly a decade and a half.

1. The first major breach in the Gulf's stability came with the July 1958 revolution in Iraq; this opened a chapter of political instability in Iraqi history that lasted until the agreement between Iraq and Iran in March 1975. In political terms, the fall of the Hashimite monarchy initiated three processes: first, it led to a period of protracted governmental instability in Baghdad with four successive military regimes (1959–63, 1963, 1963–68, 1968–) and with several other *coup* attempts; second, it opened up the dispute with the Kurds which took a military form from 1961 to 1970 and again in 1974–75; third, it led to a worsening of relations between Iraq and its neighbours in so far as, throughout the 1960s, Iraq presented itself as, and was seen as being, a threat to Western interests in the Gulf. From having been the centre of the Baghdad Pact, a central member of the system, Iraq appeared to have become the main source of opposition to Western interests in the Gulf; and Baghdad further provoked the major oil companies by nationalising 99 per cent of the territory of the Iraqi Petroleum Company in 1961.

These three dimensions were resolved only with the agreement with Iran in 1975. That agreement therefore marked the end of the consequences of the 1958 *coup*, at least in their previous form, and drew a line beneath the earlier phase. The Baathist government in Baghdad was now secure in a way that no Iraqi government since 1958 had been and did not face any new internal threat until 1979. The rivals within the Baath party were for the time being silenced for, although the last serious *coup* attempt had been in 1971, the government could not feel secure as long as there was war in the north; the country was, at the same time, economically much stronger as a result of the rise in the price of oil and the discovery of much larger reserves. Some of the preconditions now existed for the kind of concerted economic development that had been precluded by almost two decades of conflict and weak government; the major remaining obstacles lay in the social character of the new Baathist state.[2] A major constituent of this new political stability was the elimination of the Kurds as a serious threat and the concomitant accommodation with Tehran. By reaching agreement with Iran, the Baghdad government closed the frontiers and effectively ended armed opposition. Resistance was now on a small scale, and serious Kurdish military action could only restart once Turkey or Iran or Syria decided to sponsor such an endeavour. Since all had substantial Kurdish minorities of their own, which they were concerned to suppress, they were unlikely to do so. Hence, whereas until March 1975 the Kurdish problem posed a major threat to the stability of the Baghdad government, this issue had now been temporarily, if brutally, resolved.

In settling its specific disagreements with Iran, Iraq also paved the way for a more general opening towards the other states in the Gulf. Baghdad stopped supporting opposition elements in Iran as well as in Pakistani Baluchistan; within months of the March agreement, Iraq established diplomatic relations with the Sultanate of Oman, where Baghdad had previously supported the People's Front guerrillas. There was always, of course, considerable doubt as to how far Iraq's militant 'anti-imperialist' stands of the 1960s and early 1970s really corresponded to its practice but, even if there was more proclamation than real action, it was nevertheless true that the 1975 agreement with Iran marked a significant step in Iraq's reintegration into the politics and diplomacy of the Gulf. Issues of dispute certainly remained: Iraq had a border dispute with Kuwait, and had criticised the Iranian-backed plan for a Gulf security pact. Yet, over all, Iraq was now at peace with its neighbours and was discreetly strengthening its relations with Saudi Arabia; it was not actively supporting opposition to any other Gulf governments and was concentrating its disagreements at the diplomatic level. In 1974–79 the Arab rejection of Sadat brought Iraq even more into the mainstream. Hence, in terms of three key elements – governmental stability, relations with the Kurds and regional politics – 1975 marked the end of the period of unrest which began with the July 1958 *coup*.

2. The second major breach in the Gulf's stability was the North Yemeni revolution of September 1962. This led to an eight-year civil war in North Yemen in which Egypt and Saudi Arabia backed the two opposing sides. It contributed to the start of a guerrilla movement in British-dominated South Yemen in 1963 where, as a result of this guerrilla struggle, an independent People's Republic was established in 1967. Moreover, after South Yemen, the guerrilla movement spread in 1965 to the Dhofar province of the Sultanate of Oman.[3] The strategic implications of this event were in some ways greater than those of Iraq. The war in North Yemen, a war fought by Egypt and Saudi Arabia at one remove, polarised Arab politics. Through the Egyptian intervention in North Yemen, Arab nationalism generally had a major impact on the Arabian Peninsula for the first time. Yet it was also here that the conservative system in the Gulf was able to fight back and indeed use the Egyptian failure in North Yemen to build the future Cairo–Riyadh alliance. For, after the Israeli defeat of Egypt in 1967, King Faisal of Saudi Arabia forced Egypt to pull out of North Yemen in return for the financial aid that Egypt so desperately required. Henceforward, Egypt was to cease supporting opposition movements in the Arabian peninsula, and from Nasser's death in 1970 until 1978 the Cairo–Riyadh axis became the most influential in the Arab world.

The consequences of 1967 were equally important in the Peninsula itself, in differing ways. In North Yemen the war dragged on for another three years, until a conservative coalition in 1970 involving representatives of both sides was established. Although an independent republic in name, North Yemen was from then on effectively under the political and economic domination of Saudi Arabia and many royalists were reintegrated into the state. In South Yemen the guerrillas of the National Liberation Front were provoked by 1967 to turn against Egypt and began, amidst immense economic problems, the most consistent socialist transformation of any country in the Arab world. South Yemen has had, however, to pay the price of being the only non-capitalist state in the area, especially one with no oil or other substantial economic resource of its own. It has been debilitated by divisions within its own leadership and has been involved in armed conflict with all three neighbours (North Yemen, Saudi Arabia, Oman). It has been able only very slowly to improve the living conditions of its people, and the conditions of siege and scarcity that have so ravaged other countries attempting to make a transition to socialism have been seen here in a most acute form.[4]

The third country affected by the 1962 *coup* in North Yemen was Oman, and here the counter-revolutionary character of the Gulf restabilisation has been most evident. If 1967 marked the withdrawal of Egypt from North Yemen and the turnaround there, 1973 was the comparable year in Oman. For, in the aftermath of the rise in oil prices, Iran dispatched several thousand counter-insurgency troops to attack the guerrilla-held areas of Dhofar and to impose a stabilisation that was, in the Shah's eyes, all the more necessary because of the threat which the success of the guerrilla struggle in Dhofar posed to the Gulf states. The guerrillas of the People's Front for the Liberation of Oman fought bravely against the thousands of well-armed troops sent to crush them, but were by the end of 1975 compelled to abandon the liberated territories they had held since the late 1960s. Henceforward, they were forced to resort to underground political work, whilst the few military forces remaining in the mountains posed no serious threat to the establishment of counter-revolutionary control. In retrospect, the reconquest of the Dhofari mountains by the combined Omani and Iranian forces in 1975 put an end to the thirteen years of armed conflict that had begun in North Yemen in 1962 and, at least temporarily, stemmed the tide of revolution emanating from that event at the Oman–South Yemen border.[5]

3. A further country in which 1975 marked a watershed was Saudi Arabia, where King Faisal was assassinated in March of that year, and where development programmes based upon the increased oil revenues were initiated under the five-year plan which began in that year. Faisal himself had come to power under the uncertain conditions of the early 1960s, when the twin republican *coups* in Baghdad and Sanaa had removed two of the Saudi family's fellow monarchies in the area. Under pressure from the USA and from more concerned members of the dynasty, the incumbent King Saud was displaced and Faisal installed: although the formal accession of Faisal to the throne was in 1967, the decisive date was October 1962, when, less than a month after the North Yemeni *coup*, executive power in fact passed

into Faisal's hands. Under his guidance, Saudi Arabia underwent a number of changes designed to consolidate the existing political system: slavery was abolished, a more modern army was built up, education was cautiously expanded, the budget was balanced and some of the more wasteful family expenditure cut. But, despite these changes, Faisal was still in some respects a transitional character. In domestic affairs he was loath to share power with other than a very few members of his family, whilst in foreign policy it was Islam rather than any supposed 'Arab dimension' which predominated in his thinking. In the mid-1960s he mobilised international opposition to Nasser under the guise of an Islamic Pact, and his concern about Palestine after 1967 seemed to concentrate more on the al-Aqsa mosque than on the fate of the Palestinian refugees. In Saudi funding of the Palestinian resistance, it was noticeable that the more Islamic and conservative elements were those who received encouragement. In regional affairs, Faisal maintained a stubborn and hostile attitude to several neighbours, for outmoded dynastic reasons: he refused to recognise the United Arab Emirates when they were declared independent in 1971 and, long after it was a feasible prospect, he tried to harass, if not bring down, the South Yemeni government by backing exiled supporters of the pre-independence regime.

Faisal's death was in itself an individual event: he was assassinated by a disaffected and apparently isolated member of the ruling family. But his disappearance at a time of more general change put an end to the transitional period represented by his reign. A new more decentralised family team came to power, under the joint leadership of King Khaled and Emir Fahd. At the same time, the new development plan, ten times larger than the previous one, was introducing economic changes of a far more widespread kind; and in foreign policy, the anomalies of Faisal's period were soon removed. Within a year of his death, working diplomatic relations had been established with the UAE and South Yemen, whilst the Islamic emphasis of Saudi pronouncements was toned down in favour of a more specifically 'Arab' orientation. Faisal's death, therefore, marked the end of an era.

4. To a lesser extent, 1975 was also a year of transition in another Gulf state, Iran. It marked the slowing down of the increasingly rapid economic and political changes originally launched by the Shah in 1962 under the title of the White Revolution and gave the first signs of the crisis that was to explode three years later. Although in certain

respects more rhetoric than reality, the changes did reflect real alterations in the society and economy of Iran. During the 1960s, the Shah put through a land reform programme, promoted industrialisation and expanded his armed forces. The rise in oil prices between 1971 and 1973 gave this process a boost at an opportune time, and by 1974 the Shah was announcing that Iran would, within a decade, catch up with the major industrialised powers and become a second Japan. A year later all this had changed. Iran, from being a new lender on the international markets, had become a net borrower. Agricultural output, rising at 2–3 per cent a year, was lagging far behind demand, rising at 14 per cent a year. Accusations of waste and corruption in government-backed industrial projects were on the increase. Economically, the country had begun to slow down and to be limited by major problems: the dynamic period of the White Revolution was over and there was less talk about becoming a new Japan. At the same time, the regime was clearly faced with new problems on the political front: although the outright opposition, whether secular or religious, was no immediate threat to the regime, there was growing disaffection among the Iranian bourgeoisie, both those in state employment and those in private business, about the economic problems which were looming. In this context, the Shah suddenly set up a new mass party, the Rastakhiz or National Resurgence Party, which within a year had an alleged membership of over five millions. This development, a radical departure from previous rather half-hearted attempts to set up government parties, registered the regime's concern about the loyalty of its supporters and about the cohesion of the Iranian bourgeoisie in general. In an attempt to win some support from sections of the working class, the Shah also launched an anti-corruption drive in which 8,000 bazaar merchants were imprisoned and he ordered that shares of 320 top companies be sold to the workers in those firms. Yet the main consequences of these actions were further to enrage his political opponents, antagonise the artisans and traders of the bazaar and alarm the private business sector: the long-term problems of Iranian politics and industry remained and, as the oil boom subsided, they became more palpable to the Iranian population. Hence while 1975 did not mark as evident a break as it did in Saudi Arabia, it both clearly highlighted the limits of the Shah's transformation policy and set in train the crisis that was to destroy his regime. In the end the Shah was overthrown by a movement created by the White Revolution – a new urban mass – yet led by precisely those opposition elements – Khomeini and the Muslim forces – he had crushed in 1963.

5. Iran was closely involved in bringing to an end another process which had begun in the early 1960s and which culminated in or around 1975: this was decolonisation, more specifically British decolonisation. The first British colony in the region which Britain left in this period was Kuwait, in 1961. South Yemen followed in 1967 and in 1971 Britain gave up its last formal colonies in the Gulf, handing independence to Bahrain, Qatar and the seven statelets of the United Arab Emirates. Yet Britain remained as strong as ever in Oman: since this was never an official colony, British domination was unofficial, if obvious, and the British withdrawal was of a similar character. Whilst no flags were lowered and raised, Britain in effect ceased to be the dominant power in the Sultanate in 1975; on the other hand, Iranian domination increased so that it, rather than Britain, was now the most powerful outside military influence. Britain retained military bases in the area up to March 1977 and after that it provided military assistance, as it did to the other states in the Gulf which it had once ruled. But, although unofficial, a real decolonisation had taken place and by 1979, when the British Queen visited Muscat, relations between the two countries had become strained.[6]

Oman exemplifies two aspects of this decolonisation process which affected the character of the change in the Gulf as a whole. While the British maintained close ties with these independent states, other states came in part to play the regional role which Britain had previously played. In all Britain's former colonies, with the exception of South Yemen, the USA acquired a stronger political and military position than it had previously had, whilst at an intermediate level the USA fostered the 'twin-pillar' policy, whereby Iran and Saudi Arabia adopted responsibility for security in the area. On the one hand, Saudi Arabia had the main financial power, which it used in the Gulf and Middle East generally. Yet its armed forces were insignificant. Iran, on the other hand, had little money to spare but had the armed might to patrol the waters of the Gulf, to send troops to Oman and to guarantee the Kuwaitis in the event of a further Iraqi menace. Iran also sent helicopter gunships to Pakistani Baluchistan after an armed resistance movement began there in 1973. Indeed, through its expanded role and its aim to become the main military power in Western Asia, Iran came to play a much larger part in regional politics generally, and in Arab politics in particular. Throughout the 1960s Iran maintained a close relationship with Israel, supplying oil and sending officers to be trained there. That relationship continued up to 1979, but Iran now had an active policy in the Arab world too.

While in no way able to challenge Saudi political predominance, Iran built a special relationship with Egypt: there were plans that, in the event of the Egyptian army switching to US equipment, Iranian instructors were to be used in training Egyptian personnel. The decolonisation process, the gradual removal of British official political control, had therefore been accompanied by the strengthening of other powers under US guidance and by the construction of a new regional counter-revolutionary system.[7]

The system that evolved to replace the previous colonial one goes a considerable way to explaining the rather curious, and apparently unsuccessful, history of the Gulf security pact. This project was advocated by the Shah in the mid-1970s and was given varying degrees of support by other Gulf states, Iraq excepted. It was justified on the grounds that the states of the region needed to unite in order to confront the threat of 'outside interference'. At first sight, it was a rather mysterious proposal since: (a) there seemed to be no obvious outside threat against which the Gulf states had to unite; and (b) there was already massive outside interference in the Gulf, to the tune of thousands of military personnel and many tens of billions of dollars, from the USA. It was also initially unclear why no agreement on this project could be reached since, given political will, the other states could have signed a pact overriding Baghdad's objections.

The solution to this conundrum is provided by the form decolonisation took, for the rhetoric about a largely non-existent 'outside' (by which was meant Soviet) influence was designed to divert attention from the reality of an unmentioned US military deployment. Similarly, the talk about outside threats covered over the facts that: (a) the main threats were internal, from the populations of these countries themselves; and (b) that, if there was any likelihood of conventional war or threats to local states, this came from other, regional, powers. The only conflicts in the region had been civil wars (Dhofar) or inter-state (Iran–Iraq, Iran–Arab islands). Finally, the pretence of a search for a multilateral solution in a pact concealed the existence of a *de facto* unilateral solution – by the Shah's legions. For it was Iranian military might that in practice guaranteed the Shah's conception of security and, even had agreement on a pact been reached, there is little that the comparatively minute forces of the Arab monarchies could have added. There was therefore no real reason for a formal Gulf security pact, but the debate surrounding it was a convenient screen for the other, post-colonial, system being established.[8]

6. The final distinct process which reached a certain watershed in 1975/76 relates back to something that occurred in 1960 and which was then said to be rather a joke. In the board rooms, cabinet meetings and seminars of the Western world it was considered to be unimportant for almost a decade, until the institution in question finally showed its power. The event that occurred in 1960 was the founding of OPEC. OPEC was intended to protect oil producers' revenue, yet the price of oil in fact remained stable for a decade: it was only in 1970/71 that the oil states were able to redress the balance of power which had prevailed up to that time. The quintupling of prices between 1970 and 1974 and the rise in OPEC revenues from $5.2bn in 1970 to $75bn in 1974 was a momentous and generally unexpected revenge for the inertia of the previous decade. Inevitably, it provoked alarm in the advanced capitalist countries and high hopes in the developing world. In 1974 there was speculation about a US invasion of the Middle East, about a collapse of the world financial system, about a rapid and successful economic transformation of the Middle East. There was also considerable discussion about what would happen if the oil states tried to repeat their actions of 1973, either by multiplying the price or by again cutting off supplies.

Two years later the situation appeared to be somewhat different. The advanced capitalist countries had proved capable of absorbing the changes, and had accorded the OPEC states a somewhat different place in the international economic system than that which they previously had. But it was also obvious that events of the kind which had occurred in 1973 could not happen again. In the first place, nationalisation is a once-and-for-all process: once completed, it cannot be done again. Having displaced the companies, the OPEC states could now decide on the price and output of oil but, precisely because they were more directly integrated into the world market, they were therefore forced to accept, on their own behalf rather than *via* the companies, the limits of this system and of what the market could bear. In the period 1974/76, prices held steady and the attempt to increase the price of oil by 15 per cent at the end of 1976 only divided OPEC in the precise manner for which the advanced capitalist countries were hoping. The price began to rise substantially again only in the new situation that opened up in 1978.

The 1973 situation was a fortuitous one, whereby the oil producers were able to benefit from a world shortage to push the price of oil up to its market level. In such conditions it was also possible for the Arab states to institute an embargo, which had in practice very little effect. The problems surrounding oil after this date were of a rather different kind and involved not so much dramatic changes in the pre-existing structure, or multiplications in the price, but issues posed by the new system worked out between OPEC and the major importing nations: the degree of industrialisation and agricultural development of which oil-producing states were capable; the direct access by producers to the markets of the advanced capitalist countries, i.e. without having to sell their oil through the major companies; the problems of unity within OPEC itself as the conflicts between those with surplus revenues (Saudi Arabia) and those with revenue shortages (e.g. Iran and Algeria) became sharper. The prominence which these issues acquired indicated that a new chapter in the politics of oil had begun, that the conflicts of the future would reflect but not repeat the radical changes of the 1971/73 period.[9]

The New Regional Role

It is against this background of dissolution and reconstitution that the Gulf states came to play a greater role in the affairs of Egypt and the Mashreq. As we have seen, the dissolution of the post-1918 system began a decade later in the Gulf (1958) than it did in the Mashreq and Egypt (1948) and in the following decade (up to 1967) the main influence was by Egypt and the Mashreq on the countries of the Gulf rather than the other way around. 1967 marked the turning-point as far as this aspect of Arab politics was concerned. From then on Egypt supported the conservative monarchies of the Gulf, whilst Saudi Arabia acquired an increasingly strong foothold in Egypt's politics and economy. If the Gulf rulers had anyone to thank for the restabilisation of the region, then it should have been Israel, since it was the latter's victory in 1967 which put an end to Egypt's support for nationalist oppositions in the Peninsula. In this perspective, 1973 was a continuation of a process that had begun in 1967; although the outcomes of the two Arab–Israeli wars were different, the effects on inter-Arab relations were similar. The economic price of victory is often as high as that of defeat, and the need for money from the oil states on the part of the confrontation governments was as great in the post-1973 period as it had been in the years after 1967.

The capacity of the Gulf states, Iranian and Arab, to play a larger role in the region was not, however, merely a function of their relative economic strength or of the needs of the confrontation states, since it rested upon two other political preconditions: first, the restabilisation of the Gulf itself in the mid-1970s and, second, the support of the USA. It was because the Saudis, Iraqis and Iranians had been able to quell their opponents nearer home that they were in a position to pursue an active foreign policy: in a very definite sense, the price of the intervention by Iran and the conservative Arab states outside the Gulf was paid by the local opposition forces, and in particular by those in Oman and North Yemen. The relative inactivity of these states at the pan-Arab and regional level in the two decades after 1948 reflected their internal weaknesses and, later, the conflicts raging inside and nearby them. By contrast, their more active role in the 1970s reflected the consolidation which had now taken place.

The relationship with the USA was the other essential precondition of this new regional influence and involved a political–military alliance, as well as a broader coincidence of interests in promoting capitalist relations in the surrounding countries. Although the USA had had privileged relations with both Saudi Arabia and Iran since the mid-1940s, it acquired a new predominance in the 1970s, as a result both of the British withdrawal and of the rise in Gulf states' revenues which made them more able to purchase US military equipment. In the wake of the British withdrawal the US implemented its 'twin-pillar' policy, hoping to ensure peace in the region and the protection of Western interests by building up these two countries. Beyond the much-publicised military dimension, this policy also involved the construction of a new system at the political and economic levels, one particularly evident in the US economic role in Saudi development projects. It was hoped that Saudi Arabia and Iran would ensure that the flow of oil would not be cut off, and that Saudi Arabia at least would keep down pressure within OPEC for rises in the price of oil. Both countries were encouraged to counter revolutionary movements whether by force of arms, in the Iranian case, or by financial aid, as in the Saudi case, and the Arab oil states as a whole used their new wealth to endorse conservative trends in Egypt, Sudan and Jordan.

This encouragement of conservative political trends was accompanied by the use of oil money to open Middle Eastern countries to a greater degree of private business activity than had been the case hitherto, thereby undoing the various degrees of protectionism, rather misleadingly called 'socialism', which had grown up in the 1960s. The financial power of the oil states not only affected other Arab countries, but also spread to some of the poorer Asian and

African countries (e.g. Pakistan); these were being integrated into the economies of the oil-producer states through the supply of labour and through investments by the oil states designed to supplement their own economies. This process reflected the growth of capitalist finance within the oil-producing countries themselves; the generalisation of this growth, which covered other states on the periphery of the oil-producing area, determined the character of their development and structured their economies to meet the needs of the producer states. Beyond the strictly identifiable political–military alliances between governments – between Washington and Tehran or Riyadh – there therefore developed a more general community of interests through which the financial resources of the oil-producing states were being deployed to encourage the spread of capitalist relations into the poorer developing countries affected by the oil boom.[10]

In the light of these changes, the continued failure to resolve the Palestinian question has increasingly appeared as a threat, something that could in various ways upset the growing alliance between the West and the oil states and the reintegration of the other countries in the region into the West's designs for a new political and economic system. This is why the USA, and to a lesser extent the EEC countries, which could in the past circumvent the issue, have intervened more actively since 1973 to prevent a fifth Arab–Israeli war and to promote a peaceful settlement of the Palestinian question. The reasons for this are, in particular:

1. another war could disturb the economic relations developing between the oil states and the advanced capitalist countries;
2. it could provide a diplomatic context for the Soviet Union to reverse the decline in its influence in the Middle East;
3. it could lead to popular unrest in pro-Western Arab states, especially Egypt, which would worsen the conditions for continued US influence;
4. it could, if the war went badly for Israel, force the USA to intervene even more directly than it did in 1973, and thereby stimulate anti-US feelings throughout the Arab world.

Much is now at stake, as far as the Western world is concerned, far more that was at stake twenty or ten years ago. Palestine therefore presents itself as an obstacle which must be solved, rather than circumvented, in order to ensure success of the over-all relationship which is being built between the West and the oil producers.[11]

The US diplomatic initiatives since 1973 are, therefore, 'genuine' in the sense that, as in southern Africa, there are pressing political and economic reasons for their working to resolve a problem that they could, in previous decades, safely ignore. Even the question of a separate Palestinian state is a secondary issue in such a perspective: if the establishment of such a state would better guarantee the over-all aims which US policy is pursuing, then Washington can have no real objection to its being established.

The Arab oil states' interest in the Palestinian question is, in part, the same as Washington's. With the partial exception of Iraq, they do not want other issues to interrupt the construction of the new relationship with the West but, knowing the increased bargaining power which they have, they are also trying to strengthen the hand of the Arab states at the bargaining table. However, it is too simple to argue that regimes such as those in Kuwait or Saudi Arabia are unconcerned about the Palestinian question: for reasons of political convenience, if on no other grounds, they have to present themselves as opponents of Israel. Moreover, they know that through manipulating the Palestinian question, and through the reliance of the confrontation states on oil money, they can increase their influence in the Arab world and therefore counter radical and revolutionary forces which may arise.

Nevertheless, there are two points of divergence between the USA and its Gulf allies on the question of Palestine which have prevented the execution of the policy on which Washington had been intent since 1973. There remains, first of all, an unmistakable difference between the view these states hold on the Palestinian question and that held in Washington: whilst the USA has always accepted the existence of a separate Israeli state (as has the USSR), the oil producers, except for Iran under the Shah, have not made any such commitment. Indeed, one of the components of the ideological stance of the Peninsula states is that they are far less willing explicitly to countenance the existence of Israel than some sections of the Palestinian resistance. The other factor, one most evident in the aftermath of Camp David, is that the championing by the Peninsula states of the Palestinian cause is a reflection of their deep internal insecurity. So as to divert attention from political repression at home they seem to feel a need to pose as the proponents of militant Arab interests; by doing this they hope to pre-empt the left throughout the Arab world, of whom they have an often exaggerated apprehension, from taking the lead on the issue. This, in a sense, 'exporting' of their political weaknesses is evident in the way in which the Palestinian communities are treated within the oil states themselves, indicating that fear rather than fraternal sentiment is uppermost in these rulers' minds. For example, independent activities by representatives of the resistance movement were severely restricted in 1975/76 in order to prevent overt solidarity with the Palestinians in Lebanon and earlier, in Bahrain in 1972, one of the only two political weeklies in the country was closed down and its editor put on trial for criticising King Hussain's suppression of the Palestinians in Jordan – at the very moment when Bahrain's Foreign Ministry was loudly proclaiming his country's loyalty to the Palestinian cause.[12]

This two-sided policy, of support and containment, reflects the ambiguous power of the Gulf states themselves. They are, financially and now politically, strong enough to assert a certain influence in the Arab world as a whole, yet the motivation behind this assertion is in some measure an awareness of weakness, a fear of the politically unrepresented within their own countries – native and immigrant – and an anxiety about the potential for political upheaval in the Arab world as a whole. Militarily, no Peninsula Arab state, including Saudi Arabia, can significantly alter the balance of force *vis-à-vis* Israel. Such is the two-edged price they have paid for their political integration with the other more turbulent sectors of the Middle East. That price, and the cost of the conflicts within the oil-producing countries generated by the recent boom, have become starkly evident since the early months of 1978.

The New Instability

The present set of problems has affected the Gulf states in their relations with the Western world, in their relations with other Arab states and in their internal political situations. In the case of each country, one can discern both the maturing of problems born from the earlier reorganisation and boom and the much greater degree of interrelationship between events in the Gulf and events elsewhere in the Middle East.

The Iranian revolution was in the long run a product of the political policies pursued by the Shah's regime over the previous 25 years and of the manner in which the country's oil revenues were being spent. Among the immediate causes can be counted the policies which the Shah began to pursue in 1975/76 (as mentioned above), which increased the level of active political opposition as well as dealing Khomeini, exiled since 1963, back into the game: the anti-inflation measures angered the bazaar merchants, and the new more strident official political tone indicated a new element of uncertainty at the top. International factors also played a significant role. The Iranian revolution involved a marked nationalist rejection of Iran's foreign policy alignment – of the way in which Western culture was being introduced into Iran, and of the Shah's links with Western countries and Israel. Yet it also received a certain impulsion from another international factor, the downturn in the Iranian economy which occurred in 1977 and which was brought about, in part, by the recession in world markets. At the same time, this revolution has itself had an international impact inconceivable 25 years ago. To make the obvious comparisons: Mosadeq's policies did not have any comparable effect on the other countries of the Middle East, and the reduction in oil output and refining capacity was compensated for by increases elsewhere (in Kuwait and Aden respectively). The fall of the Shah, however, has had a series of major consequences: the reduction in Iranian oil output has, combined with the general oil shortage, facilitated a new series of OPEC price rises, and the decline of Iranian military potential in the Gulf and Iran's break with the West has in effect ended the 'twin-pillar' policy. The USA has been forced to go back to before the Nixon Doctrine of 1969 to produce plans for a direct intervention in the Gulf with its announced 110,000-strong mobile strike force.

The political situation within the Arabian states themselves has also been noticeably unsettled. Kuwait has lost its military protector against a possible Iraqi annexation and faces a new Shia dissent as well as pressure for a return to elections. In Bahrain, where some of the Shia population has evinced sympathy for Khomeini, the al-Khalifa family must be wondering if they too will be cast as Yazids, in the manner of the Shah. In the emirates the fall of the Shah has upset the previous balance between Dubai and Abu Dhabi by depriving the former's ruler, Shaikh Rashid, of his Iranian patron. In Oman the removal of Iranian troops – and even more so of Iranian military guarantees in the event of any substantial conflict in the future – has deprived the Sultan of his main military support at a time when his support for Sadat is causing him international difficulties and when some dissent is becoming evident as a result of his wasteful spending policies.[13] Saudi Arabia may also be concerned by events in Iran, though there is no evidence as yet of any direct impact of events there on the Wahhabi Kingdom, the main preoccupation of which is the state of relations with the USA. Iraq, on the other hand, is certainly concerned, since it shares a substantial border with Iran and has many of the same political and economic problems as Iran itself: a new conflict inside the Baath was revealed in August 1979 and, since the Shah's departure, Iraq has not been able to elaborate a stable relationship with Iran. Like Afghanistan to the east, it is exposed to pressures from Iran which combine ideological conservatism and appeal to the Shia population with a stimulation of the nationalities issue, especially, in the Iraqi case, the Kurds.

It is, however, difficult to see how Iran can play a substantial and concrete role in the Arab world, and in particular *vis-à-vis* Palestine, despite the new militant rhetoric of the Tehran government. Iran could give some moral, financial and political support to the PLO, but this will not materially alter the balance of forces *vis-à-vis* Israel or the other Arab states; and the debilitated condition of the Iranian armed forces means that it is very unlikely that Iran could in the next few years play more than a symbolic role in a war with Israel. The dispute with Iraq, which is unlikely to be resolved quickly, further weakens the impact of the new Iranian regime on the Arab world.[14]

Developments in Iran since the Shah's overthrow strongly suggest that no centralised government comparable to that which previously existed will emerge for some time. Whilst this means that no strong and coherent foreign policy is likely to take shape, it does not mean that events in Iran will not have an impact elsewhere; indeed, there are a number of ways in which the very lack of unity in Iran could increase its destabilising effects. The rise of a militant pan-Iranist nationalism, with a stronger irredentist tinge than in the last years of the Shah, will affect the Gulf states, especially in regard to Bahrain, and, despite Arab hopes, it is highly unlikely that any government in Tehran would surrender the three islands taken by Iran in 1971. The revival of the nationalities issue within Iran itself will affect all the neighbouring countries, either because they have similar minorities – Kurds, Baluchis, Azerbaijanis, etc. – or because, as is the case with the Arabs of Khuzestan, the Arab states will feel drawn into the conflicts in that region. The new Iranian government has renounced the 'gendarme' role played by the Shah and has withdrawn from CENTO, but Admiral Madani, the Navy Commander and Governor of Khuzestan, has stated that Iran will remain ready to intervene in the Arab states if there is a threat of 'communism'. This suggestion, which could be extended to cover possible protection for the Persian communities in the Arab states, is at least a plausible one, given the fact that the Iranian Navy has been the part of the armed forces least affected by the recent upheavals. The over-all lesson of the Iranian revolution in the Gulf context is therefore one familiar from history: diplomatic resolutions are much easier with highly centralised states than they are with decentralised, democratic or turbulent ones. Whilst the government in Tehran may not be in a position to pursue an activist foreign policy, this very weakness at the centre may, in other ways, generate more difficulties for Iran's neighbours.

Three other elements of the new strategic situation affecting the Gulf can be discussed more briefly. The first is the situation around the lower reaches of the Red Sea, in the two Yemens and the Horn of Africa. The decisive event here has clearly been the Ethiopian revolution which removed another component of the pro-Western alliance system and where, after some delay, a novel international alignment has been established. The turn by Ethiopia's rulers away from the West and towards the Soviet Union did not occur in 1974 immediately after the fall of Haile Selassie, but in 1977, and was a response to the increasingly active role being played in the Horn against Ethiopia by the conservative Arab states and Iraq. More precisely, the new relationship between the Soviet Union and Ethiopia resulted from the Somali military offensive of June 1977 – an initiative carried out with the active encouragement of the Arab states. The claim repeated in much of the Arab press that the Somalis and Eritreans are 'Arabs' is without foundation, but it has served to alarm the Ethiopians all the more and thereby make them the more determined to consolidate their relationship with the Russians, the only people willing to provide the weapons for Ethiopia's defence. Whereas the Saudi Arabians present events in the Horn as an ominous threat to them, it is in fact the interventionist policy of the Arab states, in particular Saudi Arabia, which has brought about the very result they most fear.[15]

At the same time, the situation in both parts of Yemen has escaped from the controls which, in the mid-1970s, it was believed Saudi policies had imposed. The Saudi attempt to entice South Yemen over with financial aid after the establishment of diplomatic relations in March 1976 did not succeed; relations between the two countries deteriorated in late 1977 under the double impact of events in the Horn of Africa and the assassination of North Yemeni President al-Hamdi, an act carried out by people generally believed to have been sympathetic to Saudi Arabia. Although the South Yemenis paid a price for the cessation of Saudi aid, the focus of conflict was in North

Yemen where the killing of al-Hamdi initiated a new round of unrest within the army and within some parts of the countryside. This led, *via* the June 1978 crisis in which the Presidents of both parts of Yemen were killed, to the February 1979 war between the YAR and the PDRY. The March 1979 unity agreement between the two states is, like its 1972 predecessor, little more than an agreement not to wage war against each other, and there is no indication that the instability in North Yemen has finally ceased. Once again the conflict in North Yemen, the most populous state in the Peninsula, with probably greater direct influence on Saudi Arabia than any other, has become an active component in the politics of the Arabian Peninsula.

The next major new factor is the Camp David agreement which has, at least for some time, driven a wedge between Egypt and most of the other Arab countries, and between Saudi Arabia and the USA. Coming at a time when the powerful pillar of Iran has been removed, this disagreement represents a serious setback to US policy; the creation of a new US intervention force is as much a response to this development as it is to the disappearance of the Shah. As with the menacing discussions in the aftermath of the 1973 war of a possible US 'invasion' of the Gulf, the announcement that this force has been created is two-sided: it is designed both to reassure the Saudis that the USA could come to their aid and to remind the Riyadh government that its licence to disagree with the USA has certain limits. The tenor of the Saudi response to Camp David partly reflects a sense that the popular response in the Arab world to Sadat's initiatives will be such as to undermine their own position. It involves a disagreement with the USA on tactics rather than on the over-all aim, but the Americans have held to their view that failure to continue with the current Egyptian–Israeli negotiations will run the risk of generating greater long-run destabilising effects.

The short-run impact of Camp David at first appeared to have been such as to close the gap between radical and conservative states in the region. If it led to a reconciliation of Baghdad and Damascus, which appears to be temporary, it also led to a reconciliation of the Saudis with the more radical states, and the anathema pronounced on the PDRY by the Arab League in July 1978 was lifted in the following November as a result of the shared need to 'confront' Egypt. The Saudis must also be reassured by the reconciliation that Sadat has provoked between the PLO and King Hussain. Yet if, whatever the state of Syrian–Iraqi relations, radicals and conservatives have come closer together, recent events have reopened divisions within these two camps themselves. Iraq's new policies have fostered major disagreement with the Soviet Union, which has been accompanied by a crisis in Iraq's relations with South Yemen. At the same time Sadat's policies have divided the conservative camp: not only has the Riyadh–Cairo axis been broken after eleven years, but a fresh breach has emerged between Oman and the other Peninsula monarchies. Alone among the Gulf states, Oman has sided with Sadat and has indicated that it might bring Egyptian forces to replace those repatriated by Iran. Whilst this may be in the immediate security interests of Sultan Qabus, it must further expose him to criticism from the other Peninsula states with which, even at the best of times, he has not enjoyed close relations. It may well also encourage his opposite numbers in the United Arab Emirates to give the middle-class opposition in Oman the encouragement which it has recently been seeking.

What Sadat's initiatives have done is to expose a divergence that always existed between the priorities of Egypt's rulers and those of the Gulf states. Sadat's policy is a logical one for any Egyptian government of his political stamp to pursue. Talk about his 'treason' and 'betrayal of Arab interests' is, in this sense, of only passing relevance. The economic and social cost of continued confrontation with Israel is too high. The Israeli state is not going to disappear, and the Palestinian resistance movement has long since ceased to be an ally of Egyptian policy. Probably the Gulf states would also agree with this calculation, but the relative weight of the different considerations is different as far as they are concerned. They do not pay a comparable price for continued confrontation of Israel, they do have oil, and the benefits which they reap from the continued conflict with Israel, in terms of a certain respectability, are greater than Egypt's. The Saudis have made clear, since King Faisal's death in 1975, that they are in favour of some settlement with Israel, but they are not at this time prepared to endorse a policy which runs the risks involved in Sadat's initiatives.

All of these political developments – Iran, the Red Sea, Camp David – are set against a less overt but in the end determinant backdrop, namely the state of socio-economic development in these countries and of their international economic links. Since 1973 a very large amount of money has been poured into the oil-producing states, representing a transfer of wealth from the industrialised world to the rulers of these countries. Yet this has not been accompanied by a comparable transformation of their socio-economic or political structures; in some ways, as the Iranian case showed, the influx of ready money has, rather, enabled states to postpone reforms which would otherwise have become imperative. At the same time, a large amount of money has been wasted – on arms, on corruption, on luxury imports – and the long-run development of productive resources which could substitute for oil has been neglected. Oil produces economic and social opportunities, but it can also be a curse, as economists like Yusuf Sayigh have pointed out, generating inflation, a rise in income inequality, new forms of social parasitism and a neglect of the non-oil sectors of the economy.[16] This has been an experience not only in the Middle East but in a host of other developing oil producers – Indonesia, Nigeria, Venezuela, Ecuador and now, potentially, Mexico. In the case of the Middle East countries, the availability of oil has given the monarchical rulers time to postpone changes in the distribution of power and to counter tendencies towards democratisation which have arisen in recent years. Ironically, by creating rather brittle political systems, these rulers may be storing up greater dangers for themselves in the future. The Shah of Iran has already paid the price for this kind of postponement, for it is at least arguable that, had he allowed a greater degree of political opposition in the 1960s or early 1970s he might have been able to avoid the ignominious ejection which was finally visited upon him. In Oman, the Sultan has for a time at least fought off the rebels in Dhofar, but in the nine years since coming to power his economic record has been lamentable and the indications are that political oppositon, distinct from that in Dhofar, is growing in the north of his country. The emirates have failed, after eight years of independence, to establish a central army or a central bank, and the wasteful competition on prestige projects (ports, airports, etc.) within what is supposed to be one state makes a mockery of regional development. In Bahrain and Kuwait the limited experiences of elected assemblies were abolished under Saudi pressure in the mid-1970s and, despite their show of outward calm, it is known that the Saudi rulers, like their associates in the smaller Gulf states, are more than disturbed by events in Iran and by the possibility of continuing political turmoil there.

The uncertainty of the Gulf rulers is, however, related to the new round of difficulties encountered in their relations with the major industrialised countries. The latter are undergoing a recession which is not caused by the oil price rises but which can conveniently be blamed on the periodic increases decreed by OPEC. All parties involved now realise that the problem of oil prices and supply levels will remain for a very long time, even if the extent of the strictly energy crisis is at times exaggerated. Faced with the recession, and with growing public disagreement between the industrialised countries themselves, the latter are bound to be less tolerant of the actions of the OPEC states than they were previously, especially if Saudi Arabia and the Gulf producers oppose US policy in the sphere of Arab–Israeli relations. Yet, at the end of the day, the Saudi Arabians and the other Gulf states are to a great extent dependent on the USA for military and economic support and will allow their fear of 'communism' to prevail over their distaste for Israel. Before this point is reached there is considerable room for dispute, and the alliance system established in the late 1960s and consolidated after 1973 will be subjected to major stress.

Conclusion

It is now possible to summarise how recent developments in the Gulf have affected the components of the 1958–75 period, as listed above. For Iraq, the Iranian revolution has reopened its eastern flank, creating the possibility of conflict with Iran itself, not only from possible Iranian involvement with the Iraqi Kurds and Iraq's Shia population, but also from the temptation for Iraq to give support to the Iranian Arabs. This is not a return to the pre-March 1975 period, in that the Iranian government will not be pursuing single-minded policies comparable to those of the Shah, but the very uncontrolled nature of the Iranian process could be as dangerous for Iraq as was the Shah's hostility. For the Yemens, the impact of the Ethiopian revolution and the renewed unrest in North Yemen have rekindled conflicts which were dormant following the unity agreement in 1972. Saudi Arabia, by overplaying its hand in the Red Sea, has reactivated this crisis area and has ensured that the revolutionary dynamic that began in south Arabia in 1962 has now returned to the country of its origin, North Yemen. For Saudi Arabia itself, the recent events mark a serious setback – its alliace with Cairo broken, its initiatives in the Horn and South Yemen frustrated, its fellow monarchy in Iran swept away, its domination of OPEC defied by other members, its relations with the USA now the object of public contention and of the first major division in the ruling family since the early 1960s. For its part Iran has, most spectacularly, broken the pattern of monarchical dictatorship established half a century ago and has embarked upon a protracted and unpredictable path of transformation. For the Western powers, these events cannot mean a return to some policy of direct colonialism, which is inconceivable, but they have destroyed the basis on which the 'twin-pillar' policy rested – Iranian military might – and have forced the US government to envisage a return to direct military intervention.

Finally, the OPEC countries now find themselves in a very different situation from that existing prior to, or immediately after, 1973: their price rises are being eroded by inflation in the price of their imports, and their own policies (plus market shortages and the recession) have placed the question of oil at the very centre of economic debates in the industrialised countries, just at a time when the problems generated by oil-based development are becoming more apparent in the producer countries themselves.

The reorganisation of the 1958–75 period was an attempt to find a solution to the Gulf's problems which would guarantee the stability of the existing governments and of their continued relations with the West and Japan. The events of 1978 and 1979 have shown not only that such a solution is an ephemeral one, but that, in resolving the issues in the way they did, the states bordering the Gulf have in fact generated new problems which may prove even less surmountable.

Notes

1. This bloc of four post-1918 monarchies was, fortuitously, extended at either end by two more monarchical regimes which were consolidated in the same historical period. On the north-east, in Afghanistan, the radical faction of the ruling Mohammadzai family were able to oust the incumbent Emir Habibullah in early 1919 and, taking advantage of Britain's weakness in the aftermath of World War I, to launch the Third Afghan War. This campaign, led by the new Emir Amanullah, broke the Protectorate agreement which had linked Afghanistan to Britain since the 1880s and by so doing rallied nationalist sentiment behind the Afghan throne. The Mohammadzai were then able to rule as independent monarchs over their paralysed country until the republican *coup* of 1973, and indeed the real break came only with the revolutionary rising of April 1978. At the other extremity, on the south-west, the protracted divisions within the reigning Solomonian monarchy of Ethiopia were overcome in 1916 with the advent to power of Ras Tafari Makonnen: he ruled as heir apparent until 1930 and, from then until his deposition in 1974, as Emperor Haile Selassie, by far the longest tenure in any of the six monarchies under discussion. Both Afghanistan and Ethiopia were independent kingdoms which none the less ensured stability on the fringes of the region – a fact which became rather more obvious once the Mohammadzai and Solominian dynasties were overthrown.

2. See Mohammad Jaafar, 'Les limites de l'industrialisation du monde arabe: études du cas d'Irak', *Khamsin*, no. 4 (1977), and the data in Keith McLachlan and Narsi Ghorban, *Economic Development of the Middle East Oil Exporting States* (*Economist* Intelligence Unit, London, 1978).

3. The political preparation for the Dhofar movement was laid among the Omani emigrant community in the Gulf – but the supplies which made the movement possible, as well as the over-all regional conjuncture, came through South Yemen.

4. For background on post-1967 developments in the PDRY see Shahid Chaudhry, *People's Democratic Republic of Yemen, A Review of Economic and Social Development* (World Bank, Washington, 1978), and my own 'Socialism in South Yemen', *MERIP Reports*, no. 83 (Washington, October 1979).

5. I have tried to give an analysis of the final period of the Dhofar war in *Mercenaries and Counter-Insurgency in the Gulf* (Nottingham, 1977). For a study by the commander of the British forces, see Maj. Gen. K. Perkins, 'Oman 1975: The Year of Decision', *Journal of the Royal United Services Institute* (March 1979).

6. *The Guardian*, 1 March 1979. The British did, however, continue to maintain a significant presence in Oman and at the end of 1977 there were still 196 serving British officers in Oman, flanked by at least an equal number of mercenaries on contract. The most influential Briton in the country was the Sultan's *aide-de-camp*, a former British intelligence officer, Tim Landen, who was believed to exert a special weight on matters of foreign policy.

7. Details of the growth of US relations with Gulf states are given in US House of Representatives, Committee on International Relations, *United States Arms Policies in the Persian Gulf and Red Sea Areas: Past, Present, and Future* (Washington, 1977). The US presence in Oman has been especially significant, given the manner in which it has been used by the Sultan to offset the influence of the British, using the CIA-financed military police force. Following the disagreement between Britain and the Sultan in 1979 and the fall of the Shah, US–Omani military co-operation was increased.

8. For a radical Arab evaluation of the debate on Gulf security, see al-Jabhah al-Shaabiah fi al-Bahrain, *Al-Sira' lil Khalij al-Arabi* (*Struggle for the Arab Gulf*) (Beirut, 1978).

9. A comprehensive discussion of the international significance of the new oil revenues can be found in *Critiques de l'Economie Politique*, no. 22 (October–December 1975). Ernest Mandel argues the case for there being a new Arab and Iranian financial bourgeoisie, whilst S. Jaber stresses the continuing dependence of these countries on the West. An additional factor which helped to pave the way for new and unmediated relations between the oil producers and the major capitalist industrialised nations was the destruction of Lebanon's financial institutions in the civil war. These had previously played an intermediary role in the Arab world. (See M. Jaafar in *Inprecor*, French edn, no. 45 (February 1979).) Mandel has also shown (*The Second Slump* (London, 1978), pp. 35–8) how the oil price rises were not the main cause of the world recession but came into operation after an underlying crisis of overproduction in these countries themselves had already begun.

10. Whilst the complaints of the industrialised world are somewhat specious, the OPEC price rises and the consequent boom in the producer states have certainly had serious and negative consequences for the poorer, 'fourth world' countries. They have meant not only much higher import bills but also a draining of scarce human resources, of skilled labour, to the producer states. This is the ugly side of the 'New Economic Order' presaged by OPEC's advances *vis-à-vis* the industrialised world, and neither the producers' aid policies nor third-world rhetoric have mitigated the disastrous impact of this new set of exploitative relations on the world's poorest nations. As a result mainly of oil price rises the current account deficit of the non-oil third world reached $21 billions in 1977, $32 billions in 1978 and is expected to reach $50 billions in 1980. The vulnerability of these countries is all the greater because their dependence on oil as an energy source is higher than that of the industrialised world (59.5 per cent as opposed to 50 per cent) (*Le Monde*, 29 September 1979).

11. The generally held view that Israel is, in some way, the *main* bastion of

Western interests in the Middle East is rather a simplification. Economically Israel is a net recipient of monies from the advanced capitalist world – not a source of profit. Militarily, despite its capacity to hit its neighbours, it has not been able to play a significant counter-revolutionary role in the rest of the Arab world apart from some minor undercover operations (aiding the North Yemeni royalists, the southern Sudanese separatists, the Iraqi Kurds). Israel's links to the West are largely of a political and affective character and the real bastions – in economic and strategic terms – have always been Arab states, especially Saudi Arabia. In strictly material terms, Israel has therefore never been a significant defender of Western interests in the region and has, if anything, been an embarrassment. This is why a shift in US and EEC policy is less difficult than theories of Israel-as-the-imperialist-agent would imply.

12. Emile Nakhleh, *Bahrain* (London, 1976), p. 71.

13. An excellent insider's account of the misuse of Omani oil revenues is given in John Townsend, *Oman* (London, 1977).

14. In an interview with the author in August 1979 Iranian Foreign Minister Ibrahim Yazdi indicated that Iran would not send troops to fight in future Arab–Israeli conflicts: 'They do not need us', he said. The grave apprehension felt by the Arab rulers about Khomeini's victory finds its obverse in the enormous hopes and enthusiasm which this has raised in many parts of the Arab world, where it has encouraged a return to religious militancy among the young. The Palestinians in particular have placed great and, it would appear, unfounded expectations upon the Iranian revolution.

15. The Ethiopian government claim that it has been the object of a concerted NATO-backed invasion plan is certainly an exaggeration, but there exists substantial evidence of a conservative Arab and Western exacerbation of the Horn of Africa situation. See my 'US Policy in the Horn', *Review of African Political Economy*, no. 10 (September–December 1978).

16. Yusuf Sayigh, *The Economies of the Arab World* (London, 1978), pp. 180ff. See also Townsend, *Oman*, p. 13, and 'The Case of Kuwait', *Monthly Review* (November 1978). The pervasive corruption of the oil states is something not normally included in academic literature on their economies but is of considerable importance, not just for commercial transactions but for popular perceptions of the ruling groups. Events in Iran should, by now, have made this clear. For journalistic accounts see Gabriel Dardaud and Simonne and Jean Lacouture, *Les Émirats Mirages* (Paris, 1975), pp. 182ff., and Andrew Duncan, *Moneyrush* (London, 1979).

Index

For Product Safety Concerns and Information please contact our EU
representative GPSR@taylorandfrancis.com
Taylor & Francis Verlag GmbH, Kaufingerstraße 24, 80331 München, Germany

www.ingramcontent.com/pod-product-compliance
Ingram Content Group UK Ltd.
Pitfield, Milton Keynes, MK11 3LW, UK
UKHW050050200926
475702UK00019B/2765
* 9 7 8 1 1 3 8 8 2 0 3 2 6 *